The Legal Side of
Private Security

The Legal Side of Private Security

WORKING THROUGH THE MAZE

Leo F. Hannon

Q

QUORUM BOOKS
Westport, Connecticut • London

Library of Congress Cataloging-in-Publication Data

Hannon, Leo F.
   The legal side of private security : working through the maze /
Leo F. Hannon.
      p.   cm.
   Includes bibliographical references (p.   ) and index.
   ISBN 0–89930–790–6 (alk. paper)
   1. Police, Private—United States.   2. Private security services—
Law and legislation—United States.   I. Title.
KF5399.5.P7H36   1992
344.73′05289—dc20
[347.3045289]   92–15685

British Library Cataloguing in Publication Data is available.

Library of Congress Catalog Card Number: 92–15685
ISBN: 0–89930–790–6

First published in 1992

Quorum Books, 88 Post Road West, Westport, CT 06881
An imprint of Greenwood Publishing Group, Inc.

Printed in the United States of America

The paper used in this book complies with the
Permanent Paper Standard issued by the National
Information Standards Organization (Z39.48–1984).

10 9 8 7 6 5 4 3 2 1

To my family—
Everything else is in second place

Contents

Introduction

The tensions between an employer's right to run a business in a profitable way and an individual's rights to do his or her own thing have dramatically increased over the past decade. Numerous articles have chronicled various aspects of these forces in conflict. In the interest of becoming more competitive, employers have cut their workforces. Employee loyalty has eroded in reaction to loss of job security. Industrial espionage has created a shortcut to technical advancement. A "what's in it for me" mentality has altered old value systems. Drugs have entered the workplace. Employee theft has increased.

Employers have responded to increasing threats to profit margins and safety by increasing security measures. Drug-sniffing dogs, undercover agents, cameras, searches, and physical and psychological testing have become part of their defensive programs. Individuals have responded to perceived excesses by both challenging them directly in court and getting new legislation passed to make them illegal.

Hundreds of cases reflecting these conflicts have been reported out of numerous judicial systems including federal, state, and local courts, private dispute resolution, and administrative agencies. In processing such cases, courts have interpreted a maze of laws including constitutional mandates, criminal and civil statutes, the National Labor Relations Act, the Civil Rights Act, and arbitration decisions. The results sometimes appear contradictory and often shed more shadow than light. For example, it might be proper under state trespassing laws to have union handbillers removed from private property, but that action might be a violation of the National Labor Relations Act. A locker search conducted by a law enforcement officer might require a search warrant, but the same search conducted by a private security officer might not.

The confusion created by the legal resolution of these conflicts has created an unusual burden for security professionals, human resources people, and lawyers giving advice on these issues. It is the intent of this book to unravel apparent legal complexities by considering a wide range of security-related issues, exploring the basic rights that are involved, and examining how the various legal forums are balancing these rights. This approach is based on the premise that complexities can only be understood by first understanding basics. The hoped-for product will be a thinking process that generates legally sound decisions that solve problems.

The Legal Side of
Private Security

1

Private Security and Law Enforcement

CONFUSION IN THE APPLICATION OF THE LAW

The maze of legal issues that confuse and frustrate people involved in the private security sector is in part created by the unusually wide cross section of problems to which they are exposed. A plant theft may have criminal law aspects but it most likely will also have serious employee relations elements and, possibly, the potential for some kind of civil action such as a defamation suit. However, the law has not developed in a way that can generate simple coordinated answers; rather, it has grown vertically in separate columns or specialized areas such as criminal, constitutional, civil, and labor law. This often means that the security issue has to be first addressed in pieces and not as a whole.

If these separate areas of the law have anything in common it is that they all involve the balancing of rights. The problem is that these rights will vary from one area of the law to another. While the rights of an individual will get the highest priority in a criminal case, they might be important but of less weight in a civil or labor case. The final decisions might appear contradictory until it is understood what the different courts were trying to do. Understanding the reasons for the differences in conclusions on the separate legal elements of a multi-faceted security issue should put a decision-maker in a better position to create a balanced solution for the whole problem. Probably the best way to start gaining some sense of perspective is to focus on the public sector, more particularly law enforcement. The many similarities between the kinds of work done and the techniques used by security in the private sector and law enforcement have created a natural tendency to think along similar lines in the application of the law. Many people in the private arena were trained by law enforcement agencies and certainly the media and entertainment industry have highlighted the criminal law. Unfortunately, this identification with law enforcement is at the heart of the confusion in the private security sector.

ROLE OF THE GOVERNMENT

Despite the similarities, private security and law enforcement are geared to completely separate legal premises. First, law enforcement is an arm of the government, and as the name indicates, has a mission of enforcing the criminal laws of the government. While private security might be controlled to some extent by government regulations, its role as an agent of a private party is to protect private property and enforce the rules and regulations that have been created by that private party. For example, police will not be interested if an employee takes beer into a chemical plant because it is not against the law. But plant security will be interested because it is against the plant rules.

It is worthwhile to pursue these distinctions in some detail in order to better understand the close attention law enforcement has received from the courts. To properly set the scene it is necessary to take a brief refresher course in American history.

The founding fathers made it clear that the people were the only legitimate source of power and the people create, control, and direct the government. The fundamental purposes of government include establishing justice, insuring domestic tranquility, and promoting the general welfare—in short, providing for the interests of the people. Of course, nothing is said about making a profit.

While some felt it would be redundant to add a Bill of Rights to the Constitution, most were still so fearful of government excesses that they insisted that the first ten amendments be added to assure the protections they felt were necessary. The knock on the door in the middle of the night was still on their minds.[1]

This paramount interest in protecting the rights of the people, however, did not exist in a vacuum. The government still had to carry out its mission of providing for the general welfare, and it could not do so without having some degree of authority. It has been said that, "In the entire realm of public affairs, there is no more basic or difficult problem than that of maintaining a proper balance between authority and liberty."[2]

This balancing of liberty and authority is engaged in at all levels of government—federal, state, and local—and is best understood by following developments in the federal Bill of Rights. While each state has its own constitution, most of the protections set out in the first ten amendments have been selectively incorporated into state law by federal court action. The vehicle for incorporation has been the fourteenth amendment.

The Supreme Court has concluded that once it has decided that a particular provision of the Bill of Rights is "fundamental to the American scheme of justice," that standard will apply both to state and federal governments.[3]

Since the fourth amendment, which pertains to search and seizure, covers both federal and state government activity and since it draws considerable attention in both the public and private sector, it is worthwhile to follow some of its recent developments. It reads as follows:

The right of its people to be secure in their persons, houses, papers and effects against unreasonable searches and seizures shall not be violated, and no warrants shall issue but upon probable cause supported by oath or affirmation, and particularly describe the place to be searched and the person or things to be searched.

Most of the case law relating to this amendment, both federal and state, focuses on the words "unreasonable," "warrants," and "probable cause." The Supreme Court made it clear in *Mapp v. Ohio*[4] that the security of one's privacy against arbitrary intrusion by the police is basic to a free society. This concept is applicable to state and local governments as well as to the federal government. The courts have attempted to deter unlawful searches and seizures by excluding materials obtained through illegal searches and seizures from admission into evidence. The idea is that police will not waste their energy getting evidence they know they will not be able to use in court. The courts also understand that by so doing there is a social cost, in that otherwise relevant information is kept from the trier of facts.[5] But this again is part of keeping a balance between liberty and authority.

The exclusion of evidence, or as it is called, the exclusionary rule, is based on the premise that there is a constitutional preference for searches to be conducted pursuant to a warrant. Searches conducted outside the judicial process, without a warrant, are considered on their face to be unreasonable[6] and some courts still zealously guard that principle.[7] There are in theory only limited exceptions to the exclusionary rule such as consent, abandonment, search pursuant to a legal arrest, and the plain view doctrine, but recently the numbers and kinds of exceptions have increased.[8] For example, these exceptions have been extended to the non–law enforcement sector of government activity. An explanation of a few of these cases will help highlight the roles that are being played by police, government administrators, and non-government people.

ANALYSIS OF NON–LAW ENFORCEMENT
GOVERNMENT CASES

In attempting to understand the court's search for the balance between liberty and authority in several fourth amendment cases, our interests will be keyed to three questions: Who is doing the search? Who is the subject of the search? What are the rights and interests of each of the parties?

In 1980 a New Jersey public high school assistant vice-principal searched a freshman student's purse to determine whether or not she had been smoking contrary to school rules. In the course of the search, he found evidence of drug use and trafficking. The state brought delinquency charges against the student and, in a subsequent hearing, the student requested that the evidence obtained in the search be excluded. *New Jersey v. T.L.O.*[9]

On review, the Supreme Court discussed the state's obligation to educate the young and the obligation to protect the student's constitutional freedoms. The court first made it clear that the fourth amendment was not limited to activities of law enforcement people but covered all public officials. Under the circumstances, there was no question, then—the fourth amendment applied to this case. But that created a dilemma.

The court recognized that the official's real interest was carrying out the day-to-day business of the school and not enforcing the criminal law. How could he go about administering school rules and maintaining discipline if he had to be continuously concerned about the need for warrants? How then to strike a balance that would let school officials do their job and still not jeopardize the students' legitimate expectation of privacy?

First, the court decided that the warrant requirement was not applicable to school officials conducting searches of students. Next, it decided that the probable cause burden was too heavy for school administrators and concluded that, in the interest of striking a better balance, the new test for a search by school administrators would be the less onerous one of reasonableness.

The public official theme was again pursued by the Supreme Court in the 1987 *O'Conner et al. v. Ortega* case.[10] This time the setting was a state hospital and the person whose office and files were searched was a hospital employee, Ortega. The persons conducting the search were hospital administrators including a state-employed security officer. The search was related to possible employment misconduct by Ortega and pursuit of a criminal action was not involved. Ortega sought damages on the premise that his rights guaranteed under the fourth amendment had been violated by the search.

It should be noted that while the exclusionary rule is often the issue in fourth amendment cases, there is also considerable litigation over the subject of damages. Damages are only discussed at this point to help explain the nature of the litigation. These damages cases can take either one of two routes depending on whether the defendants are federal or state agents. In 1971 the Supreme Court decided that federal officers could be liable for damages suffered in connection with an illegal search.[11] But what about state officers? One hundred years earlier, in 1871, Congress passed a civil rights law, 42 U.S.C. Sec. 1983, which gives any person who is deprived by state activity of federally guaranteed rights the right to sue the parties involved. In this case, since Ortega believed that his fourth amendment rights were violated by California state agents, he sued the agents, including the security officer, under 42 U.S.C. Sec. 1983. Section 1983 is, in short, a mechanism or vehicle for obtaining damages.

The court in *Ortega* had no problem in finding that the search by public officials brought the case within fourth amendment parameters. This time, though, the court was faced with striking a balance of rights in the public workplace. The court noted that public employees, like private employees, can have an expectancy of privacy in their places of work. On the other hand, the court recognized the realities of the workplace, stating, "In the case of searches conducted by a public employer, we must balance the invasion of the employee's legitimate expectation of privacy against the government's need for supervision, control, and the efficient operation of the workplace."[12] Enforcement of the criminal law was not in the balance.

As in the *T.L.O.* case, the court decided that warrants and probable cause requirements created an intolerable burden. In the court's judgment, public employer searches for non-investigatory, work-related purposes, as well as for investigations of work-related misconduct, should be judged by the "standard of reasonableness under all the circumstances."[13]

Thus, the Supreme Court, for fourth amendment purposes, has identified two classes of searchers—enforcers of the criminal law and administrators of schools and workplaces—and assigned different legal burdens to them. In both *T.L.O.* and *Ortega* the searchers were public employees. Does it make a difference if the searcher is a private employee?

Over the years, the courts have made it clear that the Bill of Rights is only applicable to government action. These first ten amendments and the fourteenth erect no shield against private conduct, however discriminatory or wrongful.[14] In order to encumber private activity with the burdens of the fourth amendment, it is necessary to prove that the private party engaged in some kind of government or state action.[15]

Following *T.L.O.* and *Ortega*, the Ninth Circuit in 1987 considered a case in which the search of a civilian Navy Department employee's office and desk was conducted initially by a private contractor's security investigator.[16] The employee, Schowengerdt, sued not only Navy personnel for damages but also the contractor, General Dynamics, and the investigator, Kessel.

The court in *Schowengerdt* approached the case as one involving a workplace search and one triggering the reasonableness tests set out in *Ortega*. It had difficulty determining whether the search was work-related based on facts in the record. Without these facts, it could not weigh the government's needs against the employee's expectancy of privacy. The case was remanded for further inquiry along those lines.

While this took care of the *Ortega* balancing of rights issue, the court still had to address the involvement of the private parties. General Dynamics and Kessel contended that they were not involved in federal action and even if they were, as private parties, they were not subject to liability for damages.

The court considered the numerous tests that have been used to determine whether or not a private party has engaged in government action and focused on two: joint participation and engagement in a public function or assumption of a police activity.[17] Without making any findings, it advised the district court in its remand to consider that if the government action requirements were met, General Dynamics and Kessel could not rely on their private-party status as a basis for dismissal.

In this still-evolving area of the law, it might be that the nature of some government-private party contracts is such that it will be very difficult to avoid government and state action findings and consequential fourth amendment obligations. But, even if these obligations are assumed, it seems that under *Ortega* and its application to the public sector workplace, "reasonableness" will be the watchword and not "probable cause" if the searches are carried out by non–law enforcement people.

As mentioned, the constitutional provisions that create burdens for law enforcement are not normally applicable to the private sector. However, there are numerous situations in which the courts find that private parties have become involved in government activity to the point that there is a real question as to whether they should be forced to meet the same legal standards applied to government action. The effect of government regulations in this area will be discussed in more detail in chapter 10.

Schowengerdt sets out a case in which, because of contractual relationships, a private party allegedly finds itself involved in government activity. There are many instances in which private parties unintentionally create the legal linkage with the government by either using off-duty law enforcement people to do private security work or developing such a close working relationship with law enforcement that it is difficult to tell where one ends and the other begins.

The interest in creating these kinds of relationships is understandable. By hiring law enforcement officers to perform private security work, the business immediately acquires a trained, experienced workforce. By creating a seamless relationship with the police, the business expedites the processing of its cases. The downside is that the legal burdens normally only carried by law enforcement may be shared with the private sector.

As noted in the *T.L.O.*, *Ortega*, and *Schowengerdt* cases, the search and seizure issue can focus on the exclusionary rule or damages. In cases involving federal government activity, there is a direct connection through the fourth amendment for both. In state situations, the connection is through the fourteenth amendment. As noted, the *Ortega* case is an example of the use of a civil rights statute, 42 U.S.C. Sec. 1983 to pursue damages. This statute is used to pursue monetary satisfaction for the deprivation of a federally guaranteed right by some state action or action under color of state law. Again, private parties are not subject to Section 1983 liability unless they have somehow become involved in the state action.

INVOLVEMENT OF THE GOVERNMENT IN PRIVATE SECTOR ACTIVITIES

Many courts have wrestled with establishing tests to determine whether there is sufficient linkage between private and government activity to warrant a finding of state action or color of law. Though these two phrases, *state action* and *color of state law*, have different roots—the fourteenth amendment and Section 1983 respectively—they are considered to mean the same thing. Numerous courts have probed their meaning but the Supreme Court in *Lugar v. Edmondson Oil Co.*[18] did set up a two-prong test to help provide an answer to whether a private activity amounts to state action or color of law.

First, the deprivation of the federal right must be caused by the exercise of some right or privilege created by the state or by a person for whom the state is responsible. This means that there has to be some kind of state policy involved in the problem.

Second, the party charged with the deprivation must be a person who may fairly be said to be a state actor. The state actor requirement ensures that not all private parties "face constitutional litigation whenever they seek to rely on some state rule governing their interactions with the community surrounding them."[19] Both elements of the test have to be met for there to be state action.

Several cases will be reviewed to help understand this difficult area of linkage between private and government activity. The cases will include several for damages under Section 1983 and several for exclusion of evidence under the fourteenth and fourth amendments. In 1989 the Ninth Circuit in *Collins v. Womancare*[20] considered a situation in which anti-abortion picketers contended they were deprived of federally protected rights when they were subjected to citizen's arrests by Womancare agents for picketing contrary to a court injunction. The federal right at issue was the right of free speech and assembly.

Before private parties can be enmeshed as defendants in a first amendment matter, it must be shown that they were acting under color of law, per Section 1983. The court proceeded to apply the two-part *Lugar* test. Focusing on the state policy issue, the court decided that by making a citizen's arrest, the health services agents were not carrying out a state function. The citizen's arrest policy did not deprive anyone of a protected right.

Looking at the citizen's arrest policy by itself was not enough, though, because the next contention was that Womancare people had *violated* the state citizen's arrest statute and that satisfied the first prong of the *Lugar* test requiring a state policy issue. The court stated that the legality of the state policy was the thing being tested and a private party violation of it did not provide the linkage to state activity.

But what would happen if a state actor had violated the state policy and the private party had acted in conjunction with the state actor? Would both tests be met? The court pointed out that the state and its agents cannot get off the hook if the state's agents abused their power. This clearly distinguishes the situation from that in which a private party misused a statute or policy.

The issue, then, was whether the Womancare employees and law enforcement people carried out the arrests as a joint action. The joint action inquiry focused on whether the state had so far insinuated itself into a position of interdependence with the private entity that it had to be recognized as a joint participant in the challenged activity. In this case the idea for the arrests came from Womancare people, when a police officer, after conducting an independent investigation, refused to arrest the protestors on his own authority. There was no evidence of any pre-arranged plan or customary procedure or policy that substituted the judgment of the private party for that of the police. Under the circumstances, there just was not any state action. It should be kept in mind that while the facts were insufficient to make a deprivation of freedom of speech case, the demonstrators could still pursue a theory of false arrest.

A discussion of *Womancare* leads naturally to a discussion of *People v. Zelinski*, a 1979 California case.[21] This was probably the high water mark of encumbering a private party with law enforcement standards. The California court was concerned with the development of law enforcement characteristics by private security forces and viewed this as a potential threat to the public. In response to this concern, it decided that a private security officer who made a citizen's arrest was acting on behalf of the public and not his employer. As a consequence, evidence he had acquired in a search was not allowed into evidence in a subsequent criminal trial. The security officer had no law enforcement affiliation and had not acted pursuant to police instructions or in a joint operation with the police. In the court's view he had taken on a public function.

How does this square with *Womancare*, a federal case that came down ten years later? First, it should be understood that *Zelinski* involved the interpretation of a state constitutional provision relating to the exclusion of evidence. But even so, the *Womancare* court said that "insofar as

Zelinski held that action by a private party pursuant to but in violation of a state statute can constitute state action, *Zelinski* directly conflicts with and is superseded by *Lugar*."[22] The court added that the California constitution had been changed since *Zelinski* and that the state exclusionary rule now tracked the federal rule.

This seems to have put an end to the viability of *Zelinski*, but the California court made it official in 1990 in *People v. Taylor*.[23] This court stated explicitly: "The fact that a private citizen makes a citizen's arrest does not automatically transform this individual into an agent of the state."[24] Taking the next step, the court found no evidence that the security officers involved had engaged in a joint operation with the state. The security people had decided to make an arrest on their own and in no way conducted themselves as law enforcement officers. The court made note of the fact that the security guards were trained under state regulations to understand that they were not police officers and did not have the same duties as police officers. The security people had at no time asserted the power of the state and as a consequence, evidence they had acquired in a search was allowed into evidence. The California courts further buried *Zelinski* in *In Re Christopher H.* in 1991 and allowed evidence obtained by private security people into evidence in a criminal trial.[25]

How do the courts handle a case in which the security officer also had some law enforcement affiliation? In *Lusby v. T.G.&Y. Stores Inc.* the Tenth Circuit Court of Appeals considered a Section 1983 damages case in which activity of an off-duty policeman employed by a store as a security guard provided the linkage to state action.[26] In response to a perceived shoplifting incident, the guard-officer flashed his badge, identified himself as a police officer and made an arrest for shoplifting. An altercation broke out and local police arrived on the scene. Based on the report of the officer-guard, the police took into custody the alleged shoplifter and two of his brothers who had joined the fray. As it turned out, the shoplifting suspect apparently had not shoplifted.

The three brothers filed, among other things, a Section 1983 action against the store, the guard-officer, the local police, and the city on the contention they were deprived of due process of law, a federally protected right, by the joint actions of the private parties and law enforcement officers.

Under the *Lugar* two-prong test, was the guard-officer a state actor? The court stated that the store was not liable for a civil rights violation simply because it employed the off-duty officer as a guard, but it came to a different conclusion when it analyzed the guard-officer's conduct. He had flashed his badge, identified himself as a police officer working as a guard, finished his paperwork at the police station, and considered filing charges against one of the brothers for assault on a police officer.

This was sufficient in the court's view to establish his status as a state actor. The court could then have tested to see if there was a legitimate state policy that had been abused.

The court stopped at this point in its analysis of the guard-officer's activity and shifted to a new point. It said that even if the guard-officer had not taken on a police role there was sufficient evidence of joint activity to pass the *Lugar* tests. The court then focused on the police policy of accepting the merchant's contentions at face value and not conducting an independent investigation before making an arrest. As far as the court was concerned this policy allowed a private citizen such as a security officer or store manager to substitute his or her judgment for that of the police. Such cooperative activity between the police and a private party was sufficient to make the store and guard-officer parties acting under color of state law even if the guard-officer had not acted as a policeman.

The point is that there has to be cooperation between private security and law enforcement but that cooperation should not extend to situations in which private security people exercise judgments that should be solely within the province of law enforcement. Separate and apart from the joint engagement with law enforcement aspects, *Lusby* should be remembered because of its analysis of the status of an off-duty police officer employed as a guard. How much police-type activity is necessary to tip the scales toward state action is a difficult call, but in *Traver v. Meshriy*[27] state action was found when a bank guard responded to a problem as a police officer by identifying himself as such and showing his police identification. In *Watkins v. Oaklawn Jockey Club*[28] no state action was found when an officer made no pretense that he was acting under color of state law. Part of the problem in *Lusby* was that no one in management ever told the guard-officer what his role was.

These cases have dwelt on whether certain private party activity amounted to state action. But what happens when state action is not contested but assumed? *Faulkner v. State*,[29] a 1989 Maryland case, involved a situation in which an employee contested the introduction of evidence at a criminal trial on the premise that it was seized unconstitutionally at his workplace without benefit of a warrant. A private employer, after becoming aware of drug activity at its plant, decided to conduct a locker search. Believing it might uncover controlled substances and possibly firearms, the plant asked local police to attend the search. The locker searches were conducted with the police in a standby position. After an employee, Faulkner, disclaimed use of a second locker although it had his name on it, the lock was cut off by management and a needle was found in the locker and turned over to police. The police arrested Faulkner, and in a follow-up search found cocaine in the locker. In the subsequent criminal trial Faulkner tried to keep the needles and drugs out of evidence.

After assuming the participation of the police constituted state action, the court proceeded to apply fourth amendment standards to the search. In doing so it focused on the expectancy of privacy and noted that the lockers were owned by the company, the company had reason to believe that there were drugs at the plant contrary to plant rules, the company had reserved a right to search lockers in such circumstances, the searches were carried out in accordance with plant rules in the presence of a union steward and the employee, and Faulkner had disclaimed use of the locker. The court stated that "under all of these circumstances, particularly Faulkner's disclaimer of any expectation of privacy in the second locker, Haysbert (a management agent) acted reasonably in entering the second locker, even if there were state action."[30] This disclaimer element was of consequence to the court because one of the exceptions to the need for a warrant is abandonment.

One can speculate how the court would have decided the case if a few facts were changed. Suppose there had been no rule preserving management's right to conduct a search, or suppose the questioned material had been found in the locker Faulkner agreed was his. Would these slightly different expectancy of privacy factors have convinced the court that the search was illegal? Of course the fourth amendment issue would have been avoided completely if the police had not been present at the search and the materials had not been turned over to them during the course of the search. This case can be read in conjunction with non–law enforcement search cases in the organized and unorganized workplaces discussed in chapters 5 and 6 to get a better feel for management's rights in such situations.

It should be kept in mind, also, that if law enforcement is invited into a situation as a participant and knows that a search might involve some expectancy of privacy they can come prepared with an appropriate warrant. It is the misunderstanding of the roles to be played that often causes the problem.

A number of state action cases involve confrontational situations, and a question often arises as to whether a person is owed a warning of some kind. Thus, attention to the *Miranda* cases is helpful. Again, they evidence the special distinct interest courts have in protecting people from law enforcement activity.

The Supreme Court in *Miranda v. State of Arizona*[31] discussed its concerns about the inherently intimidating nature of interrogations conducted by police while an individual is in their custody. In the interest of leveling the playing field, the court decided that any evidence derived from these kinds of situations will be inadmissible unless the individual is "warned that he has the right to remain silent, that anything said can and will be used against him in court, that he has the right to consult with a lawyer and to have the lawyer with him during interrogation, and that if he is indigent, a lawyer will be appointed to represent him."[32]

The source for this rule is the fifth amendment, the constitutional safeguard against self-incrimination. As with the fourth amendment, it is normally not applicable to private parties. However, numerous defenses to the admission of confessions have been raised on the premise that the warnings requirement is applicable to private security people. With limited exceptions the courts have refused to extend the coverage of *Miranda* after noting that it was designed to prevent oppressive police tactics.[33]

As in the search and seizure cases, a few courts have decided that the procedural relationships between store security and police were so close in matters of arrest and interrogation that *Miranda* would have to apply to avoid an absurdity. In *People v. Glenn*, a court recognized a store's problems with thefts and in the interest of helping the store, suggested that it either give *Miranda* warnings or somehow change its procedure to show a line of demarcation between security and police.[34] In that case, as a practice, the store security officers started an interrogation but had a police officer hovering in the wings. The police officer's regular, immediate availability is what gave the court the problem. This is the same kind of joint activity that bothered the courts in *Womancare* and *Lusby*.

The *Zelinski* line of cases bootstrapped *Miranda* and applied it to a citizen's arrest by a private security person, on the premise that the arrest was for public purposes and not in the interest of the employer. As noted, this theory has been discarded by the Ninth Circuit in *Collins v. Womancare*[35] and by a California court in *People v. Taylor*.[36] While this theory's continued viability is seriously questioned, it does not eliminate the perception of some courts that private security is a growing threat that for legal purposes should be equated to law enforcement. At this point, though, absent federal, state, or local law enforcement entanglements amounting to state action, *Miranda* is not applicable to private security.

While the *Taylor* case is significant because of its discussion of the public service issue, it is also of value in learning what courts look for in establishing joint operations. In *Taylor*, the security guards decided to make a citizen's arrest on their own; the security company had no contracts or agreements with the government; there was no prearranged plan, customary procedure, or policy that substituted the judgment of a private party for that of the police; and the state agents in no way coerced or encouraged the security guards to effect the citizen's arrest. Further, the private security officers' uniforms were unlike those of local policemen and their badges and shoulder patches were marked "security."

OBLIGATIONS TO NOTIFY LAW ENFORCEMENT OF CRIMINAL ACTIVITY

If it is decided to conduct an investigation without benefit of law enforcement involvement, does law enforcement have to be advised if the investigation makes it clear that a certain person has committed a crime? During investigation can private security attempt to cut a deal with a suspect by offering a promise not to prosecute in exchange for the return of stolen property? Assuming a deal is cut and management goes back on its word and seeks prosecution, will those admissions be admitted into evidence in a criminal proceeding?

Misprision of Felony

The first question leads to a discussion of an old common law crime called misprision of felony. In the early days in England prior to the development of any police capability, the government put a burden on citizens to report the commission of any crimes. It was the only way the government had to manage criminal activity. This concept, along with much of English law, was brought to the United States in its infancy, but misprision has never really taken hold. A Maryland court in *Pope v. State* traced the history of the crime both in the United States and England and concluded that "maintenance of law and order does not demand its application, and, overall, the welfare of the inhabitants of Maryland and society as enjoyed by us today, would not be served by it."[37]

Some states and the federal government have codified the old common law of misprision of felony, but even in those situations the mere failure to give information on the commission of a felony will not constitute a crime unless there also was an intentional concealment of facts. This concealment might include untruthful statements, suppression of evidence, harboring of a criminal, or intimidation of witnesses.[38] There are very few misprision of felony cases that are prosecuted.

Compounding Crimes

Although there might not be a legal obligation to report a crime, can a promise not to report it be used as leverage in getting back stolen property? This area of interest is called compounding crimes and the answer to the question, not surprisingly, depends on the circumstances under which the promise not to report the crime is made and the scope of the promise.

Compounding a felony or compounding a crime has been described as an agreement with a criminal not to prosecute him, in return for a benefit. This benefit can include such things as the criminal returning stolen property to the victim. While misprision just involves concealment of a crime, compounding involves concealment for a price.[39]

What could be wrong with promising not to report a theft if the property is returned? The property owner gets his or her property back and isn't that what it is all about? Why should a business get involved in a difficult criminal proceeding that might turn out to be embarrassing if it can solve its real problem, the return of its property, without any fanfare?

The response was set out in a 1971 New Jersey case, *In Re Friedland*, where the court said:

At common law, compounding an offense in agreeing not to prosecute it was a crime—a person wronged by the criminal act of another may accept restitution for the civil wrong done to him, but he cannot lawfully agree not to prosecute the crime. The reason is that private vindication of the injury done to the victim does not vindicate the public interest in securing justice. Procuring compensation for the victims of a crime is subordinate to the State's interest in causing crimes to be punished.[40]

This statement sets the tone—private interests do not necessarily coincide with public interest and if they do conflict, private interests take second place. The *Friedland* statement represents the thinking of a majority of states but there is a growing minority of states where it is not a crime if the victim cuts a deal in which he or she gets back only what it lost—not more.[41] For example, a Delaware statute reads:

In any prosecution for compounding a crime, it is an affirmative defense that the benefit did not exceed the amount which the accused believed to be due as restitution or indemnification for harm caused by the crime.[42]

In 1975, forty-five states had compounding statutes and in two others the crime was covered under common law. There is considerable variance among the states as to whether the crime covers misdemeanors as well as felonies, whether it is applicable only after criminal proceedings have been instituted, and whether the crime is committed by the promise-maker or the promise-taker or both. In any event, there has been very little litigation in the compounding crimes area and one reason is likely that the primary witness for the government is usually the thief and juries' sympathies normally are with the victim.[43]

ADMISSIBILITY OF COERCED ADMISSIONS IN CRIMINAL PROCEEDINGS

Separate and apart from whether or not management violated the law in investigating a case is the issue of admissibility of any confessions or admissions in a subsequent criminal action. As already stated, *Miranda* is not applicable to the private sector, but are criminal courts concerned about the way in which admissions are obtained?

Consider these facts in a Texas case, *Fisher v. State*.[44] An employer, while investigating the theft of tires, told a suspected employee that if he divulged who had stolen the tires and where they were located, he, the employer, would help pay for the tires if they had been sold, would not press charges, would not call the police, and would not fire the employee. After the employee admitted that he had taken the tires, he was fired and prosecuted.

The question before the court was whether the admissions made by the employee to the employer should be accepted into evidence. The court referred to a well-established general rule affirmed by a Texas statute that a confession of guilt is admissible only when it was freely and voluntarily made without having been induced by the expectation of any promised benefit, or by the fear of any threatened injury or by the exertion of any improper influence. As to the promised benefits aspect, the court indicated the promise must be positive, must be made or sanctioned by a person in authority, and must be of a character likely to influence the defendant to speak untruthfully.

Focusing on the test of whether the person making the promise was a person in authority, it must again be noted that this is not a *Miranda* test. As far as this court was concerned, an employer can be such a person. In this court's judgment, the employer's inducements created a jury issue on the voluntariness of the statements.

The message is that once all the legal jargon is stripped away, courts are interested in fair play. This underlying concept should help guide actions taken in order to avoid legal pitfalls.

OBSERVATIONS

In sum, private security people and those in law enforcement ply somewhat similar but fundamentally different trades. The law recognizes these differences and assigns legal burdens accordingly. If private security assumes the role of law enforcement, the courts will assign it law enforcement burdens. Private security, then, has to think about such things as probable cause, warrants, *Miranda*, entrapment, deprivation of civil rights, and so on. Recognizing and understanding the differences between private security and law enforcement is a critical step in making sound security decisions that relate to the business of enforcing the rules and regulations of private employers, not the criminal law.

NOTES

1. *The Federalist Papers*, No. 49 (J. Madison), Nos. 22 & 84 (A. Hamilton); Introduction to American Government, Ogg & Ray (1945).

2. Introduction to American Government, supra, at 136.

3. *Constitutional Law*, 16A Am. Jur. 2d Sec. 453–457.

4. *Mapp v. Ohio*, 367 U.S. 643 (1961).

5. *Rakas v. Illinois*, 439 U.S. 129 (1978).

6. *Coolidge v. New Hampshire,* 403 U.S. 443 (1971).

7. *State v. Muegge,* 360 S.E. 2d 216 (W. Va. 1987).

8. 22A C.J.S., Criminal Law, warrantless search or seizure Sec. 789 (1989).

9. *New Jersey v. T.L.O.,* 469 U.S. 325 (1985).

10. 480 U.S. 709 (1987).

11. *Webster Bivens v. Six Unknown Named Agents of Federal Bureau of Narcotics,* 403 U.S. 388 (1971).

12. 480 U.S. 709 at 719.

13. 480 U.S. 709 at 725, 726.

14. *Shelley v. Kraemer,* 334 U.S. 1 (1948).

15. *Collins v. Womancare,* 878 F.2d 1145 (9th Cir. 1989).

16. *Schowengerdt v. General Dynamics,* 823 F.2d 1328 (9th Cir. 1987).

17. *Schowengerdt,* 823 F.2d 1328 at 220, 221.

18. *Lugar v. Edmondson Oil Co.,* 457 U.S. 922 (1982); see also *Collins v. Womancare,* 878 F.2d 1145; *Flagg Bros., Inc. v. Brooks,* 436 U.S. 149 (1978); *Carey v. Continental Airlines Inc.,* 823 F.2d 1402 (10th Cir. 1987); *Howerton v. Gabica,* 708 F.2d 380 (9th Cir. 1983).

19. 457 U.S. 922, 937.

20. *Collins v. Womancare,* 878 F.2d 1145.

21. *People v. Zelinski,* 24 Cal. 3d 357, 594 P.2d 1000 (1979).

22. 878 F.2d 1145, 1154.

23. *People v. Taylor,* 271 Cal. Rptr. 785 222 Cal. App. 3d 265 (1990).

24. 271 Cal. Rptr. 785, 790.

25. *In Re Christopher H.,* 278 Cal. Rptr. 577 (1991).

26. *Lusby v. T.G.&Y. Stores, Inc.,* 749 F.2d 1423 (10th Cir. 1984), *vacated on other grounds,* 474 U.S. 806 (1985).

27. 627 F.2d 934 (9th Cir. 1980).

28. 183 F.2d 440 (8th Cir. 1950).

29. *Faulkner v. State,* 317 Md. 44, 564 A.2d 785 (1989).

30. 564 A.2d 785, 788.

31. 384 U.S. 436 (1966).

32. 23 C.J.S. *Criminal Law, Warnings* Sec. 918 (1989).

33. *State v. Kelly,* 61 N.J. 283, 294 A.2d 41 (1972), 666.

34. *People v. Glenn,* 435 N.Y.S.2d 516.

35. *Collins v. Womancare,* 878 F.2d 1145.

36. *People v. Taylor,* 271 Cal. Rptr. 785, 222 Cal App.3d 625.

37. *Pope v. State,* 396 A.2d 1054 (1979).

38. 18 U.S.C. Sec. 4; *Lancy v. United States,* 356 F.2d 407 (9th Cir. 1966), *cert. denied,* 385 U.S. 922 (1966); 21 Am. Jur. 2d *Criminal Law* Sec. 34 (1981).

39. 15A C.J.S. *Compounding Offenses* Sec. 1–2 (1967).

40. *In re Friedland,* 59 N.J. 209 280 A.2d 183, 188 (1971).

41. Lipson, *Compounding Crimes,* 27 *Hastings L.J.,* 175, 176 (1975).

42. Del. Code Ann. tit. 11, Sec. 1247 (1953).

43. Lipson, *Compounding Crimes,* 187–195.

44. *Fisher v. State,* 379 S.W.2d 900 (1964).

2

A View of the Maze of Laws
That Impact Private Security

Highlighting the law enforcement paths in the legal maze confronting private security people is a significant achievement but is still only a beginning point in understanding and dealing with those remaining parts of the legal network. The purpose of this chapter is to give a brief introduction to some of the legal issues encountered by private security people and to discuss some of their interrelationships.

As described in chapter 1, for fourth and fifth amendment purposes, the law deals with the individual and government and the balancing of rights and interests between the two. To a large extent, the individual may change his or her identity in the private sector and take on new names and new roles. The new names might be employee, guest, customer, visitor, student, or demonstrator. On the other side of the scales in place of the government there are new identities such as employer, innkeeper, merchant, property owner, and private school administrator. The balance that is struck by the courts in conflicts between these various parties is made only after an evaluation of the rights and interests of all those involved. An examination of the basic combinations of parties and the laws that attempt to balance the rights in those combinations is the next critical step in working through the maze. Again, the idea in this chapter is to explore the range of legal issues involved in private security and to set the scene for more detailed discussions in later chapters.

EMPLOYER-EMPLOYEE RELATIONSHIPS

The logical relationship to start with is that between employee and employer because nearly all elements of the private security sector deal with this interface.

Consider the following as a problem that has to be solved. A black, female employee, on entering the workplace, is stopped and asked to submit to a search. She refuses to comply. What happens in this confrontation? Whose rights are involved? What are the legal issues and where might they be tested? Is it going to the National Labor Relations Board? Is it an Equal Employment Opportunity Commission case, an arbitration case, or if the refusal to comply results in discharge, could it be heard as a state court wrongful discharge action? What are the possibilities that it could result in civil litigation over alleged defamation or invasion of privacy? Are there any federal or state constitutional issues involved? The confrontation might even be resolved in several forums at the same time: Do you call a labor lawyer or one who specializes in discrimination matters, or constitutional issues, or tort litigation, or all four? If so, would each know what the other was talking about? At least, it is not a criminal matter and law enforcement advice does not seem to be needed. So, how do you get started on the problem?

For analysis purposes, the legal forums that consider these kinds of relationships will be divided into three areas: administration, arbitration, and civil. The two primary administrative laws that warrant attention are the National Labor Relations Act (NLRA) and Title VII of the Civil Rights Act of 1964.

Administrative Laws

National Labor Relations Act

This act is administered by the National Labor Relations Board (NLRB). The NLRB is a separate federal agency that is unrelated to the Labor Department. While the Labor Department covers numerous workplace-related matters such as occupational safety and health, wage and hour issues, and internal union affairs, the Board focuses on collective bargaining. The NLRB's mandate is to minimize the impact of labor unrest on interstate commerce by balancing the rights of employees to bargain with the rights of employers to run an efficient business.

Its work takes it into two areas: supervising elections to determine whether or not employees want to be represented by a union, and investigating and deciding unfair labor practice charges against employers and unions. To carry out its mission, the Board is divided into two segments— the election-running and investigatory activity is conducted in the various field offices and the judicial activity is carried out by a five-member board in Washington. Petitions for election and unfair labor practice charges are filed in regional offices and the final legal decisions are made in Washington. Board decisions are appealable to federal circuit courts and can ultimately be heard by the Supreme Court.

Civil Rights

Civil rights legislation in a sense is a maze within a maze. The phrase *civil rights* is often used in a generic way without any reference to the specific laws that might be involved. In the course of their duties, private security people might be involved with one or several different civil rights laws. The best way to understand the different elements is to explore some of their history and consider their purposes.

The first such piece of legislation that is of interest is the Civil Rights Act of 1866. It was geared to cleaning up the vestiges of slavery. In its present form, it is generally referred to as Section 1981,[1] and it covers race or color discrimination—not discrimination based on sex, age, handicap, or other factors. Its focus is on making and enforcing contracts, and since employment is often considered to be contractually based, it has been extended to the employment area. Courts had limited its coverage to hiring situations, but the Civil Rights Act of 1991 amended Section 1981 so that it now covers all aspects of the employment relationship.[2] Section 1981 is still a very viable piece of legislation and is often found in litigation as a companion action to Title VII.

The Civil Rights Act of 1871 spawned two sections that are still of current interest, Sections 1983 and 1985(3). The 1871 act was passed to deal with terrorism by the Ku Klux Klan. Section 1983 has been covered to some extent in chapter 1 in discussing government activity. It is the vehicle for recovering damages incurred by the loss of federally protected rights through some kind of state action. In short, it might be interesting that the constitution has been violated, but Section 1983 puts a little meaning in it by putting money on the line. As already noted, considerable case law has developed over what types of private party activity will result in Section 1983 coverage being extended to non-government entities.

Section 1985(3), like its companion Section 1983, is a mechanism for recovering damages; it does not establish a new set of rights. The section focuses on conspiracies intended to deprive people of equal protection or equal privileges or immunities. Many of the Section 1985 cases concern the identification of classes protected by the law. It clearly covers race but its full range has yet to be defined. The Supreme Court seems to look for "class based invidiously discriminatory animus behind the conspirator's action" and refers back to congressional intent in 1871 to combat the then-prevalent animus against blacks.[3]

The subject of state activity is also involved in Section 1985 cases. In *Griffin v. Breckenridge*[4] the Supreme Court applied the section to a private conspiracy that involved the general right to travel and the prohibition of slavery, the thirteenth amendment. The court concluded there was no need to find state action in situations where individuals could commit the violations. Then, in *Carpenters v. Scott*, the court decided that violence and vandalism by union adherents against non-union employees involved the first amendment right of association and fourteenth amendment rights and accordingly triggered the need for state action of some sort. Again, it has to be kept in mind that most of the first ten amendments can only be violated by the government, not private parties. The need to find state action will depend on the nature of the violation but for the most part state action must be involved.

The court obviously does not want Section 1985 to become a mechanism for resolving economic or commercial conflicts that could be better handled in other forums. This yet to be fully defined section has been the subject of numerous law journal articles.[5] It now sometimes seems to be included in complaints when no other vehicle for alleging a violation appears to be appropriate. Such litigation is one way of establishing the full scope of Section 1985 applicability.

Title VII of the Civil Rights Act of 1964 makes it unlawful to discriminate in employment on the basis of race, color, sex, national origin, or religion. Title VII does not supersede Section 1981 and, as noted, very often the two causes of action will be alleged in the same lawsuit. Title VII has procedural limitations not shared by Section 1981 but is broader in coverage. Of course, Section 1981 stands on its own and a Section 1981 action can be taken directly to court.

Title VII was not designed to operate the same way as Section 1981, as it set up a whole new structure for eradicating discrimination. Among other things, it authorized the establishment of the Equal Employment Opportunity Commission (EEOC). Under Title VII a person can file a charge with either the EEOC or an appropriate state or local agency. Following an investigation, the commission issues a right-to-sue notice indicating that the case either lacks merit or that it has been unable to settle the case and does not want to file suit itself. The charging party can then pursue the case through the court systems. In some limited situations, the EEOC files the court action itself. The hope is that most cases will be resolved through the EEOC without going to court. The Civil Rights Act of 1991 made a number of procedural amendments to Title VII including increased, but still capped, monetary relief and the availability of trial by jury.

Title VII cases often cover areas of interest to private security people including pre-employment inquiries such as arrest and conviction record requests, reference and prior employment checks, and honesty tests, as well as sexual harassment, discipline, and discharge investigations. Very often the same set of facts might be of interest to the NLRB, but the reasons for the interest will be different. The NLRB will focus on collective bargaining issues and the EEOC will focus on discrimination. Was the employee fired because of his union activity or because he was black?

In some situations, an employee will file a charge with both the NLRB and the EEOC.

Other civil rights–related statutes and regulations such as the Age Act, the Equal Pay Act, and Executive Order 11246 will not be covered here because of the limited potential for their involvement in security-related matters.

Arbitration

While arbitration covers an increasing number of business situations, for these purposes it will be restricted to the organized or union-represented sector of the employer-employee relationship. Arbitration is the creature of an agreement between an employer and a labor organization and its purpose is to minimize labor unrest. The arbitrator's role is to determine whether or not one of the parties to the contract violated that contract by its actions. The NLRB and the EEOC weigh the rights of employers and employees based on federal statutes; the arbitrator establishes the balance based on a private contract.

Generic contract clauses such as "just cause" for discharge cause an arbitrator to examine not only employer practices but also industry practice. What has evolved is a so-called common law of the workplace and this serves as the guideline for rendering decisions.[6]

It is not unusual to have overlap between arbitration, NLRB, and Title VII issues, in that an employee might file an action in all three forums based on the same incident—for example, discharge for alleged theft. While the arbitrator weighs just cause, the Board looks only to whether the employee was engaged in protected concerted activity—was he really discharged because he was a union activist? Despite these differences, the NLRB, under its *Collyer* doctrine,[7] will defer to the arbitrator's decision and find it binding on the Board case if it appears that arbitration will resolve the unfair labor case in a manner compatible with the purposes of the NLRA.

However, in discrimination cases, the federal courts follow the *Gardner-Denver* theory[8] and will not allow an arbitrator's decision to block litigation of the same issue under Title VII. The premise is that the two forums are considering different sets of rights and interests. The arbitrator is evaluating just cause and the court is looking for statutory discrimination. What explains the lack of deference in Title VII cases, while the NLRB seems to favor deference to the arbitrator's ruling? Perhaps it is because the NLRB and arbitrators are pursuing the same objective— labor peace, whereas Title VII involves something completely different— discrimination.

Arbitration decisions are enforceable in federal district court under Section 301 of the Labor Management Relations Act. Courts put a heavy burden on parties opposing enforcement of an arbitration decision, requiring them to prove that the decision was clearly contrary to public policy or outside the scope of the contract.[9] The courts are interested in finality in labor relations disputes, because finality enhances the chances of labor peace. The idea is that the arbitrator might have made a bad decision but the parties should put it behind them and get on with running the business.

Civil Actions

Civil actions are lawsuits that involve harm to individuals, not to the public as in criminal cases. This section only deals with their application to the employment arena. For the most part, these civil actions, which include alleged contract violations and torts, have much broader application than just the employer-employee relationship, and will be treated in detail at several later points. The torts include defamation, assault, battery, false imprisonment, false arrest, and infliction of mental or emotional distress. However, a very limited review of two defamation cases at this time will help show why elements of the law should not be looked at in isolation in the employer-employee context.

In one case an employer issued a written communication to its employees in order to meet its obligations under Title VII. As a consequence of this action, a former employee filed a defamation suit. The former employee had been terminated following an alleged sexual harassment incident and the employer issued a management information bulletin generally referring to the termination and restating its policy against sexual harassment. The court accepted the employer's position that it had a legal duty to restate its policy and was only concerned whether some supervisors might have communicated the contents of the bulletin to non-employees.[10]

A former employee in another case filed an action that combined alleged violations of Title VII with defamation. The contention was that the former employee was constructively discharged because of his race and in the processing of work evaluations management had injured his reputation.[11] The court did not find merit in either contention. But the point is that laws can be intertwined to the point they can become not only multiple parts of a plaintiff's case but also legitimate parts of a business defense.

Wrongful Termination

Historically, employees were terminable at the will of the employer. This is generally referred to as the employment-at-will doctrine. Obvious exceptions to the doctrine included the protections in the NLRA, various pieces of federal and state civil rights legislation prohibiting discrimination, labor contracts that included arbitration clauses with just cause for discharge requirements, and individual employment contracts limiting employer action. Still, a significant number of employees had no legal protection from employer termination action. The idea was that employees could quit employment at any time they wanted, so it was only fair that employers had a reciprocal right to discharge an employee at any time.

Starting in the early 1980s, a growing number of states, either through their courts or legislatures, began to seriously question this doctrine. The interest in protection was likely the product of a number of developments. Those were the days of merger mania and downsizing employment rolls. Numerous law and labor journal articles were written suggesting a rethinking of the old doctrine.[12] One article noted a concern over the absence of job security for over 60 percent of the American workforce.[13] At the same time, employers were responding to increased thefts and drugs in the workplace by intensifying security measures, and some employees were upset by perceived overaggressiveness and wanted to challenge employer decisions.

These new limitations on the old employment-at-will doctrine can be placed into three categories: terminations contrary to public policy, implied contractual rights to employment, and terminations that violate implied agreements of good faith and fair dealing.

Public policy cases are often geared to situations in which an employee is fired because he refuses to violate the law, for example, fix prices, but some relate to non-specific public policies. In *Palmateer v. International Harvester*,[14] a supervisor was fired because he informed local police of possible criminal activity by other employees. The employer defended the termination on the premise that such reporting could jeopardize ongoing security investigations. In the court's judgment, however, it was more important to encourage citizens to report crimes and, accordingly, this employee was protected from retaliatory acts by the employer.

If *Palmateer* represents one end of the public policy range, *Smith v. Calgon Carbon Corporation*[15] might be closer to the middle. In that case, the Third Circuit in interpreting Pennsylvania law commented that the state was concerned that the threat of lawsuits might inhibit employers in making critical judgments on employee conduct. This concern for employer prerogatives led Pennsylvania to narrowly limit the public policy exception. The state would "insist at least that the employee be charged by the employer or by law with the specific responsibility of protecting the public interest and that he or she be acting in that role when engaging in the discharge causing conduct."[16] As far as this court was concerned, the public's interest in harmony and productivity in the workplace prevailed over the public's interest in the employee's right to express his views, particularly where the employee did not have specific responsibility for protecting the public interest in health and safety. The balancing of rights by this court was considerably different from that done by the *Palmateer* court.

Public policy cases often incorporate so-called whistle blower provisions. It has not been uncommon for both the federal government and the states to provide some kind of protection from retaliation for employees who blow the whistle on their employers. In some of these cases recourse is not through the civil courts but through the agency that administers the act involved; for example, Section 11(c) of the Occupational Safety and Health Act provides protection from retaliation for employees who file charges with that agency.

It would be counterproductive at this point to try to establish how all the various states are interpreting public policy. The idea to keep in mind is that there is continuing change as the debate goes on over balancing the rights of otherwise unprotected employees against "the interest of a corporation in commanding the loyalty of its employees to pursue its economic well-being."[17]

Probably the most common exception to the employment-at-will doctrine is the theory of the contract right to continued employment. This exception is not based on the existence of a specific fixed term contract but the accumulation of oral or written data that suggests an employee may only be discharged for cause or some other limiting reasons. Written data often includes handbooks or company policy statements.[18]

The third wrongful termination theory does not require a search for public policy or indicia of a contract for continuing employment. It operates on the premise that in every employment contract there is an implied agreement of good faith and fair dealing. In *Cleary v. American Airlines*,[19] a California court considered a case in which an eighteen-year service employee was discharged for theft. The court decided that the employer could not take away the employee's employment benefits without just cause even though there was no written just-cause termination policy or standard—such a requirement was implied.

It is interesting that while all three of these evolving theories imply some ultimate need for a just- or good-cause termination, there are no fixed formulas for determining what just cause or good cause means. The Ninth Circuit had a heated discussion on the subject in 1990 in a discharge for drug possession case, and the courts might in the future be using the definitions for just cause or good cause that labor arbitrators use. But in these cases juries will be making the decisions and the costs of losing will be considerably higher.[20] Further, there will be a real question whether courts will understand the common law of the workplace that has been established in workplace arbitration.

Since 1980 these theories of unjust termination have spread in one form or another to most of the states. At this time only Delaware, Florida,

Georgia, Louisiana, and Mississippi still appear to strictly follow the old employment-at-will rule.[21] While at one time workplace-related security practices and investigations were only challenged in NLRB, EEOC, and arbitration cases, they are now often the subject matter of litigation in this new and growing area of the law.

For whatever reasons the growth has taken place, it has introduced another element—substantial remedies. Administrative laws and arbitration are normally geared to make-whole remedies, with employers facing liability for return to work and back pay. As noted, Title VII has recently been amended so that a plaintiff may recover up to an additional $300,000 of compensatory and punitive damages. This new wrongful discharge theory has brought with it many of the tort law remedies including compensation for emotional distress, pain and suffering, and punitive damages. Courts continue to shape the elements that enter into these remedies.[22] (A 1988 study indicates that despite average jury awards of $650,000 for wrongful termination, most plaintiffs finally can only expect to pocket $30,000.)[23]

Invasion of Workplace Privacy

The *T.L.O.*, *Ortega*, and *Schowengerdt* cases were reviewed in chapter 1 in order to contrast public and private sector legal exposures. These cases dealt with fourth amendment search and seizure issues, and clearly the element in the balance that most concerned the courts was the individual's right to privacy. This concern by the federal courts over privacy is not limited to search and seizure but is also an element in first, fifth, and ninth amendment cases.[24] But again, the concern has been over government activity.

Some states, either indirectly through constitutional provisions not specifically mentioning privacy or directly through statutes that refer to privacy, have provided protection against invasion of employees' privacy by employers. As in the federal situation, most only cover government action[25] but some extend to the private sector as well.[26]

In addition to these constitutional protections, invasion of privacy, like defamation, has been considered as a tort action for some period of time and has been a standard vehicle for gaining relief.[27] The not-surprising development is that very often the separate privacy tort action becomes merged with the federal or state protections in unjust termination cases. Separating out the various elements that make up violations of contracts, state laws, and public policy becomes very difficult. It has been suggested that this merging of actions was probably created by the recent financial successes of wrongful termination cases. Prior to the 1980s, employees had little interest in or success with separate tort actions for invasion of privacy, but it now makes sense to include them in a wrongful termination action on the possibility that they might help increase damage awards.[28]

Preemption

What happens, then, if an employee is covered by a collective bargaining contract that includes an arbitration clause and he or she seeks relief in state court under a wrongful termination or tort theory? The key word is preemption and the key question is whether this issue is of such federal importance that the states will not be allowed to decide it. If the federal interest outweighs the state interest, the state interest will be preempted by the federal.

In discussing preemption in labor matters, two legal areas have to be considered: the National Labor Relations Act and arbitration. Congress and the courts have given them a dominant role in labor issues in the interest of preserving labor peace. The NLRA covers a wide range of unfair labor practices and arbitration focuses on labor contract violations. In some situations there might be an overlap of interests, in that a contract violation might also be an unfair labor practice. However, for the most part, if a contract violation issue is involved, the tendency is to think in terms of arbitration. So when the issue of federal supremacy arises, it will usually be an NLRB test if it involves non–contract violation subjects and an arbitration test if it involves contract violations.

This idea will be enlarged on in a limited way with a focus on arbitration. Section 301 of the Labor Management Relations Act provides for the enforcement of labor contracts in federal courts. As early as 1957 the Supreme Court saw the potential for conflict between arbitration and state law and concluded that Section 301 authorizes federal courts to fashion a body of federal law for the enforcement of these collective bargaining agreements.[29] The idea again was that it was of major importance to the country to promote peaceable, consistent resolutions of labor disputes. The desire for labor peace was to be the critical factor in the balance of rights—state versus federal.

Over a period of years this principle has received further refinements and in a real sense today if a state tort action can only be resolved by interpreting a collective bargaining contract, the state action will be preempted in favor of arbitration.[30] The reason that one route through the maze of rights and interests is preferred over another is because not all rights and interests are equally valued. Here, and in other situations where Congress has spoken, the federal interest will prevail.

Negligent Hiring and Negligent Continuation of Employment

Considering the possibility of unfair labor practice charges, discrimination charges, wrongful discharge allegations, and tort actions for defamation, invasion of privacy, an so on, it might seem the safe thing to do in the event of employment problems is nothing. Separate and apart from probably ruining a business, doing nothing is not legally safe because of potential tort actions for negligent hiring or negligent continuation of employment.

These tort actions are not children of the 1980s but they certainly came to adulthood during that period of time. First, it should be noted other cases in this section have dealt with balancing the rights of employees and employers, but at this point a third party is introduced into the balance, in the form of customers or users of services.

For many years in cases involving the injury of a third party by an employee, the courts looked to see if the employee was acting within the scope of his or her employment before the employer would be found liable. In some situations people were seriously injured by rape and assault but uncompensated by the employer because the employee who caused the injury was found to be acting on his own. It became apparent in some of those situations that if the employer had made reasonable inquiries before it hired the employee it would have uncovered a record that indicated a propensity for violence. In a way, then, the courts, out of sympathy for injured persons, were looking for a mechanism to compensate them. The premise that developed to permit recovery in these situations was that the employer had an obligation to hire safe employees. Thus was born the tort of negligent hiring.

The courts have not established a fixed formula of inquiry or mandated background investigations in all hiring situations, but have more or less established a sliding scale. First, they determine if the employer owes any duty to the injured person and second they assess whether the employer's lack of inquiry caused the injury.

The first test appears to be geared to the degree of exposure to the public and the nature of the job performed. The more public exposure, the greater the need for inquiries. Obviously bus drivers who have the care of many people during the course of the day and security persons who have access to hotel rooms are high public-exposure occupations.

Causation, the second test, turns on the nature of the exposure. Injuries in a bus accident would probably be attributable to the bus company if the driver had a drunk driving record and the company never bothered to find out about it, but the fact that the company did not know he had not made alimony payments probably would not reasonably connect the company to the accident.[31]

The negligent continuation of employment, negligent training, and negligent supervision theories are just logical extensions of negligent hiring. They become factors after the employment relationship has been established. In short, the liability potential does not end once the pre-hiring investigations have been completed. In discussing negligent training, a federal district court in 1981 noted that, even though there was no case law guidance in the area,

we believe that general negligence concepts would apply. Depending on this particular job in question, it seems incumbent upon the employer to provide a reasonable amount of training to an employee so as to allow him to carry out his duties without endangering himself, fellow employees, or third persons.[32]

In sum, legal exposures shift in the employment relationship depending on whether an employee is organized or unorganized or protected under a civil rights or whistle-blower statute. Even if an employee is unorganized and statutorily unprotected, he or she might have access to state court systems to challenge an employer action on some tort or contract theory. An employer cannot isolate itself from legal exposures by ignoring employee activity because it might be liable to a third party for injuries caused by an employee it should not have hired or should have fired.

PROPERTY OWNER-PROPERTY USER RELATIONSHIPS

The tensions in employer-employee relationships are shared by a major segment of the private security sector. Other pressures and concerns are not equally distributed but to some extent are dictated by the nature of the business. Some businesses introduce new parties—customers, for example—and the law gives certain weight to their interests and puts certain burdens on businesses to accommodate those interests. The legal avenues for challenging management actions in security-related areas are as many and varied as in the employer-employee relationship and they are also in a state of change.

Injuries Caused by Owners

First, though, it is important to identify and analyze those elements that businesses share in common. Generally, all businesses are occupiers of land and more particularly they all have obligations to people that come onto their land. Over a period of many years, courts generally have placed people that come onto land into three categories and have assigned different degrees of duty owed to the people in each category. These classes are often referred to in personal injury cases but the terms carry over into security-related areas. To understand the legal developments that impact security, it is worthwhile to have some appreciation of the scope of these three classes.

The lowest degree of duty is owed to *trespassers*. A trespasser is usually defined as a "person who enters or remains upon land in the possession of another without a privilege to do so."[33] In general, property owners owe no duty to trespassers. In layman's terms, the owner's only duty is to not go out of his way to hurt a trespasser. Or in legal terminology, the owner must refrain from willfully or wantonly injuring the trespasser. As one might expect, there are a number of exceptions, including trespassing children.[34]

Next up the scale is the *licensee*, who is usually considered to be one who comes onto property with consent but for his own purposes. This would include people taking shortcuts, taking cover from the rain, conducting business with employees of the possessor of the property, or soliciting money for charities. A licensee, as does a trespasser, assumes the risk of whatever he may encounter, but the owner must refrain from intentionally injuring the licensee. The owner does not have to give a warning or protection against conditions which are known or should be obvious to the licensee. The licensee receives the use of the property as a gift and accordingly may not look a gift horse in the mouth.[35]

The *invitee* or business visitor is on the highest level of duty owed. These include customers in stores and patrons of restaurants, banks, theaters, and other service establishments. There are two theories used for defining this class. The economic benefit theory looks toward the property possessor having the potential for some kind of profit. It has been used to include people who are shopping in the hope that they find something they want. Courts have extended the coverage to children and friends who accompany customers, people visiting patients in hospitals, and users of restrooms and telephones that are open to the public. The second theory does not require a search for economic benefit but a check to see if there had been acts of encouragement or invitation to enter the property. This would include people going to free concerts, parks, playgrounds, and the like.

The owner-occupier is not an insurer of the safety of invitees and his or her duty is to exercise reasonable care for their protection. The owner-occupier must take care not to injure invitees or visitors by negligent acts and must warn them of known hidden dangers.

Some states have attempted to merge these three categories into one and assign the same duties for all. Other states have merged the licensee and invitee categories and have assigned the same common duties of reasonable care. The changes took place during the 1960s and 1970s but at present most states still make decisions based upon the traditional categories.[36] It is only intended to introduce the concepts of trespassers, licensees, and invitees at this point. The duties owed to persons entering onto land play a major role in private security and will be discussed at numerous points throughout this publication.

Injury Caused by Criminal Activity of a Third Party

For many years it was generally understood that property owners had no duty to protect people on their property from the criminal acts of third parties. This approach was probably based on the belief that the government had the duty of protecting citizens. The costs of businesses providing appropriate protection would be considerable, and foreseeing criminal activity and maintaining the degree of security necessary to offset it would be very difficult burdens.[37]

As with most legal premises, this one of no duty had exceptions. A duty could arise if there were special relationships or special circumstances. Special relationships included situations in which a party entrusted himself to the protection of another and relied on that person to provide a place of safety. For a long period of time this extended to only a few relationships such as common carriers and passengers, innkeepers and guests, and sometimes schools and students. It is of interest that the latter group, at least in some jurisdictions, might no longer include college students because since the 1960s they have been granted more independence and have been under less control;[38] more about that later. Special circumstances include those situations in which a known dangerous or violent individual is present or where an individual has conducted himself so as to indicate the existence of a dangerous situation and there is sufficient time to prevent injury.[39]

Starting in the 1960s, the old formulas did not seem to be working. Crime moved to places like shopping malls and parking lots and the victims did not seem to fit into either the special relationship or special circumstances categories. If property owners did not owe these victims a duty, they could not be found to owe them any damages. Certainly the criminals were not paying for the injuries they caused, and many courts became concerned that innocent victims were left uncompensated for their injuries.

Some states passed laws extending protection to school children,[40] and others developed new case law approaches to solving the duty problem. At one time, courts did not consider the issue of foreseeability of a criminal event until they found a duty to protect;[41] foreseeability was an element in determining whether or not the duty had been breached. To extend liability, some jurisdictions introduced foreseeability as an element in or the sole means of establishing a duty to protect. Foreseeability may be geared to prior similar incidents or to the totality of the circumstances.[42] Other routes have also been found in order to establish a duty; for example, a Delaware court found that incidents of criminal activity provided a duty to foresee specific criminal conduct.[43] In a college rape case a Massachusetts court found a duty "in existing social values and customs."[44]

Once the legal duty has been established, the next step is to determine whether or not the property owner was negligent in meeting that duty. Inquiry is made into the level and kinds of crimes committed in the area and the security techniques that were applied in trying to protect patrons, customers, students, or others to whom a duty was owed. Juries decide whether or not enough was done.

Commentators have questioned the value to society of the old limited duty or no duty approach and have noted the confusion caused by the growing differences in standards applied by courts. Their proposals to solve the problem invariably put more of an economic burden on property owners to help defeat crime. The idea is that the burden has to go somewhere and property owners are in the best position to accept it.[45]

These proposals stop short of putting private security in the law enforcement business but strongly suggest there is a need for closer cooperation between these two groups. Cooperation, of course, does not mean assuming each other's roles.

Protection of Property

While providing for the protection of people is a very important part of the private security person's role, he or she obviously also has to be concerned about protecting property. In terms of value, the law does not put property on the same level as people, and laws are adjusted accordingly. An assault in defense of property will not be measured in the same way as an assault in defense of a person. Still, the law adjusts to societal changes and with the increase in thefts from stores, states have passed shoplifting statutes to better protect merchants. Merchants, then, are in a better position legally to protect their property but of course they have more exposure than the usual business location.

If an employer is faced with employees picketing on its property, it is reasonable to assume that the matter can be handled through the National Labor Relations Board. But then again, if the picketing turns violent, it will be a matter for local police. If similar picketing is carried out by non-employee demonstrators in the furtherance of some social interest, will the same rules apply? Who will make the judgments? Of course if it is not a labor matter it will not be the NLRB; and if it is not a constitutionally based matter it will not be of interest to the federal government. But it could involve a state constitutional issue or it could be just a garden-variety trespass case. These variables are discussed at length in chapters 4, 6, 7, and 8 but the general theme is that employees have more rights than trespassers, licensees, and invitees, and the federal constitution does not apply to the private sector even if it involves what appears to be some public places such as shopping malls. This latter generalization, of course, does not cover the whole subject because, as noted, there is a possibility that a state constitutional provision might be applicable. For example, the California constitution extends the protections for free speech to the private sector.[46]

It seems easy enough to define property while thinking in terms of tangible land or materials. But is an idea, or some other intangible, considered to be property? And if so, what rights exist to protect them? For example, trade secrets can be considered to be intellectual property, and the real measure of their value is the degree of care the owner takes in protecting them. The courts in trade secret cases are underwhelmed with the argument that the best way to provide protection is hide them in plain sight.[47]

Some things such as the intangible right to honest and faithful service by employees do not measure up to being property, but under certain circumstances they can be protected. The protection is offered under federal mail and wire fraud statutes and it is available because the federal government does not want its services to be used as a vehicle in carrying out a scheme to defraud.[48] The focus, then, is more on the misuse of the government than it is on defining and protecting property.

STATUTORY VIOLATIONS INVOLVING IMPRISONMENT OR MONETARY REMEDIES

It is evident that private security activity can be challenged and assisted in a number of forums and under a number of different theories. At the same time it has to be kept in mind that at least two potential security-related investigative techniques can trigger either imprisonment or monetary fines as remedies: electronic eavesdropping and use of the polygraph.

Electronic Surveillance

The average person does not have too much trouble tolerating the use of physical surveillance to gain evidence. There is not much problem, either, with accepting the use of personally overheard conversations. But once electronic devices are introduced into the process of gathering information, the general public gets its back up. In 1968 Congress passed the Omnibus Crime Control and Safe Streets Act, which included restrictions on interception of conversations by wire and electronics.[49]

This act, among other things, makes it a crime to intercept telephone conversations unless one party to the conversations has given consent. Individuals violating the statute are subject to criminal penalties of up to five years in prison and fines up to $250,000. Organizations can be fined up to $500,000.[50] Recovery in civil actions is also permitted. Many states have adopted similar laws.[51] Pennsylvania, for example, is even more stringent, requiring all parties to a conversation to give consent.[52]

At one time these statutes were of primary concern to those security people taping conversations in kickback, extortion, and drug abuse cases. However, the recent surge of interest in workplace monitoring has been a reaction to businesses taking advantage of new, sophisticated electronic technology in keeping track of workplace activity. Computers allow employers to better gauge productivity and assure the proper use of telephone sales techniques. Employees, clearly concerned about the growth of "big brother," have caused state and federal legislatures to seriously consider curbing perceived incursions into areas of privacy. Many state and federal legislative sessions regularly consider new bills addressing the subject.[53] Only time will tell how the legislatures and courts will balance management's interest in becoming more competitive and employees' interest to be freed from the stresses these new procedures create.

Polygraph

The intrusion of the polygraph into peoples' minds has always caused some apprehension on the part of the general public. This apprehension increased as businesses made more and more use of the polygraph in screening applicants and solving workplace problems. Management, of course, was only reacting to the acceleration of thefts and drug use in the workplace during the 1970s and 1980s. Push finally came to shove, and the Employee Polygraph Protection Act of 1988 was enacted, generally banning the use of all lie detector tests by private employers. Lie detectors were defined to include polygraphs, deceptographs, voice stress analyzers, psychological stress evaluators, and any other similar device (whether mechanical or electrical) that is used for the purpose of rendering a diagnostic opinion regarding the honesty or dishonesty of an individual. Certain exceptions were carved out for the polygraph but it was banned in the use of applicant screening except in the security and drug industries. Further, the act placed critical restrictions on its use with present employees. For example, if there is an ongoing theft investigation, a polygraph exam may be given if there is reasonable suspicion of guilt, but the results of the test cannot on their own justify discharge.[54]

This, of course, was not the first piece of legislation involving the use of polygraphs. About twenty-six states and the District of Columbia had already seriously restricted their use. The Delaware statute is fairly representative; it prohibits requiring, requesting, or suggesting an employee or prospective employee take a polygraph examination as a condition of employment. The federal Employee Polygraph Protection Act does not negate these more restrictive state statutes.[55]

The Federal Polygraph Act provides for civil penalties up to $10,000 for violations but does not indicate whether it preempts any separate civil actions. It has to be kept in mind that, like the Omnibus Crime Bill, some state restrictions on polygraph use are criminal in nature and provide for fines and imprisonment.

OBSERVATIONS

It was the intent of this chapter to describe the wide range of legal exposures faced by private security people and the large number of paths that lead through the legal maze. At this point, they may seen disjointed, overlapping, contradictory, and unrelated. Trying to understand and harmonize the different pieces is a necessary step to making good decisions. The concept, again, is that security problems cannot be solved by focusing on a single issue of law. There are just too many that might apply. Once a general feel for the law has been acquired, areas of specific concern may be targeted. But even then there is a reasonable chance that more than one area of the law will be involved in coming up with answers.

A suggested approach for coming to grips with these multi-faceted issues is to first identify the players, determine what they are trying to do, consider what rights and duties are in the balance, and then create a plan of action. For example, appropriate questions could be: Is the security person or problem-solver employed by a retail store, a hotel, an industrial plant? Is property involved, and if so, what kind—real, personal, intangible? Who are the other people involved in the problem—employees, customers, trespassers, law enforcement agents? If they are employees, are they represented by a union or are they in a protected class?

Once these preliminary inquiries have been answered, attention can be given to some of the specific areas of the law and observations can be made as to what legal forums are involved, what rights are being balanced, and what factors enter into the balancing. In attempting to work through the maze by starting with security-related problems, identifying the players, and then examining applicable laws, some legal issues, such as defamation and privacy, will be discussed at several different points and not just one. This approach might not make it possible to put tidy bows on one area of the law before moving on to the next but it will emphasize the multi-sided legal aspects of private security problem-solving.

NOTES

1. 42 U.S.C. Sec. 1981.
2. Civil Rights Act of 1991, 42 USC 1981, Prohibition Against All Racial Discrimination in the Making and Enforcement of Contracts.
3. *Carpenters v. Scott*, 463 U.S. 825 (1983).
4. 408 U.S. 88 (1971).
5. K. Gormley, *Private Conspiracies and the Constitution*, 64 Tex. L. Rev. 527 (1985); Case comment, *Private Conspiracies to Violate Civil Rights*, 90 Harv. L. Rev. 1721 (1977); note, *The Class-Based Animus Requirements of 42 U.S.C. §1985 (c)*, 64 Minn. L. Rev. 635 (1980).
6. F. Elkouri & E. Elkouri, *How Arbitration Works* (4th ed. 1985).
7. *Collyer Insulated Wire*, 192 N.L.R.B. 837 (1971).
8. *Alexander v. Gardner-Denver Co.*, 415 U.S. 36 (1974).
9. *United Paperworkers v. Misco Inc.*, 484 U.S. 29 (1987).
10. *Garziano v. E. I. du Pont*, 818 F.2d 380 (5th Cir. 1987).
11. *Boze v. Branstetter*, 912 F.2d 801 (5th Cir. 1990).

12. J. De Guiseppe, Jr., *The Effect of the Employment-At-Will Rule in Employee Rights to Job Security and Fringe Benefits*, 10 Fordham Urb. L.J. 1(1981); T. Olsen, *Wrongful Discharge Claims Raised by At-Will-Employees, A New Legal Concern*, 32 Lab. L.J. 265 (1981); Note, *Protecting Employees-At-Will Against Wrongful Discharge: The Public Policy Exception*, 96 Harv. L. Rev. 1931 (1983).

13. *Reforming At-Will Employment Law: A Model Statute* 16 J. L. Reforms 389, 394 (1983).

14. 85 Ill. 2d 124, 421 N.E.2d 876 (1981).

15. 917 F.2d 1338 (3rd Cir. 1990).

16. 917 F.2d 1338, 1345.

17. *Novosel v. Nationwide Ins. Co.*, 721 F.2d 894, 903 (3rd Cir. 1983).

18. *Foley v. Interactive Data Corporation*, 47 Cal. 3d 654, 765 P.2d 373 (1988).

19. III Cal. App. 3d 443, 168 Cal. Rptr. 722 (1980).

20. Dertouzos, Holland, & Ebener, *The Legal and Economic Consequences of Wrongful Termination* 25 (1988).

21. H. Perritt, Jr., *Employee Dismissal Law and Practice* Sec. 1.12: Current Status of the Employment-At-Will Rule in 50 States (2d ed. 1987).

22. *Foley v. Interactive Data Corporation*, 47 Cal.3d 654, 765 P.2d 373 (1988).

23. J. Dertouzos, E. Holland, P. Ebener, *The Legal and Economic Consequences of Wrongful Termination* 44 (1988).

24. *Griswold*, 381 U.S. 479 (1965).

25. *Luedtke v. Nabors Alaska Drilling*, 768 P.2d 1123 (Alaska 1989).

26. *Porten v. University of San Francisco*, 64 Cal. App. 825, 134 Cal. Rptr. 839 (1976).

27. 62 Am. Jur. 2d Premises Liability, I (1990) Sec. 1–4.

28. Dertouzos, Holland, & Ebener, *Legal and Economic Consequences* 10 (1988).

29. *Textile Workers v. Lincoln Mills*, 353 U.S. 448 (1957).

30. *Lingle v. Norge Division of Magic Chef Inc.*, 486 U.S. 399 (1988); *Stikes v. Chevron USA, Inc.*, 914 F.2d 1265 (9th Cir. 1990), *cert. denied*, 114 L. ed. 2d 101 (1991).

31. Minuti, *Employer Liability Under the Doctrine of Negligent Hiring*, 13 Del. J. Corp. L. 501–532 (1988); Gregory, *Reducing the Risk of Negligence in Hiring* 14 Employee Rel. L.J. 31 (Summer 1988).

32. *Focke v. United States*, 597 F. Supp. 1325, 1341 (1982).

33. *Restatement (Second) of Torts* Sec. 329, 333–339 (1965).

34. *Restatement (Second) of Torts* Sec. 330, 341, 342 (1965).

35. W. Page Keeton, et al., *Prosser & Keeton On the Law of Torts* Sec. 58, pp. 393, 394, Sec. 60, pp. 412, 413 (1971).

36. Keeton, et al., *Prosser & Keeton*, Secs. 61, 62, pp. 419–434.

37. Yelonsky, *Business Inviters Duty to Protect Invitees from Criminal Acts*, 134 U. Pa. L. Rev. 883, 889 (1986); Bazyler, *The Duty to Provide Adequate Protection: Landowner's Liability For Failure to Protect Patrons from Criminal Attack*, 21 Ariz. L. Rev. 727 (1979); *Goldberg v. Housing Authority of Newark*, 38 N.J. 578, 186 A.2d 291 (1962).

38. *Meadows v. Freedman R.R. Salvage Warehouse*, 655 S.W.2d 718 (Mo. App. 1983); *Rabel v. Illinois Wesleyan University*, 161 Ill. App.3d 348, 514 N.E.2d 552 (1987); *Mullins v. Pine Manor College*, 389 Mass. 47, 449 N.E.2d 331, 335 (Mass. 1983).

39. *Pizzuro v. First North County Bank & Trust Co.*, 545 S.W.2d 348 (Mo. App. 1976).

40. *Chavez v. Tolleson Elementary School District*, 122 Ariz. 477, 595 P.2d 1017 (1979).

41. *Goldberg v. Housing Authority* 38 N.J. 578, 186 A.2d 291.

42. *Isaacs v. Huntington Memorial Hospital*, 38 Cal.3d 112, 695 P.2d 653, 211 Cal. Rptr. 356 (1985); Annot., 49 A.L.R. 4th 1257, *Parking Lot, Duty Owed to Patron*.

43. *Jardel Co. v. Hughes*, 523 A.2d 518 (1987), *Craig v. AAR Realty Corp.*, 576 A.2d 688 (1989).

44. *Mullins v. Pine Manor*, 389 Mass. at 51, 449 N.E.2d at 335.

45. *Bazyler, The Duty to Provide Adequate Protection, Yelonsky, Business Inviters Duty.*

46. *Prune Yard Shopping Center v. Robbins*, 447 U.S. 74 (1980).

47. *J.T. Healy & Son, Inc. v. Murphy & Son, Inc.*, 357 Mass. 728, 260 N.E.2d 723 (1970).

48. *McNally v. United States*, 483 U.S. 350 (1987); 18 U.S.C. Sec. 1341, 1343, 1346.

49. Omnibus Crime Bill and Safe Streets Act of 1968 (18 U.S.C. Sec. 2510); Annot. Fed., 67 A.L.R. 429, *Interception of Telecommunication* (1984).

50. 18 U.S.C. Sec. 2510–2521.

51. N.Y. Penal Law, Sec. 250.05; McKinney (1988); *United States v. Vespe*, 389 F. Supp. 1359 (D. Del. 1975).

52. 18 Pa. Cons. Stat. Ann. Sec. 5725 aff'd, 520 F.2d 1369 (3rd Cir. 1975); *Barr v. Arco Chemical Corp.*, 529 F. Supp. 1277 (1982).

53. *House Bill Would Curb Employee Monitoring, Individual Employment Rights*, Individual Employment Rights (BNA), May 9, 1989; *9–5 Report on Electronic Surveillance Details Stories of Monitored Workers*, Daily Labor Report, February 15, 1990, 4–12; *Curbs Proposed on Electronic Monitoring*, 135 Labor Relations Reporter 229, October 22, 1990; Senate Bill 2164, Privacy for Consumers and Workers Act, introduced by Sen. Paul Simon, February 22, 1990; Susser, *Electronic Monitoring in the Private Sector: How Closely Should Employers Supervise Their Workers*, 13 Employee Rel. L.J. 575 (1988).

54. *Employee Polygraph Protection Act of 1988*, Law & Explanation Labor Law Reports, No. 81, July 15, 1988.

55. I. Shepard & R. Dustin, *Thieves at Work: An Employer's Guide to Combating Workplace Dishonesty* 179–213 (1988); Fitzpatrick, *Polygraph Testing of Employees in Private Industry*, Fed. B. News and J., March 4, 1988; Del. Code Ann. tit. 19, Sec. 704; *Lie Detector Tests*, Daily Labor Reports, January 14, 1983.

3

Security-Related Matters in Collective Bargaining

Understanding the origins of the National Labor Relations Act is necessary in order to understand how it fits in with other areas of the law. During the 1930s, Congress grew concerned with labor turmoil that was having an adverse effect on the general public. In its judgment, labor peace could only be brought about if labor was put on an equal footing with management. As Congress saw it, this balance could be best achieved through fostering collective bargaining. The key word is *collective*, because it was believed that effective employee bargaining strength could only be achieved through the group and not the individual. This is a cornerstone in labor law thinking and distinguishes it from many other areas of the law that emphasize the individual.

The NLRA was passed with these ideas in mind and it is the role of the NLRB, as pointed out in chapter 2, to balance the rights of employees to bargain collectively with the rights of employers to run an efficient business. In the process of discussing the application of the NLRA to security issues, there will be some comment on drug programs, gate and locker searches, interrogations, surveillance, polygraph use, and similar issues, but these issues will be viewed only in connection with the National Labor Relations Act.

The heart and soul of the NLRA is Section 7. Under that section, employees are given the "right to self organization, to form, join or assist labor organizations, to bargain collectively through representatives of their own choosing, and to engage in other concerted activities for the purpose of collective bargaining or other material aid or protection." They also are given the right to refrain from many of these activities. These rights are implemented and protected through Board-conducted elections and through unfair labor practice charges investigated by the Board.

REPRESENTATION ISSUES

A key element in the representation process is the establishment of appropriate collective bargaining units. There are many variables in the types of employees that will be included in or excluded from a given bargaining unit. For example, plant clerical workers may either be included in or excluded from production and maintenance units, depending on their community of interest. But one thing is certain: guards will not be included in any unit but their own. Guards have received special attention under the NLRA. Under Section 9(b)(3), the NLRB is precluded from finding a bargaining unit appropriate if it "includes, together with other employees, any individual employed as a guard to enforce against employees and other persons rules to protect property of the employer or to protect the safety of persons on the employer's premises." Further, "no labor organization shall be certified as the representative of employees in a bargaining unit of guards if such organization admits to membership, or is affiliated directly or indirectly with an organization which admits to membership, employees other than guards."

Congress' concern in enacting 9(b)(3) was to avoid the possibility of divided loyalty on the part of plant protection employees during times of labor unrest. The idea was to provide the employer with a core of security people it could count on during strikes and other employee-related strife. Although Section 9(b)(3) has been a part of the act since 1947, the Board and the courts are still fighting over its meaning.

Definition of Guards

The essential element in the definition of *guard* is that he or she is one who enforces the employer's rules against employees and others, such as visitors. The question is whether this means all rules or just security rules. The Board in a 1990 case took the position that since firefighters enforced only fire- and safety-related rules that they were not guards.[1] Meanwhile, the Eighth Circuit in a 1987 case took a broader position and said that the potential for divided loyalty is not limited to security or police-type rule enforcers but instead "exists whenever any employee is invested with rule enforcement obligations in relation to his co-workers."[2] In a real sense, the question of when a guard is a guard is not completely answered.

As the Board ponders inclusions and exclusions it is not concerned with names or titles, and as a consequence, from time to time employees called boiler tenders, watchmen, or janitors are found to be guards. Neither is the Board concerned about incidentals such as uniforms. As already noted, the Board focuses on duties and more specifically the enforcement of employer rules. If the employee's job is to refuse entry to visitors who are not properly identified, the employee is a guard. If the employee has these duties as a regular part of his or her employment, the fact that he or she is also engaged in non-guard duties will not deter the Board from finding guard status.[3]

In *Defender Security and Investigation Services Inc.* the Board placed two undercover agents in a security guard unit. The company was engaged in the business of providing guards and other security and investigative services. Two on-premises undercover investigators were frequently retained by clients experiencing property damages or thefts, in the interest of detecting which customers or employees were responsible. They worked assignments in retail and clothing stores as well as manufacturing plants and construction sites. The Board noted that "whatever minor differences may exist between the uniformed guards and the on-premises undercover investigators in terms of attire and method of compensation do not, in our opinion, destroy the community of interest which they otherwise share by virtue of their common job function, namely, the protection and security of the client's property."[4]

As another example of determining unit placement, in *Burns Security Systems, Inc.,*[5] the Board included the job category "complaints and survey sergeants" in a guard unit. These employees were involved in investigating accidents, break-ins, and thefts. They engaged in stakeouts, used electronic devices, and checked for fingerprints. The Board found that their duties were part and parcel of the statutorily described function of enforcement of rules to protect property and safety of persons.

Even if all the questions on unit placement are put to rest, there still might be a concern over what kind of labor organization can represent guards. In 1988 the Eleventh Circuit refused to enforce an NLRB finding that an appropriate guard unit could be represented by a guard union.[6] The court's decision was based on the belief that since the guard union was affiliated with a non-guard union, there was a potential for conflict between loyalty to the employer and fidelity to the non-guard union. In the court's judgment, there did not have to be actual control of one over the other. It should be kept in mind that the representation of guards by a non-guard union is not illegal, but the employer has no legal obligation to bargain with it.

The Board also determines the size of bargaining units, that is, whether a unit will include multiple locations, a single location, be statewide or metropolitan area-wide, an so forth. The Board considers a number of factors in making these decisions such as common supervision, common working conditions, interchange of personnel, bargaining history, and geographical proximity. The ultimate finding is based upon the extent of community of interest. A union does not have to ask for the most appropriate unit—just one that is appropriate.[7]

Definition of Supervisor

Supervisors are also excluded from bargaining units, but unlike guards they are excluded by the Board from all units. Guards are considered to be employees under the NLRA and have the act's protections. Supervisors are not considered to be employees and accordingly are unprotected. *Supervisor* is defined in Section 2(11) of the act as

any individual having authority, in the interest of the employer, to hire, transfer, suspend, layoff, recall, promote, discharge, assign, reward or discipline other employees, or responsibly to direct them, or to adjust their grievances, or effectively to recommend such action, if in connection with the foregoing the exercise of such authority is not of a merely routine or clerical nature, but requires the use of independent judgment.

Again, there isn't much in a name. A "security supervisor" was found not to be a supervisor because of the routine nature of the job, which did not require the use of independent judgment.[8] As noted, the "sergeants" in the *Burns* case were not excluded from the bargaining unit.[9] In a 1976 *Wackenhut* case, a lieutenant was found to be a supervisor because he responsibly directed employees in the course of their duties.[10] The emphasis, again, is on duties.

Election Conduct

In the Board's judgment, its most important function is to carry out elections. These elections are of such consequence the Board requires that they be conducted under laboratory conditions. If these conditions are violated, the Board will rerun the election or if the conduct is heinous enough, will issue a bargaining order without benefit of another election.[11]

ABC Liquors Inc.[12] illustrates aggravated election conduct by an employer and the Board's treatment of such conduct. Following receipt of a petition for election, the employer hired an undercover agent to report on two things, union activities and thievery. It apparently intended to use theft activity as a means to eliminate union activists. Separate and apart from the undercover agents' activities, the employer questioned employees about signing authorization cards and attending union meetings, and threatened employees with discharge if they supported the union. Following a recitation of the violative conduct engaged in by the employer, including surveilling employees, the Board ordered the employer to cease and desist from such activity and to post a notice identifying its misconduct, and directed a second election. The employer's conduct in *ABC Liquors* was typical of the 1930s; today the Board is normally faced with more sophisticated conduct, but the interests and concerns are still the same.

UNFAIR LABOR PRACTICES

Concerted Activities

Before getting into specific unfair labor practices, it should be pointed out that while the majority of Board cases involve union activity, the Board also has a broader interest. Section 7 of the Act concerns "concerted activities for . . . mutual aid or protection." There has been a long history of cases that concluded that this provision covered non-union employees who were acting together to present a grievance, threaten a strike, engage in a work stoppage, or other concerted activities.[13] These cases involved employees whose activities were pointed toward or prepared for some kind of group action.

A real question developed as to how far this concerted activity theory could be carried to protect individual employees. Would it cover an unorganized employee who was discharged for complaining on his own about the lack of safety on his truck? After considerable litigation, the Board finally said no.[14] The Board stated that it had sympathy for the employee but pointed out that the NLRB was not the forum for all injustices of the workplace. The Board determined that the individual employee's action was so remotely related to the activities of other employees that it did not amount to concerted activity. The employee might have a legal cause of action—some kind of public policy, state law, or whistle-blower provision might apply—but it was not within the Board's province. For the Board, the bottom line is that the actions of an individual employee must be linked to the actions of other employees before it will have an interest.

A non-union case somewhat on point involved a security guard who was discharged because he gave a statement relating to a security incident to a discharged employee of a contractor.[15] The statement was to be used in that employee's grievance hearing. The security guard had made a report noting that the contractor employee appeared to be drinking but nothing was said in the report about the possession of alcohol. The security guard's employer, a hospital, apparently paraphrased the report and led the contractor to believe the employee had alcohol in his possession. The guard tried to correct the misconception by going to his superior, but nothing was done about it. At the contractor employee's request, the guard gave him a statement explaining what had really happened. Without the guard's knowledge, the statement was used in the employee's grievance hearing. The hospital discharged the guard for several reasons but relied primarily on a violation of a rule prohibiting discussion of reports outside the safety and security department.

The court found that the guard had participated in concerted activity in that he had given mutual aid in a grievance proceeding. It further found that even though in this mixed-motive case the guard violated a rule, he was in fact fired because his superiors were annoyed and embarrassed that he had given another employee a statement that undermined the contractor's position in a union grievance. As far as the court was concerned, the guard would not have been fired for the rule violation if the statement had not been used in the grievance procedure.

While this case might represent a questionable stretch of the definition of concerted activity, the point is still clear: non-union employees can be protected by the National Labor Relations Act. Further, this is a good example to show that employers, such as the hospital, should not get so deeply involved in the employment decisions of others, such as the contractor. The owner of property can insure observance of its rules by contractor employees by advising the contractor that it no longer wants the problem employee on the premises. It is up to the contractor then to decide whether it places the employee on another job or discharges him. It is the contractor's decision. It was the hospital's involvement in the contractor's employment decision that convinced the court that there was a violation.

The discussion of the employer's needs for undivided loyalty by guards might create a false impression that guards are always management's agents and their rights will be less protected than the rights of other employees. Many years ago, in 1949, the NLRB made it clear that guards were not so closely allied with management that they could not be represented in collective bargaining.[16] As noted in the *Faulkner Hospital* case, they do, unlike supervisors, receive protection under the NLRA.

Another case demonstrating this legal protection of guards' employment rights involves a store detective whose primary responsibilities were detecting and apprehending shoplifters, who was discharged for refusing to do what the Board calls "struck work."[17] The store detectives were unorganized but other non-guard employees were not only organized but appeared to be going out on strike over a contract. The store detective was told to report to a store that it was assumed was going to be picketed and do non-guard work—pack meat. He refused to report and was discharged. The Board traditionally considers even a single employee to be protected from discharge for not crossing a co-workers' picket line. In this case, the Board did not hesitate in extending the same protection to the store detective. While the Board did not comment on the language and background of Section 9(b)(3), the administrative law judge stated that although that section imposes certain representation limitations on guards, he was not aware of any authority that limited their right to strike.

The Board typically protects these sympathy strikers from discharge but appreciates that if they refuse assignments they can be replaced, not discharged. This replacement feature gives the employer a mechanism for continuing to run its business.

Interference with Protected Activities

The discussion on concerted activities necessarily leads to the subject of protected activities. It is not enough that an activity be concerted to get NLRB attention; it also has to be the kind of activity that is protected by the National Labor Relations Act. For example, three employees acting together may steal from the workplace, and though it is concerted activity, it certainly is not protected. Protected activities must be related to Section 7 rights such as organizing employees, processing grievances, and filing charges. These are the types of activities the Board protects in the cases considered under the concerted activity section of the NLRA.

Interference by employers can include polling employees about their union interests, threatening or discharging them because of their union activities, or surveilling them to determine the extent of their union sympathies. Activity of this kind is usually considered in violation of Section 8(a)(1) of the act and in the case of a discharge it is covered by Section 8(a)(3).

Resolving these issues often requires the Board to balance rights. The use of a camera in a picket line situation is a good example. The Board knows that picket lines can lead to blocking entrances or other misconduct and appreciates that employers are in a better position to get needed relief if they have pictures of the activity. At the same time, the Board believes that the presence of cameras is intimidating to some employees and the use of cameras might keep them from exercising their rights. As a consequence, the Board frowns on taking pictures of peaceful employee pickets. Care has to be taken by security people in order to avoid making unjustified incursions into protected areas.[18]

A *Phoenix Newspapers* case highlights the concern the Board and the courts have in protecting employees involved in concerted activity from employer retaliation.[19] A union filed an unfair labor practice charge against the employer and in a bulletin notifying its membership of its action commented that the employer had tapped the telephone of at least one union officer. The employer in turn filed a lawsuit for libel, conspiracy, and tortious interference with business relationships. The Board was then called upon to decide whether the employer's filing of the lawsuit constituted a violation of the NLRA. It decided that it did.

The Board followed a two-prong test set up earlier by the Supreme Court in *Bill Johnson's Restaurant v. NLRB*:[20] Was it a meritless suit, and was it for retaliatory purposes? As to point one, the parties had effectively settled the suit after the court had dismissed the complaint on a motion for summary judgment and the employer did not appeal the court's decision. As far as the Board was concerned, this proved the employer's action was meritless. On the second point the Board noted that the employer sought large punitive damages from the union and its employee-members and officers because they were responsible for the communication related to the unfair labor practice charge that they in good faith felt had been committed. As far as the Board was concerned, the lawsuit was filed in retaliation for this exercise of a legitimate right. The Board did not believe that the union's conduct was so reckless or maliciously untrue as to lose the protection of the NLRA. The moral is that the Board does not want employees frightened out of engaging in concerted activity.

Interference and discharge cases sometimes raise a mixed-motive issue. The discharged employee contends he was fired because of his or her activity and the employer contends that the discharge took place because of a rule violation. In such cases the Board applies a so-called *Wright Line* test.[21] It amounts to a "but for" rule: But for the union activity would the employee have been fired? In some situations it might be that the employee did violate a rule but no one had ever been fired for such activity. The purpose, of course, is to defeat contrived employer excuses.

Collective Bargaining Obligations

It is of considerable importance that security people at unionized locations have some knowledge of management's collective bargaining obligations as they can relate to many of their activities.

To meet their bargaining obligations and not commit an unfair labor practice, employers must confer in good faith with respect to wages, hours, and other terms and conditions of employment. However, these obligations do not compel either party to agree to a proposal or require the making of a concession. These bargaining obligations are set out in Sections 8(a)(5) and 8(d) of the National Labor Relations Act.

While it might be relatively easy to determine the meaning of wages and hours, it is often difficult to determine what constitutes "other terms and conditions of employment." For a long time many employers believed that this phrase covered everything that could happen at the workplace and that they could not implement any changes without the benefit of bargaining. Today the phrase is interpreted as requiring bargaining on those things that have a direct effect on the employment relationship and a material and significant impact on the terms and conditions of employment.[22]

The intent of these comments is to set out some specific examples of mandatory subjects of collective bargaining, but they will also cover other elements of the bargaining obligation, such as requests for information. Again, it should be kept in mind that the NLRB deals with conditions of employment and concerted activity. For example, few of its cases speak directly to privacy because privacy is an individual right and the Board is interested in the rights of the group. It is these group rights that will be in the balance in the following cases.

In the *Medicenter* case,[23] during a period of time that its union employees were engaged in picketing activity, a hospital and extended care facility suffered repeated acts of vandalism. Police were called, guards hired, and other security measures implemented but the vandalism continued. Somewhat in desperation, management decided to implement polygraph testing for all employees and posted a notice to that effect. Taking the test was made a condition of continued employment. Management did not directly notify the union of its intentions but it was evident the union knew about it and took an adamant position in opposition to the plans. The examinations went forward and thirty-eight people who refused to take the test were discharged. Unfair labor charges were filed.

The Board decided that polygraph testing was a mandatory subject of collective bargaining, adopting the administrative law judge's (ALJ's) position that a change in the method by which the employer investigated suspected employee misconduct was a change in the terms and conditions of employment at the hospital. The ALJ noted that prior investigations involved the application of human skill, judgment, and experience, using interrogations and other information-gathering methods. Now the employer "was introducing a chart based on variations in bodily functions, which has never been considered sufficiently trustworthy to be deemed probative in criminal proceedings."[24]

The comments are reasonably reflective of the attitude of many legal forums toward polygraph tests. They just aren't well liked. The case was likened to cases in which the Board found that requiring tardy and absentee employees to take physical examinations was a condition of employment, and the ALJ noted that the Board had held the mere change from a system of oral warnings to one of written warnings was a mandatory bargaining subject. The ALJ concluded that since a penalty for refusing to take the test—discharge—was included within the change in policy, the total package, test and penalty, was clearly a mandatory subject for collective bargaining.

However, after making this finding, the ALJ, with Board agreement, decided that there was not a violation. Even though the employer had not formally notified the union of its plan, the union did find out about it and told the employer there was no way it could agree. In the Board's judgment, the employer was not obligated to make a formal proposal to the union if the union already knew of its plans. Once the union knew of the plan, the burden shifted to it to engage in bargaining. Sitting back and complaining were not enough to meet its burden; since the union chose not to engage in discussions with the employer, the employer could go forward and implement its plan without violating its bargaining obligation. As stated previously, *agreement* is not the key to the bargaining process; the employer can implement a proposed change once it has offered to meet and discuss the subject with the union and the bargaining had led to an impasse or deadlock and no further bargaining would be fruitful.[25]

The Board subsequently built on this precedent in a 1989 drug and alcohol program case, *Johnson-Bateman*.[26] The employer had a rule against using or possessing alcohol on company premises and against reporting for work while under the influence of alcohol or drugs. Violators were subject to discipline. The employer was concerned about an increasing number of workplace accidents and felt that alcohol or drug use might be at the bottom of it. Accordingly, it implemented a policy that anyone requiring medical treatment for work injuries would have to be tested for drugs and alcohol. The test requirement was made a condition of employment. No bargaining took place.

The Board found that the tests were germane to the working environment. It applied Supreme Court–approved thinking and concluded that testing was "not among those managerial decisions which lie at the core of entrepreneurial control."[27] These are the kinds of things that are outside the bargaining arena, and this phrase is normally construed to cover such fundamental business activities as the commitment of investment capital or the basic scope of the enterprise. This is not as limiting as it might seem, because courts have also said that to be a mandatory bargaining subject, there must be a direct effect on the employment relationship and a material and significant impact on the terms and conditions of employment.[28] Although those words were not used in this case, it is clear that drug and alcohol testing fell within the description of mandatory subjects. Accordingly, the program was found to be illegally implemented.

In a companion case to the *Johnson-Bateman* employee testing case, the Board considered similar subject matter in the *Star-Tribune* case, but made a critical distinction.[29] The drug and alcohol testing in this case involved applicants, and since applicants are not protected by the NLRA, only employees, the employer had no obligation to bargain on issues affecting them. However, the employer had refused to provide the union with names, addresses, and telephone numbers of people to whom conditional offers of employment had been made and with the identities of persons who had refused to submit to the tests. The Board found that this refusal violated the act. The Board reasoned that employers are obligated to honor union requests for information relevant to the bargaining process or the processing of grievances. The elimination of actual or suspected sexual discrimination is a mandatory subject of collective bargaining and females might have been unfairly removed from employment consideration by the tests. A union has a right to insure that discriminatory practices are not established or continued, and, therefore, is entitled to information that relates to alleged discrimination.[30]

But if the Board had just finished saying that the employer does not have to bargain over these applicants, how could anything relating to the applicants be relevant? In the Board's thinking, one reason the applicant testing did not vitally affect unit employees was that the union could propose drug and alcohol testing as soon as applicants were hired. The union could thus satisfy its concerns over providing a safe workplace for employees. But, in the sexual discrimination arena, if it waited until the hiring process had been completed, the discriminatory damage might already be done. If the union were not given the requested information, the union could not properly carry out its duties as a bargaining representative. The Board said that "possible discrimination in the hiring process is so intertwined with possible discrimination in the employment relationship that to bar a union from investigating the hiring process could bar it from effectively seeking elimination of discrimination in the employment relationship."[31]

The Board ordered the employer to turn over to the union the names, addresses, and telephone numbers of applicants to whom it had made conditional offers of employment, and to identify the people who refused to take the test. There was a Minnesota statute that prohibited unconsented disclosures of certain test-related information, but the Board analyzed the statute and concluded that its order did not force the employer to violate the statute. Furthermore, the Board noted that, "to the extent that the Minnesota statute permits the Respondent to engage in conduct that is arguably prohibited by the National Labor Relations Act, the Board has primary jurisdiction over that conduct, and the state statute is preempted by the Act."[32] Again, the congressional interest in preserving labor peace will take a higher priority than a state's interest in preserving an individual's privacy. This does not mean that once the NLRB has spoken that is the end of it. The Supreme Court limits federal incursions into areas where states have a substantial interest in protecting their citizens from outrageous conduct and there is little risk of interference with the Board's jurisdiction.[33]

The primary intent of this section has been to discuss some security-related subject matters of collective bargaining. The discourse has gone into related areas including information relevant to the bargaining process that employers must make available upon request on the premise that some of this data is of real interest to the employer's security functions. This is an area of real concern to private security because much of the information in their possession is considered to be confidential. With these thoughts in mind, it is worthwhile to explore two more "refusal to give information" cases.

In 1978, in the *Anheuser-Busch* case, the NLRB decided that an employer did not need to supply to a union a statement given to an employer
by a witness in the course of an employee misconduct investigation.[34] The
Board restated its belief that giving over information fostered collective
bargaining but added that giving over witness statements would inhibit it.
It pointed out that witnesses may be reluctant to give statements absent
assurances that they will not be disclosed at least until the time of a
hearing. Further, there was always the possibility that if this information
were made available, attempts could be made to have witnesses change
their testimony or not testify at all.

In 1990 in a *New Jersey Bell Telephone Co.* case,[35] the Board made
the company turn over to the union a security official's report describing
a customer complaint that triggered a five-day suspension of an employee.
The Board, in a 2–1 split, noted that the report did not fall into the
Anheuser-Busch class because it could more readily be characterized as
work product of the company than a witness statement. The complaining
customer did not review the reports or in any manner adopt them as a
reflection of any statement or complaint she had made. There was no
contention by the employer that the reports even approximated a verbatim
transcript of the customer's statements.

Returning to the subject matter of collective bargaining, in *Great Western Produce*,[36] while considering a number of unilateral changes made by
the employer, the NLRB found that inspections of employees' personal
lockers and vehicles were subject matters for collective bargaining. Included in the same mandatory subject matter category were a reprimand
system, an attendance policy, and mandatory overtime requirements.
After following the Board's reasoning through the polygraph and drug
and alcohol testing cases, inclusion of these practices as mandatory bargaining subjects should not come as a surprise. From a practical point of
view, most organized employers and many unorganized employers have
had long-standing policies or practices involving management's right to
search lockers and vehicles. If an unorganized employer has such a policy
and is subsequently organized, the union takes the employer as it finds
it with the policy in place. It is just a matter of making sure everyone
understands it.[37] In the *Great Western Produce* case, there were not any
pre-existing working conditions involving these practices, and bargaining
was necessary.

The case, though, does make another good point worth remembering.
If an employee is disciplined or discharged because of violating the illegally implemented work rule, the employee will be made whole, meaning
returned to work with back pay. The employer's only defense is that the
employee would have been discharged even absent the rule. In the *Medicenter* polygraph case discussed earlier, about thirty-eight people who

refused to take the test would have been returned to work if the employer had illegally implemented the testing requirement.

These cases on subject matters for which bargaining is mandated certainly do not cover all the areas of interest to private security, but they do give a flavor for those issues the Board feels should be bargained because they have a material and significant impact on employees. Gate searches and regular drug-sniffing dog patrols through working areas would probably meet the test.

But how about the use of cameras? This question can be used to illustrate the best approach to making good decisions. It should first be asked how the cameras are going to be used and what their impact on people will be. Cameras used as part of a surveillance program to establish or test production standards probably would have an intimidating effect on employees and warrant attention in the bargaining process. By the same token, if a surreptitiously placed camera is used in the course of an ongoing drug distribution investigation to help identify the parties involved, it is just one of several investigative tools that are utilized and would not likely trigger the level of concern voiced by the Board in the polygraph cases. The camera only replaces the eye of a human being, and if management could observe employee misconduct with a supervisor without bargaining, there should be no reason that it should have to bargain over the use of a camera. The same thing can be said for the use of an undercover agent. Because of the nature of these investigative functions, their use would be completely compromised by introducing them into the bargaining area. A balancing of interests should dictate that they not be designated as mandatory subjects of collective bargaining. However, a draconian use of these techniques would drive the Board to reach a contrary conclusion. A desire to be ingenious does not give one a license to be stupid.

Weingarten—Interviews Leading to Discipline

Weingarten[38] is to private security what *Miranda* is to law enforcement, and it necessarily warrants special attention. The motivation for the *Weingarten* rule is uncomplicated: it was created out of fear of private security excesses.

It all started in 1972 when an undercover security employee and a store manager interviewed an employee about taking a $2.98 box of chicken and only paying $1 for it. The employee's requests for union representation during the interview were denied. It turned out, to management's satisfaction, that she had merely put a dollar's worth of chicken in a $2.98 box. When the interview was being concluded, she sobbed that the only thing she had ever taken was a free lunch. This started a whole new line of interrogation about taking lunches without payment and again her request for union representation was denied. The security agent prepared a statement for the employee to sign, indicating that she owed the store $160. She refused to sign, and unfair labor practice charges were filed with the NLRB. In the Board's investigation it found that most of the employees, including the manager, took lunch without paying for it. As a matter of fact, the security agent had been told by headquarters during the interview that they did not know what the lunch policy was for this store.

Some facts just beg for some kind of remedy and in this case the Supreme Court agreed with the Board "that section 7 of the Act creates a statutory right in an employee to refuse to submit without union representation to an interview which he reasonably fears may result in his discipline."[39] The Supreme Court then restated the contours and limits of this new right, which had been shaped by the Board.

First, the right inheres in section 7's guarantee of the right of employees to act in concert for mutual aid and protection. . . .

Second, the right arises only in situations where the employee requests representation. In other words, the employee may forego his guaranteed right and if he prefers, participate in an interview unaccompanied by his union representative.

Third, the employee's right to request representation as a condition of participation in an interview is limited to situations where the employee reasonably believes the investigation will result in disciplinary action. . . .

Fourth, exercise of the right may not interfere with legitimate employer prerogatives. The employer has no obligation to justify his refusal to allow union representation and despite refusal, the employer is free to carry on his inquiry without interviewing the employee, and thus leave to the employee the choice between having an interview unaccompanied by his representative, or having no interview and foregoing any benefits that might be derived from one. . . .

Fifth, the employer has no duty to bargain with any union representative who may be permitted to attend the investigatory interview.[40]

In its favorable review of the Board's decision, the Supreme Court noted the recent growth in the use of sophisticated investigative techniques such as closed circuit television, undercover security agents, and lie detectors to monitor and investigate employee conduct at the workplace. The Court commented that these techniques increase not only the employees' feelings of apprehension, but also their need for experienced assistance in dealing with them. Often, as in this case, investigative interviews are conducted by security specialists. The employee is not confronted by a supervisor who is known or familiar but by a stranger trained in interrogation techniques. The Court stated that "these developments in industrial life warrant a concomitant reappraisal by the Board of their impact on statutory rights."[41]

It is the NLRB's job to adapt the NLRA to changing patterns of industrial life and, at least in the view of the Supreme Court, that is what the Board did in this case. A new factor was placed into the balance of rights.

Naturally enough, though, a force in motion tends to stay in motion, and it was not too long before the Board tried to extend *Weingarten* coverage to the non-union sector.[42] The Board retreated from that position in a *Sears Roebuck & Co.* case[43] and then more fully explained the reasoning in a 1988 *E. I. du Pont de Nemours* case.[44] The Board pointed out that it, with Supreme Court approval, struck a fair and reasoned balance in *Weingarten* between conflicting interests. Factors in the scales included the belief that a union representative might be able to safeguard interests of the bargaining unit as well as those of the employee. At the same time, a knowledgeable union representative might be of some assistance to the employer by helping it get to the bottom of the incident and avoid use of a formal grievance procedure. This was in keeping with industrial practice and did not create a significant change.

An analysis of the non-union sector indicated that the mid-course corrections set out in *Weingarten* were not appropriate for the non-union arena. There would be no guarantee that the interests of employees as a group would be safeguarded and no feeling that the representative would bring the skills, experience, and knowledge to the meeting that would more likely be made available by a union agent. Absent these and similar elements, the Board reasoned that it would not be achieving a fair and reasoned balance between the interests of management and labor by giving non-represented employees *Weingarten* rights.

Weingarten has been refined by subsequent case law. In a *Montgomery Ward* case,[45] in the course of investigating the thefts of employer property, security people interrogated several suspected employees. During the course of two separate interviews, two employees asked to have union representatives present. The Board in one situation found that the security agent stated, "Sure, you can have anybody you want. But by the time they get here, you will be in Allen Park jail." In the other interview, the Board found that the security person said, "If we do have a third person come in the room, the police will be notified." In both situations, the employees went on with the interviews and signed statements admitting that they took company property. In both situations, the Board concluded that they were coerced into waiving their rights to representation and the employer had violated the NLRA.

As an aside, it is interesting to speculate whether making the Allen Park jail or notification to police statements would constitute false imprisonment under the criteria set out in *Foley v. Polaroid*[46] and other cases discussed under that subject in chapters 6 and 8. It should be kept in mind that an employer, by detaining an employee for an interview, can commit the tort of false imprisonment. Under *Foley*, an employee is not unlawfully detained if he is told to stay or be fired. This employment coercion does not amount to tort coercion. Of course, in *Montgomery Ward* the statements were made in terms of restricting rights to representation and not detaining for the interview. The NLRA would probably preempt any tort action challenge. But by the same token, if the coercion related to detention, then at least some state courts would entertain a false imprisonment action. In *Tumbarella v. Kroger*,[47] a Michigan court considered a situation in which an organized store cashier, following a security-related interview, accused her employer of false imprisonment and the employer defended, in part, on the premise that the state tort action was preempted by the federal NLRA. The state court disagreed, finding that the state had a substantial interest in protecting its citizens from the alleged harm and that there was little risk that its actions would interfere with federal labor policy. The point, again, is that security-related activity has to be thought of in a broad framework. Getting through one legal thicket does not mean that there is no need to think of other legal brambles.

Pacific Telephone & Telegraph Co.[48] is a case of interest on another *Weingarten* aspect. During the course of an investigation the company developed evidence that one employee had installed unauthorized equipment in another employee's home. The two employees plus a union representative were called in for the next step of the investigation—interviews. All three inquired as to the purpose of the interview and were told nothing. During the first interview, the employee admitted making the unauthorized installation. Prior to the interview of the second employee, the union representative requested an opportunity to talk to him. The request was denied. During the subsequent interview, the employee denied the accusations related to the incident under investigation but admitted that he had possession of other equipment. Both employees were terminated.

At about the same time, two operators were interviewed concerning failure to pay bills for calls. The investigator advised both employees about the subject matter of the interviews but refused the representative's request for a pre-interview conference with the employees. At the conclusion of the investigations, both operators were discharged.

The Board and the court concluded that the securing of information as to the subject matter of the interview and a pre-interview conference with a union representative were within the scope of *Weingarten*. The disclosure need not be detailed but must be enough to give the employees enough information to know the purpose of the meeting. In the court's judgment, "Without such information and such conference, the ability of the union representative effectively to give the aid and protection sought by the employee would be seriously diminished."[49] The Board and court also concluded that once a union representative becomes involved pursuant to the employee request, he can speak for the employee and make the request for information and the pre-interview conference.

In a 1989 NLRB case, the Board considered a situation in which a supervisor who was also a part-time police officer approached two employees entering an automobile off the plant and asked them if they had been drinking.[50] They replied in the affirmative and asked if there was a problem. The supervisor-officer had another supervisor come to the scene and the employees related that as far as they knew, the person that asked them the questions was a police officer. They were both suspended for violating a plant rule about not drinking during the work day. The employer admitted that the supervisor-officer was acting on its behalf when he questioned the employees. The Board found that *Weingarten* obligations had not been met because the supervisor-officer had failed to disclose his supervisory status and thus deprived the employees of an opportunity to have a union representative present.

Again, identifying the parties and knowing their roles is critical in making good decisions that are legally sound.

OBSERVATIONS

Security people cannot function in a vacuum. If a security-related program, such as a gate search, is desired at an organized location, it has to be bargained before it is implemented. If it is not bargained, it can be removed by the Board. If information relative to a proposed security program or an investigation is requested by a bargaining agent, the information might well have to be made available. If the information is withheld, the program might be delayed or the results of the investigation negated. If employees are not allowed to exercise their *Weingarten* rights, an otherwise good case might be compromised.

Groping with all these aspects of collective bargaining is difficult and frustrating even for professionals long exposed to the uncertainties of the law. These uncertainties over what is concerted activity, what subjects have to be bargained, what information has to be supplied, and when employees can have a representative present, are generated by continuously placing new concerns and interests in the balance. Congress's concern over labor peace mandates that the Board constantly reconsider its evaluation of that balance and make appropriate changes to adjust to new factors in workplace life.

Legal change makes decision-making difficult for employers, but as long as there is a feel for basic rights and valuing of those rights, the mid-course corrections should be manageable without too much travail. The secret is not to know all the nuances of all the cases but to have a feel for the major factors in the balance, and then to apply common sense. Sometimes it might take a little longer to get the job done, involving going through the bargaining process, but there can be a lot of satisfaction from knowing the end result will be legally bulletproof or at least bullet-resistant.

NOTES

1. *BPS Guard Services Inc*, 300 N.L.R.B. 34 (1990).

2. *McDonnel Aircraft v. NLRB*, 827 F.2d 324 (8th Cir. 1987).

3. *Watchmanitors Inc.*, 128 N.L.R.B. 903 (1960); *Textron Inc.*, 107 N.L.R.B. 355 (1953).

4. 212 N.L.R.B. 407, 408 (1974).

5. 188 N.L.R.B. 222 (1971).

6. *Brinks Inc. of Florida*, 283 N.L.R.B. 711 (1987), *enforcement denied*, 843 F.2d 448 (11th Cir. 1988).

7. *Atlas Guard Service*, 229 N.L.R.B. 698 (1977); *Advance Industrial Security Inc.*, 225 N.L.R.B. 151 (1976); *Sentry Security Services, Inc.*, 230 N.L.R.B. 1170 (1977); *Burns International Security Services Inc.*, 257 N.L.R.B. 387 (1981); *Trustees of Tufts College*, 229 N.L.R.B. 523 (1977).

8. *Faulkner Hospital*, 259 N.L.R.B. 364 (1981), *enforced*, 691 F.2d 51 (1st Cir. 1982).

9. 188 N.L.R.B. 222 (1971).

10. 226 N.L.R.B. 1085 (1976).

11. *NLRB v. Gissel Packing Co.*, 395 U.S. 575 (1969); *United Dairy Farmers Co-operative Association*, 257 N.L.R.B. 772 (1981).

12. 263 N.L.R.B. 1271 (1982).

13. *Mushroom Transportation v. NLRB*, 330 F.2d 683 (3d Cir. 1964); *Hugh H. Wilson Corp.*, 171 N.L.R.B. 1040 (1968), *enforced*, 414 F.2d 1345 (3rd Cir. 1969).

14. *Meyers Industries, Inc.*, 281 N.L.R.B. 882 (1986).

15. *Faulkner Hospital*, 259 N.L.R.B. 364, *enforced*, 691 F.2d 51.

16. *International Harvester Co.*, 84 N.L.R.B. 848 (1949).

17. *Supermarkets General Corp.*, 296 N.L.R.B. no. 149 (1989).

18. *Ming Tree Restaurant v. NLRB*, 736 F.2d 1295 (9th Cir., 1984); *Vernon Livestock*, 172 N.L.R.B. 1805 (1968); *Struksnes Construction Co.*, 165 N.L.R.B. 1062 (1962); *Larand Leisurelies, Inc.*, 213 N.L.R.B. 197 (1974); *U.S. Steel Corp.*, ALJ Decision 13-CA-19419, 19420 (1980).

19. 294 N.L.R.B. 47 (1989).

20. 461 U.S. 731 (1983).

21. 251 N.L.R.B. 1083, *enforced*, 662 F.2d 899 (1st Cir. 1981), *cert. denied*, 455 U.S. 989 (1982).

22. *Fiberboard Paper Products Corp. v. NLRB*, 379 U.S. 203 (1964); *Seattle First National Bank v. NLRB*, 444 F.2d 30 (9th Cir. 1971).

23. *Medicenter, Mid-South Hospital*, 221 N.L.R.B. 670 (1975).

24. 221 N.L.R.B. 670, 675.

25. *E. I. du Pont de Nemours & Co.*, 268 N.L.R.B. 1075 (1984).

26. *Johnson-Bateman Co.*, 295 N.L.R.B. 180, (1989).

27. 295 N.L.R.B. 180, 182.

28. *Seattle First National Bank v. NLRB*, 444 F.2d 30 (9th Cir. 1971); *Fiberboard Paper Products Corp. v. NLRB*, 379 U.S. 203 (1964).

29. *Star Tribune*, 295 N.L.R.B. 543, (1989).

30. *Jubilee Mfg. Co.*, 202 N.L.R.B. 272 (1973); *Westinghouse Electric Corp.*, 239 N.L.R.B. 106 (1978), *enforced as modified*, 648 F.2d 18 (D.C. Cir. 1980).

31. 295 N.L.R.B. 543, 549.

32. 295 N.L.R.B. 543, 549, 550.

33. *Linn v. Plant Guard Workers*, 383 U.S. 53 (1966); *Farmer v. Carpenters*, 430 U.S. 290 (1977).

34. *Anheuser-Busch*, 237 N.L.R.B. 982 (1978).

35. 300 N.L.R.B. no. 6 (1990).

36. 299 N.L.R.B. 154, 135 LRRM 1213 (1990).

37. *Gulf Coast Automotive Warehouse, Inc.*, 256 N.L.R.B. 486 (1981).

38. *NLRB v. J. Weingarten*, 420 U.S. 251 (1975).

39. 420 U.S. 251, 256.

40. 420 U.S. 521, 256–258.

41. 420 U.S. 251, 265.

42. *Materials Research*, 262 N.L.R.B. 1010 (1982).

43. 274 N.L.R.B. 230 (1985).

44. 289 N.L.R.B. 627 (1988).

45. *Montgomery Ward & Co.*, 254 N.L.R.B. 826 (1981).

46. 400 Mass. 82, 508 N.E.2d 72 (1987).

47. 85 Mich. App. 482 271 N.W.2d 284 (1978).

48. 262 N.L.R.B. 1048 (1982); *modified in part*, 711 F.2d 134 (9th Cir. 1983).

49. 711 F.2d 134, 137.

50. Report of NLRB General Counsel on Cases Decided in Second Quarter 1989.

4

Labor-Related Demonstrations, Picketing, and Handbilling

Labor peace is not always achievable, and from time to time the wheels come off, as the saying goes. This discussion of labor activities during times of unrest will start with work stoppages and on-site demonstrations by employees and work out to activities engaged in at the borders of private property, both by employees and non-employee union agents. Since the predominant interests involved are labor-related, the bright legal light will be shed by the National Labor Relations Act. Factors in the balance will be the employees' right to engage in protected concerted activities and the employer's property rights and right to operate an efficient business.

ON-SITE WORK STOPPAGES AND DEMONSTRATIONS BY EMPLOYEES

At the risk of redundancy, the first inquiry will be into the non-union sector. Remember, the National Labor Relations Act extends its coverage to employees engaging in concerted activities, not just union activities. Such covered activities include work stoppages. A review of two venerable but still viable non-union cases illustrates the point.

In *Quaker Alloy*,[1] twenty-one unorganized employees from off-going and oncoming shifts took about ten minutes of company time to meet in a company washroom to discuss the formulation of a grievance over a change in working hours. The employees were engaged in bench work and the impact on productivity was limited. The Board and the court found that the employer's discharge of the two ringleaders was in violation of the NLRA.

By way of contrast, the employer in *Terry Poultry*[2] was engaged in a production line process. Two employees left the line without permission to present a grievance to management and were subsequently discharged. The Board noted that the employer had a well-known rule requiring employees to get permission before they left the production line and that the rule was necessary to insure the orderly and efficient operation of the business. The Board reasoned that under the circumstances, even though the employees were engaged in concerted activity, the presenting of a grievance, it was not protected and the employer's action was justified. Obviously, the nature of the business and the existence of a procedure for leaving the line made the difference. On a related matter, engaging in concerted activity alone does not create instant coverage of the National Labor Relations Act. Two employees going to a manager with a gun demanding raises for all employees might be engaged in concerted activity but it will not be protected.

On-site demonstrations are only a step up from work stoppages, which only consist of a withholding of labor. Two cases from the organized sector help establish a frame of reference. In a *Chrysler* case,[3] a union official led a group of about thirteen employees on a walk through the workplace to protest a lack of heat. This demonstration took place on their break and proceeded through several work areas accompanied by loud talk. The Board found that the demonstration was not disruptive and did not interfere with production. Accordingly, the activity was protected and the participants could not be subjected to discipline.

The facts were somewhat different in a *Ford* case.[4] A larger number of employees, fifty to eighty, participated in a lunchtime demonstration, but this time there was a loss in production as fellow employees left their workstations to observe or join in the activity. This was enough to tip the scales and the Board found that the demonstration was an unprotected activity. The administrative law judge observed that

it is the function of the Board to work out adjustments between the right of employees to organize, to bargain collectively, or to disagree with their employer or their collective bargaining representative. But this right must be weighed against "the equally undisputed right of employers to maintain discipline in their establishments." *Republic Aviation Corporation v. NLRB*, 324 U.S. 793 (1945). The institutional rights of the employer cannot be ignored but must be balanced against legitimate rights and aspirations of employees, even where the exercise of those rights is distasteful both to the employer and the union.[5]

For legal purposes then, there are demonstrations and there are demonstrations.

The Seventh Circuit gave more weight than the Board to the existence of a grievance procedure in an *Advance Industries* case.[6] Five employees who had just returned to work after a strike refused to leave work after their shortened work shift had ended. After a confrontation with management on the subject, they were arrested by the police, removed, and subsequently discharged. Unlike the Board, the court considered the employees' refusal to leave the premises, their failure to express their questions to management representatives who were present, and their attempt to dictate who the management representatives would be, to show a complete lack of respect for their employer's property rights. While the Board believed the available grievance procedure to be of little value, the court felt that its existence shifted the accommodation between employees' rights and private property rights in favor of the employer. In the court's words, "The employees cannot justify their refusal to leave the plant when ordered to do so on the grounds that they had no other method available to present their grievances."[7] The introduction of the grievance procedure argument makes sense when it is viewed against the backdrop of congressional interest in avoiding labor unrest.

In situations in which an employer and a union have agreed that there will be no work stoppages, employees engaging in such activity lose the protection of the NLRA. The Board recognizes that unions can waive employee rights during the collective bargaining process.

DISTRIBUTION OF LITERATURE BY EMPLOYEES

The Board and the courts have long accepted the idea that working time is for work and accordingly have limited solicitation, any oral activity, and distribution of literature to non-working time. Distribution creates an added problem—littering; it is understood that such activity can be limited to non-working areas where there will be less impact on productivity. Parking lots generally come under the definition of non-working areas.

This appeared to be a fairly reasonable balance. The employer could run his plant and the employees could engage in protected activity. But what about employees who are off duty—do they lose their status as employees? The *Tri-County Medical Center* case[8] established a test for the right of off-duty employees to pass out literature to fellow employees in non-working areas. The Board determined that a rule prohibiting such activity would only be valid if it (1) limits access solely with respect to the interior of the place and other working areas; (2) is clearly disseminated to all employees; and (3) applies to off-duty employees seeking access to the plant for any purpose and not just to those employees engaging in union activity. Further, except where justified by business reasons, a rule that denies off-duty employees entry to parking lots, gates, and other outside non-working areas will be found invalid.

In a 1990 *St. Luke's Hospital* case,[9] a security official ordered an off-duty employee to leave the hospital parking lot where he was distributing union literature to fellow employees and placing material on car windshields. In the Board's judgment, the vague, generalized testimony of the security official did not meet the burden of establishing legitimate business considerations necessary to justify interfering with the employees' Section 7 rights. Harder evidence might have brought about a different result.

PICKET LINE ACTIVITY BY EMPLOYEES

Neither the Board nor the courts put handbilling on the same coercive level as picketing, and the distinction between the two activities should be kept in mind in balancing rights.

Another look at the *Advance Industries* case helps frame the issue of what happens when employees engage in questionable picket line activity. After stating that picket line misconduct may be sufficient to warrant termination, the court added that "trivial rough incidents or moments of animal exuberance must be distinguished from misconduct so violent or of such a serious character as to render the employees unfit for further service."[10] This is hardly the brightest possible line but it does give a feel for the balance. The court accepted the Board's judgment that rocking a post and a single incident of pounding on a car were not egregious. It did not accept a similar conclusion of the Board relative to an employee who aimed a gun at company property for a minute or two. In the court's judgment, the word that strikers were armed could have a strong coercive effect on non-strikers. This employee had gone too far. The court also mentioned another time in which the Sixth Circuit refused to approve a Board's order to return an employee to work.[11] In that case, a striker threw gravel at a supervisor taking photographs of other employees engaging in picket line misconduct. Despite the Board's position, the court had no trouble finding this behavior outside the exuberant or impulsive conduct that the NLRA protects. Again, these are judgment calls and for the most part have to be based on common sense and a feel for the intentions of the law.[12]

TRESPASS ACTIVITY BY NON-EMPLOYEE
UNION AGENTS

The battle over the balance between a union's use of private property to engage in protected activity and an employer's refusal to allow that use in the interest of protecting its property took on new intensity in the 1988 *Jean Country* case.[13] Before getting to that case, though, it is important to first set the scene.

The Board and the courts recognize that, as a general principle, owners have a right to exclude individuals from entry onto their property. Unauthorized entry onto private property may constitute a trespass and may subject the trespasser to civil or criminal action. However, as early as 1956 the Supreme Court in *NLRB v. Babcock & Wilcox Co.* stated that "Organization rights are granted to workers by the same authority, the National Government, that preserves property rights. Accommodations between the two must be obtained with as little destruction of one as is consistent with the maintenance of the other."[14] Carrying along the same theme twenty years later, the Supreme Court in *Hudgens v. NLRB* stated, "The locus of that accommodation, however, may fall at differing points along the spectrum depending on the nature and strength of the respective Section 7 rights and private property rights asserted in any given context."[15] The spotting of the locus has been rather a turbulent process, always seeming to evoke the wrath of whatever side feels it has been abused.

These, then, are the rights to be balanced. But what were the circumstances that created these conclusions? The seminal case, *Babcock and Wilcox*, involved a refusal by the company to allow non-employee union organizers to pass out literature on the company's parking lot. In searching for the appropriate accommodation, the court commented that if employees are not accessible through feasible channels, "the right to exclude from property has been required to yield to the extent needed to permit communication of information or the right to organize."[16]

The court then looked to see if there were alternative means to communicate other than using private property. In this case, employees lived in nearby communities and could be reached by the usual means of mail, home visits, and telephone calls. In the court's judgment, the employer did not have to grant access to non-employee union oganizers because of the existence of reasonable alternative means.

This seemed like a reasonable benchmark but confusion entered the picture for two reasons. First, employers were grouping their businesses together in office buildings, industrial parks, and shopping malls, and the courts were equating some of these locations to company towns and extending first amendment rights to antiwar and other kinds of non-work-related demonstrators. Second, unions were targeting employers at these multiple employer locations, and the question was whether the first amendment privileges for these demonstrators should be extended to union activities. After a lot of marching in both directions, the Supreme Court finally stated in *Hudgens* that these semi-public locations were not covered by the constitution because there was no involvement of state action. So much for first amendment rights for any kind of demonstrator. But that did not end the discussion.

The court went on to say that if there were any rights involved it was the duty of the NLRB to identify and balance them. This reintroduced *Babcock and Wilcox* but the court noted that there were distinguishing facts. *Hudgens* involved picketing by warehouse employees of an employer, Butler, who had one of its stores at Hudgens's mall. The picketing involved contract negotiations. Remember in *Babcock and Wilcox* organizing was being carried out by non-employees. Further, while *Babcock and Wilcox* involved the employer's property, *Hudgens* involved the property of a third party. The case was sent back to the Board for reconsideration.

Of course, on remand the Board dropped its first amendment approach and applied *Babcock and Wilcox*.[17] In the Board's judgment, if non-employee organizers had certain rights, striking employees must have at least the same rights if not more. Since organizing and economic strike activity were both protected by the Act, the economic activities deserved at least equal deference. Furthermore, as far as the Board was concerned, Hudgens, the mall owner, was acting as the employer's (Butler's) agent when it told the picketers to get off the mall or be arrested. The Board then affirmed its earlier finding that this threat constituted a violation of Section 8(a)(1) of the National Labor Relations Act.

This agency relationship was created in part by the fact that Hudgens supplied security to the mall. As the Board framed it, "To the extent that the businesses on the Mall have delegated to Hudgens responsibility for the maintenance of an environment that maximizes the shopper's peace of mind, and therefore sales, those doing business at the Center are protecting their own interests through Hudgens."[18]

A detailed tracking of the evolutionary process of what might appear to be a simple balancing problem would only add confusion, as it took a number of twists and turns. It will be more productive to take a snapshot of the process as it presently exists and get a feel for where it seems to be going.

The hero or villain, depending on how one looks at it, is *Jean Country*, a 1988 NLRB case.[19] Jean Country was engaged in the sale of casual clothes in a Yonkers, New York shopping center. Its employees were unorganized. Over the protests of the mall operator, a union commenced peaceful picketing within the mall just outside Jean Country store windows. Picket signs noted that Jean Country was not union and that it was a threat to union area wages, hours, and conditions. The chief of security for the mall called the police and told them the mall wanted these people off the property, and the police told the union agent that he might be arrested for trespassing if he continued to picket in the mall. The pickets were directed to do any further picketing on the public road beyond the mall property. The union filed charges with the Board against Jean Country and Brook, the mall operator.

As part of its balancing of rights function, the Board first established that Jean Country's and Brook's conduct was based on a legitimate property interest. The Board next examined the relative strengths of their right to maintain the privacy of the property. Elements warranting Board attention included the quasi-public character of the mall. The Board noted that the quasi-public trait tends to lessen the private nature of the property "because it is apparent that the public is extended a broad invitation to come on the property, and not necessarily with the specific purpose of purchasing a particular product or service."[20]

After analyzing the width of the walkways and aisles, the Board concluded that even at peak hours, peaceful union pickets could not have obstructed movement of people, and there was no evidence that the pickets had engaged in anything but peaceful activity. In summing up these and other factors, the Board concluded that strict maintenance of privacy on the mall during business hours was not an overriding concern because the presence of the public in large numbers was intrinsic to the commercial interest of Jean Country and Brook. In short, "the private property right asserted by the Respondents in reaction to the Union's picketing is quite weak in the circumstances."[21]

In looking at labor's rights, the Board considered the picketing to be organizational in nature and conducted, at least in part, on behalf of the unionized employees of those stores that were in competition with the non-union Jean Country store. Attention was again given to the fact that the picketing was limited in scope, peaceful, and unobstructive. While the purpose of the *picketing*—organizational—did not put it on the stronger end of the spectrum of Section 7 rights, as economic strike activity or unfair labor practice picketing might have, it was still worthy of protection against substantial impairment.

Now the Board locked in the *Babcock & Wilcox* alternative method of communication test as a permanent part of its inquiry. It identified the union's audience as the potential customers of the Jean Country store and considered whether the alternative of moving the picket line to public property could satisfy its needs. The nearest public property was one quarter of a mile away from the closest entrance to the mall. In the Board's judgment, the union's message would be seriously diluted from that distance as there would be no probability of identifying the potential Jean Country customers and communicating with them. The Board also voiced concern about the unintentional enmeshment of non-involved employers in the problem as potential customers might assume the whole mall was involved in some kind of dispute; thus, picketing on public property at the mall entrance was not a reasonably effective alternative.

Following this detailed analysis, the Board found that the private property rights were weak, there were Section 7 rights to protect, and there were no reasonable alternative means for communication. This necessarily, in the Board's mind, led to the conclusion that Jean Country and Brook had violated the NLRA by refusing to permit the picketing and causing the police to threaten the pickets with arrest for trespass.

It is evident that the Board was not trying to come up with a fixed formula for establishing the balance of employer and employee rights in *Jean Country*. If an employer had an especially compelling reason for barring access, such as the manufacture of dangerous substances or explosives, the Board would more easily find that there were alternative methods of communication. As the property involved was quasi-public, it was more likely the Board would find the alternative means unsatisfactory and allow the trespass.

The Board did identify a number of factors it might consider as relevant in its evaluation of the balance. These included (1) as to the employer's property right: the nature of the interest, the use of which the property is put, any restrictions that are imposed on public access to it, and the property's relative size and openness; (2) as to the employee's Section 7 rights: the nature of the right, the identity of the employer to whom the right is directly related, the relationship of the employer to the property, the identity of the audience to which the communication is directed, and the manner in which the activity is carried out; and (3) as to the alternative means: the safety of attempting communication at alternative sites or in other ways, the desirability of avoiding enmeshment of neutrals, and the extent to which use of communication alternatives would dilute the effectiveness of the union's message.

It almost necessarily followed that most of the cases following and applying *Jean Country* involved quasi-public settings, because this is where property rights carried less weight in the balance. The triggers for many, but not all, *Jean Country* violations have been pulled by a security officer or a security officer in conjunction with other management representatives. As the following discussion shows, though, *Jean Country* had only a short and turbulent history, and should no longer be considered the standard in trespass cases involving non-employee union organizers.

Jean Country represented, in the Board's view, an updating of the 1956 *Babcock & Wilcox* case. *Lechmere Inc. v. NLRB*[22] is a *Babcock & Wilcox*-type case in a different geographical setting looked at through *Jean Country* eyes. In theory, the advent of the *Jean Country* test should not produce a different result because it is supposed to be the same test as in *Babcock & Wilcox*. Only now the Board applied the accommodation part of the test all the time in these kinds of cases. The Lechmere shopping plaza was located off a major highway in the greater Hartford area. The Lechmere store was not the only store but was the dominant one in the complex. The principal entrance to common parking lots was off the highway. The doors to the Lechmere store were posted with rules prohibiting solicitation or distribution of literature on the premises. The policy applied both to the store and the parking lots.

After an unsuccessful attempt to organize Lechmere employees through newspaper advertising, union organizers started *leafleting* cars on the primary parking lots. Store management asked them to leave and security people removed the leaflets from the cars. Subsequently organizers attempted to *distribute literature* from nearby public property to cars entering the lots. These organizers were confronted by members of management and security guards. They were told they were on private property and asked to leave. They were advised that if they did not leave, the police would be called. Police were called, who determined that the organizers were on public property and allowed them to remain there. The police noted that they were dangerously close to the highway and could obstruct traffic. The organizers left after they observed they were being videotaped by security people. Charges were filed against Lechmere.

The Board and later the circuit court went through the three-point test. While *Babcock & Wilcox* set up the test, it must be remembered that no violation was found in that case. Here the First Circuit observed that *Babcock & Wilcox* involved a factory that was the only building on a large secluded tract, it was a manufacturing facility not open to the public, the surrounding area was rural, most of the employees lived in a nearby community and drove to work in private cars, and were relatively easily identifiable. In short, the employees were in reasonable reach by methods short of handbilling on private property. In contrast, the Lechmere facility was quasi-public in nature and was located in a metropolitan area. There was considerable difficulty in identifying employees, as they lived in scattered locations and entered and left their place of employment merged in with customers and employees of other stores.

The Board, with circuit court agreement, called the employer's property rights "relatively substantial" but classified the organizing activity at the high end of the Section 7 scale. In the discussion on alternative methods, the Board and the court noted with approval that the union had first tried to reach employees through a newspaper before resorting to handbilling on the parking lot. Both added it was not necessary that all means of communication have to be tried prior to making a trespass. For example, they pointed out that use of television and radio probably would be too expensive to warrant practical consideration. In the end it was concluded that the complexities of identifying and effectively communicating with employees was such that intrusion onto private property was warranted in the interest of pursuing Section 7 rights. By barring union representatives from organizing activity on the parking lot, and by threatening to call the police to remove them from public property, management violated the Act.

As the *Jean Country* test was evolving, the Board soon came across a situation in which handbilling activity on company property was being carried out by both non-employees and employees. Should *Jean Country* be applied to both or would two separate tests be used? In *Sahara Tahoe*

Corporation,[23] a handbilling case, the Board opted for two tests—*Jean Country* for non-employees and *Tri-County Medical Center* for employees. The employer operated a hotel and casino on approximately twenty acres and employed about nineteen hundred people. The complex faced a major highway and had parking lots on all sides. The parking lots were accessed through six entrances. A certified bargaining agent for about 290 of the employees attempted to pass out literature relative to bargaining on a company parking lot. A non-employee distributor was taken into custody at the direction of security personnel and two employees engaged in the same activity were allowed to continue. The employer had a rule against solicitation and distribution but there was no rule barring off-duty employees from the property. The off-duty employees had earlier been excluded from the parking lot by security on the mistaken belief they were not employees.

First, as to the non-employees, the Board applied its *Jean Country* test. In its judgment, the employer had a relatively modest property interest in the parking lot area outside the entrance most commonly used by employees, and the employees were the primary target for the handbilling. The entrance was located in a rear corner and there was nothing to indicate it had restricted use. The employer's concern about security made little impression on the Board as it pointed out that nineteen hundred employees and two thousand customers were in and out every day and the presence of two non-employees on the parking lot did not seem to have any real impact on security.

On the Section 7 side, the Board noted that the handbilling was not disruptive and it was directly related to the bargaining process. The Board also found that there were no reasonable alternative methods for reaching employees with the bargaining information. The employer had given a list of employees to the union but it did not contain telephone numbers and only about one-sixth of the employees' numbers were listed in the telephone book. Addresses given were post office boxes or general delivery numbers without street addresses and the union had difficulty trying to make home contacts. Handbilling from the perimeter or bus stop would have made it difficult to distinguish unit employees from customers and non-unit employees. On balance, then, considering the relatively modest property interests, the significant Section 7 interests, and the lack of reasonable alternatives for getting out the message, the Board opted to find the employer's rights inferior to those of the employees. The violation necessarily followed.

As to the early exclusion of off-duty employees from handbilling on the parking lot, the Board did not use the *Jean Country* tests but went directly to *Republic Aviation*.[24] In that case the Supreme Court decided that an employer may not prohibit employees from distributing union literature in non-work areas during non-work time without a showing that a ban is necessary to maintain discipline or production. Although the two employees were off duty, the Board did not utilize its *Tri-County Medical Center* test because there the employer did not contest the employee's right to be on the property.[25] This was a straight *Republic Aviation* distribution test, and the employer agreed that the employees had a right to do what they were doing; only the security people thought they were non-employees and had not recognized them as employees. The Board said it was not concerned with the employer's motive but whether the exclusion, mistake or not, interfered with Section 7 rights. The prohibition, though isolated, was found to be a violation of the NLRA. In short, if the handbilling activity involves employees, the Board will not go through the long accommodation balancing exercise.[26]

As the Board was refining its *Jean Country* balancing act, things were happening in the court area. *Lechmere* went to the Supreme Court and the result was the end of the evolutionary process for *Jean Country*—it was emasculated. In its 1992 decision, the Court said that the Board was guilty of overextending employee protected rights to non-employee union agents.[27] It agreed that non-employee organizers had some rights in order to insure that employees could properly exercise theirs but these non-employee rights were very limited when measured against employer property rights.

Of course, this meant going back to *Babcock & Wilcox*, and this is where the Supreme Court said the Board made a mistake. The Court stated that *Babcock & Wilcox* meant that Section 7 does not protect non-employee union organizers except in the rare case where the inaccessibility of employees makes ineffective the reasonable attempts by non-employees to communicate with them through the usual channels. The court said its reference to "reasonable" attempts was nothing more than a common sense recognition that unions need not engage in extraordinary feats to communicate with inaccessible employees. So long as non-employee union organizers have reasonable access to employees outside an employer's property, the requisite accommodation has taken place. It is only where such access is infeasible that it becomes necessary to take the accommodation inquiry to a second level and balance the employees' and employer's rights. This, of course, trashed the Board's *Jean Country* doctrine of automatically applying the accommodation balancing tests.

So, under the Supreme Court's *Lechmere* ruling, you do not get to balancing accommodations until the union proves it has unique obstacles preventing it from communicating with employees. But when does that happen? The Court said that the standard is not met just because access to employees may be cumbersome or less than ideally effective. It is limited to situations in which the location of a plant and the living quarters of the employees place the employees beyond the reach of reasonable union efforts. The Court cited logging and mining camp cases as classic examples. The union's problems in communicating with Lechmere's employees did not meet the unique obstacles test and accordingly there was no unfair labor practice in not allowing union agents on the property.

In sum, the Court seriously narrowed the rights of non-employee union agents to come onto company property. These agents still have more rights than the general public but now have considerably less than an employee. The Board has no alternative but to adjust its future decisions relative to non-employee union agents to this interpretation. As noted in *Sahara Tahoe*, it had already decided that *Jean Country* did not apply to employees.

EMPLOYER ACCESS TO STATE COURTS IN LABOR TRESPASS CASES—ARE STATE ACTIONS PREEMPTED BY THE NLRA?

In non-employee union agent trespassing cases, security people are between a proverbial rock and a hard place. If they tell these people that the property is private and they should remove themselves, they are creating a potential NLRA violation. If they do not put people on notice, they probably have little, if any, chance of prevailing in a state injunction or criminal trespass case. But what chance do they have anyway of pursuing some kind of state relief, as this seems like an area where the NLRB has staked out total coverage? The subject for discussion is preemption. Preemption was discussed in chapter 2 but the focus was on arbitration and contract violations. Some comment was made in chapter 3 on the subject as a straight NLRB issue, but now is the time to look at it in more depth.

The NLRA preemption issue was met head-on in a 1978 *Sears, Roebuck & Co.* case.[28] Sears was approached by union agents who requested that carpentry work being performed at the store be performed either by a contractor using union labor or by Sears, itself, and asked that Sears agree to abide by union contract terms relative to the dispatching of and use of carpenters. When Sears did not respond to the request, the union placed pickets on both public and Sears property. Picketing was peaceful. Sears security demanded that the union remove the pickets from Sears property. The union refused, stating that the pickets would not leave unless forced to do so by legal action.

Sears went into a California state court and got a temporary restraining order against the picketing on its property. On appeal, the Supreme Court of California ruled that the picketing was arguably protected by Section 7 of the NLRA and arguably prohibited by that act. The obvious conclusion for this court was that this was a federal matter and the state had no business being involved. And so the next step was the United States Supreme Court.

Going back to the basics, the Supreme Court quoted from the grand-daddy of the labor preemption cases, *Garmon*:[29] "When an activity is arguably subject to Section 7 of the Act, the States as well as the federal courts must defer to the exclusive competence of the National Labor Relations Board if the danger of state interference with national policy is to be averted." As has been mentioned on numerous occasions herein, Section 7 deals with the right to engage in concerted activity. Section 8 is the unfair labor practice section that sets out the protections and limitations on protections. The court made it clear that the *Garmon* language was not an inflexible standard to be applied in a literal, mechanical fashion. For example, the court had permitted state court incursions into federal areas where the involved conduct touched on "interests so deeply rooted in local feeling and responsibility that, in the absence of congressional direction, we could not infer that Congress had deprived the states of the power to act."[30] Some of these cases involved violence or threats of violence.[31]

With these thoughts in mind, the Court split the case into two areas of inquiry. Was the union engaging in some kind of unfair labor practice that could only be remedied by the Board, or was it engaging in some protected activity that only the Board should protect? For the Court, the critical point of inquiry in resolving the unfair labor practice question was whether the controversy presented to the state court was identical to or different from the controversy that might be presented to the Board. As the court saw it, "it is only in the former situation (identical controversy) that a state court's exercise of jurisdiction necessarily involves a risk of interference with the unfair labor practice jurisdiction of the Board."[32]

The court then considered several unfair labor practices that the union might have committed and pointed out that the location of the pickets, the trespass aspect, would not have been a critical point in any of the charges that might have been filed with the Board by Sears. In the Supreme Court's judgment, the state court's trespass action would not have interfered with a Board case.

Now for the tough part—the potential that a state court action on a trespass case could impact on rights protected by Section 7. This could include the right to picket or distribute handbills. The court acknowledged that this was a bigger problem than the one just resolved on prohibited activity but pointed out that the state court is not deprived of jurisdiction just because the union's trespass was arguably protected.

The Court's chief concern seemed to be that the trespasser was in an ideal position unless the owner-user was given some avenue for challenging the trespass. The trespass as a trespass was not a Board matter and recourse naturally existed through the state court. If the employer could not get into state court, it could either let the pickets stay where they were or forcefully evict them with the risk of violence. Of course this legal dilemma would only be created if the union did not seek protection of its rights by filing a charge with the Board. Thus, in the Court's judgment, the trespass action would not be preempted unless the union had a reasonable opportunity to file a Board charge and had not done so.

But what happens in the state court during the trespass hearing relative to the Supreme Court's *Lechmere* decision? The court decided that it would not be an unacceptable risk for a state court to evaluate the merits of the case and decide whether or not the trespassing activity was protected. At least at that time, 1978, the court felt that "a trespass is far more likely to be unprotected than protected."[33] Certainly that statement is more accurate under *Lechmere* than it was under *Jean Country*. The court added that whatever risk that an erroneous state-court adjudication

does exist is outweighed by the anomalous consequences of a rule which would deny the employer access to any forum in which to litigate either the trespass issue or the protection issue in those cases in which the disputed conduct is likely to be protected by Section 7.[34]

Again, the union was in the key position and could forestall state court action by going to the Board when the employer told it to get off its property. As noted, the employer could not go to the Board because the trespass by itself was not a violation of the NLRA. The employer could only go to the court.

Predictably, this perceived erosion of the preemption doctrine triggered an unusual amount of reaction from the bar and academia.[35] Part of the concern was that the fifty states have many different local prohibitions, limitations, and interpretations that will make it difficult to determine whether or not a given act is a trespass. For example, when the *Sears* case went back to the California state court, the request for the injunction was denied under the California Moscone Act that directly references peaceful picketing outside a store.[36]

Sears seems to take care of trespass actions in state civil courts, but what about a criminal trespass action in a state court—does *Sears* still apply? It has to be kept in mind that most states do have two trespass actions, both civil and criminal. While the definitions vary from state to state, the egregiousness of the activity is always higher for criminal violations. Will states draw the line on intrusions of the federal government into their police activities?

Commonwealth v. Noffke is a case on point decided by a Massachusetts court in 1978.[37] A union organizer went onto a hospital parking lot and spoke to employees as they passed by. A hospital administrator asked him to leave, he refused, and two police officers placed him under arrest. The court saw it as a *Sears*-type case even though it was prosecuted as a criminal action and it assumed jurisdiction after applying the *Sears* tests.

This meant, as in the *Sears* California civil action, that a state court was first applying Board law. In *Noffke*, the court decided that the criminal prosecution was not preempted and the union's motion to dismiss was denied.

MASS PICKETING AND VIOLENCE ON THE PICKET LINE

Trespass has been the key word in *Babcock and Wilcox*, *Hudgens*, *Sears*, and *Lechmere*. Those cases and their progeny dealt with peaceful labor activity. Once violence and mass picketing are introduced into the equation, there is a significant shift in balance. While degrees of conduct might change from case to case, generally speaking these activities, particularly violence, are considered to be indefensible and are not tolerated as legitimate means of gaining Section 7 ends. As already noted, picket line violence by employees takes them outside the protection of the act and subjects them to discipline or discharge.

While one section of the act, Section 8(b)(1)(A), covers such activity, it is seldom utilized. Blocking of entrances and exits and violence that leads to the shutting down of an operation calls for quick relief and the Board cannot supply it. Once charges are filed, the Board has to conduct an investigation, and if the facts warrant it, then issue a complaint. It is only after the complaint has been issued that the Board can seek injunctive relief in federal district court under Section 10(j) of the act. Assuming that the Board has a clear-cut case, a requisite to a 10(j) proceeding, there is no guarantee the Board will decide to seek relief, and it is the Board's decision to make, not the employer's. If the Board does seek an injunction, the relief in all likelihood will not be granted until long after the initial charge was filed.

But what about preemption? Will a state court take jurisdiction over a labor matter? *Sears*, a trespass case, represents a fairly close call relative to preemption, but trespass is more of a property right and does not really involve one of the fundamental functions of the state, protection of people. In *Auto Workers v. Wisconsin Employment Relations Board*,[38] the Supreme Court said that the preemption doctrine

does not take from the States power to prevent mass picketing, violence, and overt threats of violence. The dominant interest of the state in preventing violence and property damage cannot be questioned. It is a matter of general local concern. Nor should the fact that a union commits a federal unfair labor practice while engaging in violent conduct prevent States from taking steps to stop the violence. ... The states are the natural guardians of the public against violence.

This concern about public safety, though, does not give state courts the power to make incursions into Board-controlled areas. For example, in *Youndahl v. Rainfair Inc.*[39] there was an attempt to restrain all picketing. In the Supreme Court's judgment, the state court exceeded its jurisdiction when it attempted to enjoin peaceful picketing as well as that which included violence, threats of violence, and intimidation. It would be highly unusual for a state court to ban all picketing, as the Supreme Court has reaffirmed its position that the state court's remedy must be carefully crafted to only protect matters of compelling state interests.[40] Accordingly, state court injunctions more often than not speak to numbers and distance between pickets as well as conduct of pickets.

States vary considerably in the burdens they place on employers in seeking relief and the speed with which they act. A large number of states, about thirty-three, have no statutes that set out the details of labor injunctions, and others have statutes that provide specific tests employers have to pass before an injunction will be granted. New York is an example of the latter. In New York, an employer must prove that unlawful acts have been threatened or committed, the property of the employer will be substantially and irreparably injured unless the injunction is granted, the injury to the person enjoined will be less than the injury suffered by the person seeking relief, there is no other adequate remedy at law, and the police are unable or unwilling to furnish adequate protection. The employer also is required to have complied with all its legal obligations relative to the labor dispute and to have made every reasonable effort to settle the dispute.[41] These restrictions on injunctions in New York and several other states have been circumvented in certain circumstances so that the courts have not been deprived of their fundamental interest in providing for public safety. These states tend to think that the public should not be hurt just because the employer has not dotted all its "i's".[42]

As difficult as some states make it to receive injunctive relief in mass picketing and violence cases, none of them quite measures up to the burdens placed on employers in federal district court under the Norris-La Guardia Act. The New York statute mirrors this federal statute on nearly all points, but while the state court might provide some give to get their job done, no flexibility will be found in the federal court.[43] This is probably for two reasons: one, the Norris-La Guardia Act was a reaction to long-term leniency by federal courts in giving employers too much relief, and two, after all, providing safety to the public is a state job, and the federal courts seem to believe that state courts are where the relief should be sought. Understandably, it is only in rare circumstances that employers seek injunctive relief for mass picketing and violence in federal court. In any event, wherever it is sought, it is understood that the court should not be asked for relief that the NLRA places within the domain of the NLRB. This NLRA relief covers a number of peaceful picketing situations.

SECONDARY BOYCOTTS

Absent contract restrictions, unions and employees have access to strikes and picketing as weapons to be used in disputes with their employers. The desire of the NLRA is to keep these situations contained so they do not involve neutral third parties. The secondary boycott provision of the act, 8(b)(4)(B), prohibits a union from putting pressure via picketing or threats to pickets on an employer to force that employer to cease doing business with the employer with which the union has a dispute. In short, a union cannot picket at a supplier's or customer's place of business. The union's intent in such picketing obviously would be to have the supplier or customer—neutrals—call the employer and tell him or her to solve the problem or they will have to cease doing business with the employer. This is the kind of pressure that is prohibited.

Probably most of the confusion in the application of this provision takes place at locations where there are numerous employers doing business. The law is interested in allowing a union the right to picket the employer with which it has a problem and it is equally concerned about protecting employers who are not involved in the problem. These multi-employer situations are normally managed through the use of separate gate systems so that non-involved employers and employees can enter and leave without the need to cross a picket line. The confusion comes about in identifying who is or is not involved. The questions to resolve are who can be sent through what entrance and can picketing legally take place there?

Case law has evolved along two lines in attempting to answer the questions. The first is the *G.E.* test[44] and the second is the *Moore Drydock Co.* test.[45] An analysis of the two cases is helpful in evaluating when each should be applied.

General Electric operated a manufacturing facility in Louisville, Kentucky. Ingress and egress to the site were attained through five gates or entrances. G.E. confined its contractors to the use of one gate with the intent of keeping them uninvolved in its plant union labor disputes. A sign was posted at the entrance indicating it was for contractors' use and not for G.E. employees. The plant union went out on strike and picketing took place at the contractor gate. Was the union enmeshing neutrals in its dispute or were they proper targets for its activity?

After noting that there is no bright line for resolving the differences between primary and secondary activity, the Supreme Court established three conditions to help decide the question: (1) there must be a separate gate marked and set apart from other gates; (2) the work done by the people who use the gate must be unrelated to the normal operations of the employer; and (3) the work must be of a kind that would not, if done when the employer was engaged in its regular operations, necessitate curtailing those operations.

The idea was that if the contractor's employees were integrated into the plant operation by the nature of their work, they could hardly be called neutrals. For example, did the contractor's people work interchangeably with plant people on maintenance or other jobs? Were they working on a conveyor belt, or some similar job, that was an integral part of the plant production process and would require shutting down the production operation to get the job done? The Court sent the case back to the Board to apply the tests. The Board subsequently found that the work to be done by the contractor related to the normal operation of the plant and therefore the union's picketing was legal.[46]

Moore Drydock preceded *G.E.* and concerned a slightly but critically different circumstance. This was a so-called common situs situation, in which a number of employers were carrying out their businesses at one location. The union had a dispute with a ship that was tied up at the Moore yard. It was refused permission to picket on the pier next to the ship and thereafter posted its pickets at the yard entrance on public property. Picket signs identified the employer being picketed and no attempts were made to interfere with other work in progress.

The Board asked whether the right to picket follows the situs of the dispute, in this case the ship, while it is stationed at the premises of a secondary employer. As the Board noted, "Essentially the problem is one of balancing the right of a union to picket at the site of its dispute as against the right of a secondary employer to be free from picketing in a controversy in which it is not directly involved."

And so came into being the four-part *Moore Drydock* analysis. In these kinds of circumstances to be legal, the picketing (1) must be strictly limited to times when the situs of dispute, the employer with which it has a problem, is located on the secondary employer's premises; (2) at the time of the picketing, the primary employer, the disputant employer, is engaged in its normal business at the site; (3) the picketing is limited to places reasonably close to the location of the situs; and (4) the picketing discloses clearly that the dispute is with the primary employer. In this case, the picketing met all the tests and was found to be legal.

For a person who has to make judgments on the use of entrances at his or her place of business, it would be nice to use the *Moore Drydock* tests as much as possible, because there is more flexibility on assignments. Under *G.E.*, the gate has to be marked and set apart before the dispute takes place. Under *Moore Drydock*, one can react after the fact and move contractors around to minimize the impact of picketing. Further, under *Moore Drydock*, there is no need to consider the integral relationship with plant operations. But how can one be sure which test the Board will apply?

In *Markwell & Hartz, Inc.*[47] a general contractor, M&H, was involved with other contractors in the expansion of a filtration plant. The job site was surrounded by a chain link fence and had four entrances. The union commenced picketing M&H at all the entrances. Six days after the start-up of picketing, M&H separated out one of the four gates for its use and marked it accordingly. The union continued its picketing at the three entrances that were now clearly marked that they were not to be used by M&H. The union defended on the premise that this was a *G.E.*-type case and its picketing was legal because the M&H entrance had not been set out and marked prior to the start of picketing.

The Board did not agree and opted to use the *Moore Drydock* test. As the Board pointed out, *G.E.* involved picketing at the premises of a struck manufacturer and this case involved a construction job by a transitory contractor who happened to be at the site. The Board added, "The distinction between common situs picketing and that which occurs at premises occupied solely by the struck employer has been a guiding consideration in Board efforts to strike a balance between the competing interests underlying the boycott provisions of the Act."[48] It was also pointed out that the Supreme Court in *G.E.* approved *Moore Drydock* and in no way attempted to interfere with the Board's traditional approach to common situs problems. Again, *G.E.* is limited to situations in which the disputant or primary employer occupies a premises and has numerous contractors come to its place of business. It is not applicable to the contractor who has a labor dispute and comes to that premises and brings its dispute with it. As pointed out in *Markwell & Hartz* and similar cases, that situation requires a *Moore Drydock* test.[49]

The location of entrances at a site is more often than not dictated by the size and configuration of the property, road arrangements, and traffic patterns. *Local 33 Carpenters (CB Construction Co. Inc.)*[50] is a good case in point. CB Construction, a non-union contractor, was engaged in renovation work in an eight-story Boston office building when it was picketed at the front entrance of the building by Local 33. The owners of the building excluded CB from the front entrance and designated the rear entrance for its use. Signs were posted accordingly but the union continued to picket at the front of the building on the contention that the rear entrance on a 25-feet wide public passageway was so remotely and inconveniently located that it interfered with the union's right to appeal to the general public as well as CB's employees and suppliers.[51]

The Board and the D.C. Circuit Court of Appeals found a secondary boycott violation in the *CB Construction* case, after comparing the facts to those in *Local Union 501 v. NLRB (Pond)*.[52] In *CB* there were only two choices as to where to put the contractor: in front or in the alley. Space limitations at the front entrance made it infeasible for CB's use. The Board and court concluded that the union has to take the primary employer as it finds him and it was irrelevant that the union was not provided access to the general public, a limited public or no public.

In *Pond*, the job site was located in a rural area and the disputant contractor was assigned an entrance virtually hidden from all public view. While the court did not believe that an employer has an obligation to maximize a picket's chance to reach the general public, it did feel that the Board should not presume under *Moore Drydock* that picketing at the neutral gate automatically means the union violated the Act. The Court felt the Board should at least have analyzed the facts to determine whether the union was being deprived of a public forum in the dispute. As the court said, "We believe that the Board was required to determine whether the employer's reserved gate system unreasonably operated to impair the union's legitimate interest in reaching the public."[53] In other words, an employer does not have to give a union the best spot to appeal to the public, but if it puts the union in a position where it has no access to that audience it must have a good reason for its action, in order to obtain secondary boycott relief.

Once established and appropriately marked, care has to be given to the use of entrances. A good example is set out in the *Local 323 IBEW & J. F. Hoff Electric Co.* case.[54] Hoff, an electrical subcontractor on a project, was limited to a marked gate during a dispute it had with the union. Picketing by the union was extended to the neutral gate after the union observed deliveries of electrical fixtures being made through that entrance. Charges were filed and the union defended on the premise that these fixtures were to be installed by Hoff and it accordingly had a right to picket.

It was accepted that deliveries made to a primary, the employer with the problem, as well as customers of and visitors to the primary, must go through the same entrance as the primary. The idea, of course, is that the union has a right to appeal to them and advise them of its dispute. If they enter or leave a common situs through neutral entrances, the union can legitimately extend its picketing. In this case, though, the fixtures were ordered, owned by, and delivered to the owner, not Hoff, at the job. Hoff then picked them up on the job and installed them. Did it make a difference in the union's rights? Both the Board and the court concluded that any gate used to deliver materials essential to the primary employer's normal operation, in this case Hoff, is subject to lawful picketing. The picketing was legal.

Particularly at large sites where there is significant traffic, the gates from time to time may be misused. The Board recognizes these possibilities and is not concerned with isolated occurrences that do not establish a pattern of destruction of the reserve gate system.[55] In *Local 76 IBEW and Gaylord Broadcasting Company*,[56] a guard disregarded instructions and allowed delivery of a primary disputant's dumpster to be made through a neutral gate. The guard involved was removed and the instructions on gate use reaffirmed. The Board and the court found the incident to be insignificant and not of sufficient importance to warrant the extension of union picketing.

Misuse of entrances by employers is always a possibility, and, accordingly, unions are given a right to observe entrances for improper use. A question often surfaces as to whether a union representative is at the neutral gate to observe or to signal others not to use the entrance. In some cases, the Board has considered the use of cameras and clipboards by union observers to be legitimate if they also carried signs identifying themselves as observers. Signal picketing, which is in violation of the NLRA, was found in a Board case in which a union business manager stood at a neutral entrance for several hours and spoke to entering workmen, none of whom reported for work. The Board found no legitimate reason for him to be there and concluded it must have been to signal union people to stay off the job.[57] The decision as to whether gate activity is mere observation or prohibited signal picketing is based on the facts in each case, but this again evidences the difficulty in maintaining a proper balance of rights.

The secondary boycott cases discussed to this point have involved picketing activity. A question concerning whether handbilling by a union will be found to be prohibited secondary boycott activity has been raised before the Board, numerous courts, and the Supreme Court. In 1988 the Supreme Court considered a case in which a construction company, High, was building a department store for a tenant, Wilson, at a shopping mall owned by DeBartolo.[58] The union had a dispute with High, the contractor, and distributed handbills asking mall customers not to shop at any stores in the mall until the mall's owner publicly promised that all construction at the mall would be done using contractors who paid their employees fair wages and fringe benefits. These handbills were passed out at all mall entrances without any picketing. Charges were filed by DeBartolo with the Board.

After lengthy litigation before the Board and Fourth Circuit, the Supreme Court finally decided that handbilling could not be held to be secondary boycott activity since there was no violence, picketing, patrolling, or other intimidating conduct. Handbilling by itself is not sufficiently coercive to trigger a secondary boycott finding even though all the other factors such as a "cease doing business with" objective are in place.[59]

While relief through the Board is not sought in mass picketing and violence cases it is the forum of choice in secondary boycott cases for two good reasons. First, state courts are preempted from solving these kinds of problems. State involvement in labor picketing violence cases is justified only because of the state's fundamental interest in protecting public safety, which is not at issue in secondary boycott cases. Second, Congress has recognized that there is a need for quick relief in secondary boycott cases and has provided the Board with priority access to federal district courts to gain injunctions. The priority procedure set out in Section 10(1) of the NLRA can generate relief in roughly ten days, while non-priority procedure under Section 10(j) followed in violence (and other) cases might not bear fruit for over thirty days.

Other labor activity conducted at the periphery of a work site might be covered under other sections of the act, such as Sections 8(e) and 8(b)(4)(A), which pertains to hot cargo picketing; 8(b)(4)(D), regarding jurisdictional dispute picketing; or 8(b)(7)(C), which deals with recognitional or organizational picketing. But because of the lesser potential for security involvement in these types of activities, no attempt will be made to analyze them here. It is of interest, though, that the possibility of a Section 8(b)(7)(C) violation, concerning recognitional and organizational picketing, was lurking in the background of the *Sears* trespass case.

OBSERVATIONS

In the event of picketing, handbilling, or some other kind of demonstration by union agents or employees, employers can think in terms of three areas for finding relief: (1) self help through disciplinary procedures; (2) use of police or state courts if the activity constitutes a trespass, becomes violent, or blocks ingress and egress; and (3) filing unfair labor practice charges with the NLRB to remove certain kinds of violative activity. It is common to have more than one option exercised by an employer at the same time.

While the Board is only accessed directly by employers under one of the three options, the Board might become involved in all of the three. If the employer uses the first option and discharges employees for engaging in protected concerted activity, the Board can negate the discharges if the employees or a union files charges. If the employer warns employees to leave private property, the Board could consider such warning to be violative of the NLRA, per *Sahara Tahoe*. In limited circumstances, non-employee union agents may be permitted by the Board to come on to private property. If this is perceived as a trespass and if the trespass case is heard by a state court and no charges were filed, the court may make a decision on the trespass after interpreting national labor law, in particular, the *Lechmere* case.

This means that if activity is labor related, a problem-solver has to think in terms of the National Labor Relations Act and understand that congressional interest in maintaining labor peace gives this act a key role in resolving employment related issues. Time spent in evaluating the rights and obligations of the parties involved in any labor confrontation including employers, employees, and non-employee union agents will facilitate access to effective relief.

NOTES

1. 135 N.L.R.B. 805 (1962), *enforced*, 320 F.2d 260 (3rd Cir. 1963).
2. 109 N.L.R.B. 1097 (1954).
3. *Chrysler Corporation*, 228 N.L.R.B. 486 (1977).
4. *Ford Motor Company*, 246 N.L.R.B. 671 (1979).
5. 246 N.L.R.B. 671 at 676.
6. 220 N.L.R.B. 431 (1975), *enforced. denied in part*, 540 F.2d 878 (7th Cir. 1976).
7. 540 F.2d 878 at 885.
8. 222 N.L.R.B. 1089 (1976).
9. 300 N.L.R.B. No. 108 (1990).
10. 540 F.2d 878 at 882.
11. *W. J. Roscoe v. NLRB*, 166 N.L.R.B. 618, *enforcement denied in relevant part*, 406 F.2d 725 (6th Cir. 1969).
12. *Clear Pine Mouldings*, 268 N.L.R.B. 1044 (1986), *enforced*, 765 F.2d 148 (9th Cir. 1985); *Tube Craft Inc.*, 287 N.L.R.B. 491 (1987).
13. 291 N.L.R.B. 11, (1988).
14. *NLRB v. Babcock & Wilcox Co.*, 351 U.S. 105 at 112 (1956).
15. *Hudgens v. NLRB*, 424 U.S. 507 at 522 (1976).
16. 351 U.S. 105 at 112.
17. *Scott Hudgens*, 230 N.L.R.B. 414 (1977).
18. 230 N.L.R.B. 414 at 417.
19. 291 N.L.R.B. 11 (1988).
20. 291 N.L.R.B. 11 at 16.
21. 291 N.L.R.B. 11 at 17.
22. *Lechmere v. NLRB*, 914 F.2d 313 (1st Cir. 1990), *enforcing* 295 N.L.R.B. 92 (1989).
23. 292 N.L.R.B. 812 (1989).
24. *Republic Aviation Corp. v. NLRB*, 324 U.S. 793 (1945).
25. *Tri-County Medical Center*, 222 N.L.R.B. 1089.
26. *Southern Services*, 300 N.L.R.B. 161, 136 LRRM 1066 (1991).
27. _____ US _____ , 117 L. Ed. 2d 79, decided January 27, 1992.
28. *Sears, Roebuck & Co. v. San Diego County District Council of Carpentry*, 436 U.S. 180 (1978).
29. *San Diego Building Trades Council v. Garmon*, 359 U.S. 236 (1959).
30. 436 U.S. 180 at 195.
31. *Construction Workers v. Laburnum Construction Corp.*, 347 U.S. 656 (1954); *Youngdahl v. Rainfair Inc.*, 355 U.S. 131 (1957).
32. 436 U.S. 180 at 197.
33. 486 U.S. 180 at 205.
34. 486 U.S. 180 at 206.
35. D. Avery, *Federal Labor Rights and Access to Private Property: The NLRB and the Right to Exclude*, Vol. 11 2 Indus. Rel. L.J. 145, 208–220 (1989); D. O'Connor, *Accommodating Labor's Section 7 Rights to Picket, Solicit and Distribute Literature in Quasi-Public Property with the Owner's Property Rights*, 32 Mercer L. Rev. 769 (1981); Note, *Labor Law–Federal Preemption—The Aftermath of Sears*, 27 Wayne L. Rev. 313 (1980).

36. *Sears Roebuck & Co. v. San Diego County District Council of Carpenters*, 158 Cal. Rptr. 370, 25 Cal. 3d 328, 599, P.2d 676 (1979).

37. 376 Mass. 127, 379 N.E.2d 1086 (1978).

38. 351 U.S. 266, 274–275 (1956).

39. 355 U.S. 131 (1957).

40. *United Mine Workers of America v. Gibbs*, 383 U.S. 715 (1966).

41. N.Y. Lab Law § 807 (McKinney 1965).

42. *Nathan's Famous, Inc. v. Local 1115, Joint Board, AFL-CIO*, 70 Misc.2d 257, 332 N.Y.S.2d 513 (1972).

43. *Lauf v. E. G. Skinner & Company*, 303 U.S. 323 (1988).

44. *Local 761, International Union of Electrical Radio & Machines Workers, AFL-CIO (General Electric Co.) v. NLRB*, 366 U.S. 677 (1961).

45. *Sailor's Union of the Pacific, AFL (Moore Dry Dock Company)*, 92 N.L.R.B. 547 (1950).

46. Local 761, I.U.E. (General Electric), 138 N.L.R.B. 342 (1962).

47. *Building & Construction Trades Council of New Orleans, AFL-CIO (Markwell & Hartz, Inc.)*, 155 N.L.R.B. 319 (1965).

48. 155 N.L.R.B. 319 at 324.

49. *Plumbers & Pipefitters Local 60 (Circle, Inc.)*, 202 N.L.R.B. 99 (1973).

50. *Local 33 (CB Construction Co., Inc.)*, 289 N.L.R.B. 528 (1988), *den. petition for rev.*, 873 F.2d 316 (D.C. Cir. 1989)

51. As a brief aside on the signs that are used at entrances, after reviewing a number of these around the country over the years one begins to think they were created by lawyers for other lawyers. Little thought seems to be given to the idea that they are really there to help people decide how they are going to get into a site. The signs obviously should be large enough so that truck drivers can read them without leaving their cab, and clear and short enough in text so that they do not have to spend an unusual amount of time holding up traffic as they puzzle over their real meaning. Most importantly, union pickets should know exactly where the employer with whom they have a dispute is entering and leaving the site. See, e.g., *IBEW, Local 441 (O'Brien Electric Company)*, 158 N.L.R.B. 549 (1966); *IBEW, Local 640 (Timber Buildings, Inc.)*, 176 N.L.R.B. 150 (1969); *Laborer's Local 1290 (Walter's Foundation)*, 195 N.L.R.B. 370 (1972).

52. 756 F.2d 888 (D.C. Cir. 1985), *reversing* 269 N.L.R.B. 274 (1984).

53. 756 F.2d 888 at 896.

54. 241 N.L.R.B. 694, *enforced*, 642 F.2d 1266 (D.C. Cir. 1980).

55. *Plumbers & Pipefitters Local 48 (Calvert General Contractors)*, 249 N.L.R.B. 1183 (1980).

56. 268 N.L.R.B. 230 (1983), *enforced*, 742 F.2d 498 (9th Cir. 1984).

57. *Iron Workers, Local 433 (R. F. Erection)*, 233 N.L.R.B. 283 (1977), *enforced in part*, 598 F.2d 1154 (9th Cir. 1979).

58. *Edward J. DeBartolo v. Florida Gulf Coast Building Trades Council*, 463 U.S. 147 (1983).

59. *Delta Air Lines*, 293 N.L.R.B. 736 (1989).

5

Arbitration

There is a natural relationship between the National Labor Relations Act and arbitration. Congress passed the NLRA to level the playing field between management and labor by fostering and protecting collective bargaining. The fruit of the collective bargaining process is the labor contract, and it is the purpose of arbitration to resolve disputes that arise over alleged violations of the contract. From Congress's vantage point the whole scheme of protection of the bargaining process through the NLRB and interpretation of the contract by the arbitrator is to preserve labor peace.[1] In many instances the arbitration clause in a labor contract is the quid pro quo for a no-strike clause.

THE BALANCE TO BE STRUCK

As already noted, the fundamental focus of the NLRA is on group activity and the balance of interests is between management and the group.[2] The role of the individual employee is covered in Section 9(a) of the NLRA. That section gives employees the right to present grievances to their employer and have those grievances adjusted as long as the adjustment is not inconsistent with the terms of a collective bargaining contract or agreement then in effect and further that the union representative has been given an opportunity to be present at any adjustment. Thus there is a concern about the individual, but the concern does not seriously color the NLRA's mission of fostering and protecting the collective bargaining process.

The balance to be struck in arbitration was explained this way in Fairweather's *Practice and Procedure in Labor Arbitration*:[3]

Most of the rights which are basic to an employee's claim in arbitration are acquired for the group as well as for the individual via the collective bargaining process. The group has rights which must be protected by the union and the individual employee has separate rights which must be protected by the union but which may be found to be in conflict with the interests of the group and the employer, and the employee may have separate rights to be protected by the company representatives. Hence, "due process" in labor arbitration involves a balancing of the interests of the three—individual, employment group, and employer.

In discussing the same theme, another commentator has noted:

The grievant . . . is part of an industrial community. The group to which he belongs is not merely a vessel containing the sum total of the individual interests of its members. It has independent rights and interests of its own which may be deeply affected by his actions. Moreover, a large part of the "rights" claimed by the grievant owe their existence to the group. Nevertheless, he can demand that they be given recognition and protection. But the subject matter and the necessities of the situation strike a different balance, because they have to take into account those independent rights and interests of the group.[4]

The commentator went on to say that, in balancing the interests of management, the group, and the individual, the subordination of the rights of the individual does not seem to violate the overall interest in fairness.

Since most security-related cases in arbitration involve individual employee activity, it is important to keep the individual's status in mind. He or she is obviously important, but individual rights are often subordinate to or keyed to the rights and obligations of the group.

THE WORKINGS OF THE ARBITRATION PROCESS

Background

The arbitration process is generally informal in nature and its intent is to resolve problems in an expeditious, fair, and final fashion. Arbitrators are obligated to draw their decisions from the essence of the labor contract and attempt to determine on what it was the parties had agreed. They are not supposed to make decisions based on what they think the agreement should have been. In carrying out their functions, arbitrators are interested in custom, past practice, or, as it is often called, the "law of the shop." These kinds of things give meaning to the actual words of the contract.

Basic Concepts

This section explores some basic concepts common to most arbitration cases and then analyzes them in the context of a number of cases. It should first be understood that arbitrators are not obligated to follow the decisions or thinking of their peers and there is a wide variance in the acceptance and application of the different theories. Still, there is enough of a common thread to make the exercise of value.

Discharge

Discharge is recognized to be the extreme industrial penalty, since the employee's job, seniority, and other contractual benefits and reputation are at stake.[5] As a consequence, the employer is obligated to carry the burden of proof and this is usually tested against a contract clause that provides that discharges will be only for "just cause."

The arbitrator in a *Maverick Tube Co.* drug possession case[6] discussed the meaning of just cause at some length and in turn quoted arbitrator Platt in *Riley Stoker* (7 LA 764) on the subject:

To be sure, no standard exists to aid an arbitrator in finding a conclusive answer to such a question (what constitutes just cause), and therefore, perhaps the best we can do is decide what a reasonable man mindful of the habits and customs of industrial life and of the standards of justice in fair dealing prevalent in the community ought to have done under similar circumstances and in that light to decide whether the conduct of the discharged employee was defensible and that the disciplinary penalty just.

The *Maverick Tube* arbitrator concluded that employers must act in a reasonable and fair manner—not one that is arbitrary or capricious. Reasonableness, then, is the order of the day.

Now that we have this somewhat vague definition of just cause or justifiable cause or proper cause, or whatever term might mean the same thing, it is now necessary to understand that that vagueness is in turn separated into other somewhat vague areas. In short, the degrees of proof necessary to prove just cause will vary with the circumstances. Generally arbitrators will refer to the preponderance of the evidence rule, but there may be a higher degree of proof required if the alleged activity is of a kind recognized and punished by the criminal law.

A number of years ago, Arbitrator Smith stated:

It seems reasonable and proper to hold the alleged misconduct of a kind which carries the stigma of social disapproval as well as disapproval under accepted canons of plant discipline should be clearly and convincingly established by the evidence. Reasonable doubts raised by the proofs should be resolved in favor of the accused.[7]

This theme was carried out in an *Associated Grocers of Colorado* case.[8] The company was suffering significant theft and vandalism problems and instituted an undercover program. Subsequently about fifty employees were both terminated and convicted in criminal proceedings involving narcotics as well as thefts. The grievant, in this case a truck driver, was not subject to criminal action but was terminated for on- and off-the-job use of drugs. The discharge decision was based on surreptitiously taped admissions of use to an undercover agent.

The arbitrator was faced with the problem of determining whether or not the employee was "putting on" or telling the truth when he talked about his drug use. To frame the question in terms of burden of proof, he resorted to Smith's statement about reasonable doubts resolved in favor of the accused. In the arbitrator's judgment, the employer had not met its burden. As he stated, "Despite substantial evidence of the grievant's guilt . . . I hold a reasonable doubt of such guilt based upon his testimony that such admissions were a put-on."[9]

Arbitrators will shift back and forth in the use of terminology in discussing the burden of proof in social stigma cases involving theft, drugs, or other charges involving moral turpitude. In *Maverick Tube*, for example, the arbitrator said he was using a clear and convincing standard, which was less than reasonable doubt but more than a preponderance of the evidence test. These differing standards are almost impossible to practically define, and security people should primarily keep in mind in conducting their investigations that it takes good, solid evidence to win a social stigma discharge case.

On Plant/Off Plant Activity

In determining whether or not certain on-plant activity warrants discharge, arbitrators are guided in part by the nature of the activity, the rules of the workplace, the record and service of the employee, and comparable treatment of other employees. Serious offenses include theft, falsification of business or employment records; fighting; trafficking, possession, and use of drugs; picket line misconduct; sabotage; sexual harassment; and other violations.[10]

A new set of benchmarks is used if the activity takes place away from the work site. Most arbitrators will check on three points: (1) can the behavior harm the company's reputation or product; (2) does the behavior render the employee unable to perform his duties or appear at work, in which case the discharge would be based upon inefficiency or excessive absenteeism; and (3) was the behavior of such a nature that employees refuse or are reluctant or unable to work with him?[11]

Since these cases stand more or less by themselves and seldom involve on-plant activity, several will be treated at this point to give a feel for the subject. In a 1973 *National Steel Corp.* case,[12] Arbitrator McDermott found that the employer had proper cause for suspending three employees following their indictment for possession and sale of marijuana and for discharging one of them after he was convicted. There was no on-plant activity involved.

McDermott first noted that arbitrators have generally held that the impact on business requirement was not met where the disciplinary action was for an arrest because of possession of marijuana off company property. He then moved to the subjects of suspension as a result of indictment for possession and sale and discharge for conviction on the same charges. In his judgment, possession of the substance for purposes of sale for profit constitutes a far more serious violation than mere possession and use.

In discussing the fact that the activity took place off company property he stated:

This distinction I find to be rather arbitrary where it is dealing with this matter of possession for sale for profit. What it implies is that the Company must wait until the individual seller is caught engaging in the illegal act on Company premises before it can act to protect its interests and the welfare of its employees. It also implies that persons who engage in the sale of drugs for profit will necessarily refuse to sell on Company property or to fellow employees, even if they had an opportunity to do so.

The nature of drug sales is such that it is not easily detected, and to require that a company cannot act against employees who engage in the sale of illegal drugs for profit, unless it catches them in the act on company property, would deny to the company the power to police successfully its work force either to prevent the creation of a drug problem among its employees or to combat effectively an existing problem that may have risen.[13]

The arbitrator went on to say:

Obviously, indictment on a criminal charge is not the same as being guilty of the charge, and for many criminal indictments there would not exist justification for the company to suspend an employee or take other disciplinary action against him until after he had been found guilty. However, the seriousness of the drug problem and the need for an employer to strive to prevent any drug abuse among its employees, would warrant a finding that a company has the right to act immediately to protect its own interests and the interests of its employees from the possibility that persons charged with possession of drugs for the purpose of sale for profit will not engage in such activity on company property and with fellow employees.[14]

As to the discharge case for one of the employees who pleaded guilty to possession for purpose of sale, the arbitrator stated, "If, as has been held, the company was warranted in suspending him from employment on the basis of his indictment, it must be concluded that there existed proper cause for his discharge upon his being found guilty of the charges against him."[15]

The *National Steel* case has since been cited many times by other arbitrators, but not all have agreed with its approach. In a *W. R. Grace & Co.* case[16] the arbitrator considered an off-duty possession and sale conviction and first discussed how other arbitrators have treated off-duty activity and the nexus with the job. Among other things he noted that "Misconduct which itself makes clear an individual's incompatibility with his job (a kindergarten teacher who is convicted of child abuse, a security guard of shoplifting) obviously indicated a real and direct relationship. Similarly, fears, animosities, and other negative reactions and attitudes of fellow employees respecting working with or around the individual constitute a legitimate connector."[17] However, as far as this arbitrator was concerned, there had to be more than proof that the employee had been selling drugs away from the plant. He stated, "I do not believe that it is necessary, or even plausible to assume that every individual who has sold drugs in the past will continue to do so in the future."[18] In the search for more factors, it appears that he would have been satisfied with the employer's position if, for example, there had been some evidence that the employer's reputation was being sullied. He noted with apparent approval the *Alabama Power Co.* case[19] in which there was considerable local press coverage of the employee's arrest, status as an employee, and description as a "pusher." Further, the Alabama Power contract made unlawful drug involvement off company property grounds for termination. The added factor in a *Martin-Marietta Aero-Space* case[20] was the verifiable history of drug abuse by the grievant. The arbitrator noted that, "Where Grievant has not changed after a prior conviction and has only escalated his problem by moving to a stronger and more expensive drug, it is reasonable for this Employer to anticipate a propensity exists to use and sell prohibited substances."[21]

These, again, are just examples of the kinds of exceptions to the normal rule that what takes place off site is none of the employer's business. The shadings and variations are considerable, but it is critical that the questioned conduct has some kind of connection to the workplace before discharge or discipline is warranted.[22]

Insubordination

This item is of such importance in so many security-related cases that it warrants special attention at this time. In case after case employers are faced with employees who refuse to comply with orders to open lunch boxes, cars on parking lots, purses, and such property, or submit to urinalysis or other tests. Arbitrator McGury stated the general rule in a 1964 *Simoniz Co.* case:

It is a well recognized principle of industrial relations, that in a situation where an employee is directed to do something which he feels he should not be required to do, he must follow the direction, and file a grievance on it later, unless the request involves a hazard to his health or safety, or he could be involved in an illegal or immoral act.[23]

Since employers have a right to a reasonable amount of cooperation from their employees, the refusal to obey an order constitutes insubordination.[24]

Evidence

In keeping with the informal nature of arbitration, arbitrators generally are flexible in the rules of evidence. As stated in *How Arbitration Works*:

Although strict observance of legal rules of evidence usually is not required, the parties in all cases must be given adequate opportunity to present all of their evidence, giving the parties a free hand in presenting any type of evidence thought to strengthen and clarify their case.[25]

By the same token, arbitrators are not interested in conducting endless hearings and may refuse to admit evidence that lacks relevance or probative value.

For security people a major concern is not only the admissibility of certain evidence acquired during the course of an investigation but also the weight given to such evidence even if it is admitted. This problem exists because security-related matters represent the ultimate tension between employees' privacy and personal dignity and the employer's right to run an efficient business and obligation to provide a safe workplace.

As an example, arbitrators simply do not like polygraphs. Arbitrators will not sustain penalties for refusal to take polygraph examinations, frequently do not allow the results into evidence, and seldom give them any weight if they are admitted. One arbitrator framed it this way: "The conclusion is compelling that no matter how well qualified educationally and experientially may be the polygraphist, the results of the lie-detector tests should routinely be ruled inadmissible."[26]

There seems to be an instinct on the part of some arbitrators to resort to criminal law standards to properly protect employees from what are perceived to be overly aggressive employers. More commonly, though, arbitrators recognize the fundamental distinction between criminal prosecution and arbitration proceedings. Criminal matters involve the individual and the government. The whole process is geared toward protecting the liberties of the accused while recognizing the obligations of the government to provide for the public safety. "The defendant accused of the commission of a crime struggles against his accuser, the state, with its overwhelming powers and sanctions threatening his life and liberty."[27]

In contrast, the individual in the employment setting is part of a group and gets many of his or her rights from the group. The rights of the individual may be subordinate to the rights of the group and to the rights of the employer to run an efficient business. "The difference in the relationship of an accused versus the state and the relationship of a grievant to the total work group and to his or her employer must be emphasized to encourage arbitrators from blindly adopting criminal law 'due process' rules in arbitration."[28]

Entrapment arguments have not been readily accepted by arbitrators— again, the entrapment defense is a creature of criminal law used by defendants to keep improperly gained evidence out of evidence.[29] In discussing the evidence problem, Arbitrator McGury stated in *Hennis Freight Lines*:[30]

It may be argued that the spirit of the Constitutional prohibition against unreasonable search and seizure is violated, where the fruits of what has been judicially determined to be an illegal arrest and, therefore, an unreasonable search and seizure, are nevertheless allowed to be considered by the Company or an arbitrator for discharge.

There is an essential difference between procedural and substantive rights of the parties. The constitutional principles may keep the grievants out of jail but do they guarantee them their jobs in the face of Company knowledge of extremely strong proof of dishonesty involving Company property.

The arbitrator in *Aldens, Inc.*[31] recognized the distinction between the criminal law and arbitration in a very practical way. When entering her workplace, a female employee stated, "Nobody is going to inspect my purse unless they have a search warrant." The arbitrator commented that "No Company could stay in business and continue to provide job opportunities for the membership of the union unless it protected itself against loss by theft."[32] He ignored the constitutional argument and went directly to the reasonableness and application of the company rule in searches. It is interesting that this rationale tracks that of the federal courts in the *New Jersey v. T.L.O.*, *O'Conner v. Ortega*, and *Schowengert v. General Dynamics* cases discussed in chapter 1. Even in the government sector, management carrying out non–law enforcement tasks is not encumbered with criminal law obligations. Arbitrators in the private sector can hardly expect more from employers who are not even covered by the constitution.

Weight given to evidence by arbitrators once it has been admitted can often be a problem in security-related matters, especially in cases involving the use of undercover agents. Arbitrator Goldstein in a *Modine Manufacturing Co.* case[33] noted that many arbitrators will not sustain a discharge based on the uncorroborated reports or testimony of an undercover agent, citing such cases as *ARA Manufacturing Co.* (83 LA 581), *Costing Engineering* (71 LA 949), *General Telephone Co. of California* (73 LA 531), and *General Portland, Inc.* (62 LA 709).

This is not to say categorically that such cases cannot be made. In
Consumer Plastics Corp.[34] an arbitrator tipped the scales in favor of an
undercover agent in a drug case where it was evident that the agent had
a strong background in the drug investigation business and his testimony
was lucid and clear and stood up well under cross examination. Further,
the grievants admitted they had lied in earlier unemployment compensation hearings.

As often happens in cases involving the use of undercover agents, part
of the defense in the *Consumer Plastics* case involved entrapment. In
responding to that defense, Arbitrator Garnholy quoted from another case,
Rust Engineering, in which the arbitrator said:

It must be stated that the matter at issue is arbitration, not a criminal prosecution.
The job of the arbitrator, in contrast to the function of a judge or jury, is to
interpret and apply the collective-bargaining agreement.[35]

However, just to put a belt on with the suspenders, the arbitrator added
that the grievants were not entrapped anyway. Entrapment in the criminal
law takes place when a law enforcement officer persuades a person to
commit a crime he otherwise would not have committed.

In *Dietrich Industries*[36] an arbitrator was also impressed with the fact
that the agent made daily reports, had no interest in the outcome of the
investigation, and his testimony was exact and specific as to dates, people,
and method of drug use. On the other hand, the grievant's denial was
general and self-serving, and it glossed over events.

Due Process

This concept is hard to capture in a few words, but generally speaking
in a discharge or discipline case, arbitrators will look to see if there is an
established and known rule, whether the rule is based on the legitimate
interests of the employer, whether fair procedures have been followed,
and whether there is consistency in discipline. These elements will be
explored independently to give a feel for the process.

1. *Established and Known Rule.* In *B. Green Co.* an arbitrator was
presented with the question of whether the smoking of one marijuana
cigarette during a work break on company premises and the possession
of another warranted "the severe penalty of discharge."[37] There was no
company rule expressly prohibiting the possession or use of marijuana
on company property.

The arbitrator noted that in another case a fellow arbitrator had given
controlling weight to the absence of a rule.[38] Yet, another had found the
absence no bar to discharge.[39] With this as background, he expressed his
view that the absence of an express rule, while a factor to be considered,
is not controlling. All serious misconduct need not be codified and pub-

lished in the form of a rule. An employee may reasonably be deemed to expect that criminal conduct such as theft of company property or the use of drugs that may affect employee work performance or safety may subject him to discharge. In this *Green* case the discharge was sustained.

A *Sahara Coal Co.* case[40] presents two different rules and two different results. Management officials smelled smoke in a mine area and suspected two employees of smoking cigarettes in violation of various laws and company policy. A manager requested a body search of both employees and they refused. They were subsequently asked to take a drug test and again they refused.

The arbitrator found that there was a known policy on smoking underground, the employees were on notice of the policy, and they were advised that it was believed they had violated that rule. They, accordingly, were obligated to submit to that search. However, the arbitrator did not believe the manager had reasonable cause to require the grievants to submit to a drug test, as there was no evidence that the two employees had been observed under the influence of drugs. While the drug test issue focuses on the reasonable application of a rule, it does highlight the need for a rule in most cases.

This chapter started off by noting that there is a natural relationship between the NLRA and arbitration. Sometimes, though, it is not an exact fit, and the rule-making area is one in which there is some difference between the two systems. As discussed in chapter 3, employers have an obligation to bargain over those things that have an impact on conditions of employment. In *Johnson-Bateman Co.*[41] the Board found that a drug and alcohol testing program was a mandatory subject of bargaining. The Board further found that a general management rights clause did not constitute a waiver of bargaining rights. For a waiver to be found, the Board requires that it be clear and unmistakable.

Meanwhile, in the arbitration arena, it is generally believed that employers have a right to make work rules as they see fit. Bargaining over the rule is not a necessary element.[42] These two positions can come into conflict not only in Board cases, *Johnson-Bateman* for example, but also in arbitration cases. In *Material Services Corp.*[43] the arbitrator pursued the NLRB approach and found that no bargaining had taken place on a drug policy, and accordingly, the employer did not have just cause to discharge an employee for refusal to take a drug test. A supervisor had detected marijuana smoke in the cab of the employee's end loader and asked him to take a drug test, which he refused.

The point to keep in mind is that an employer's security-related program can be challenged either with the Board under a refusal to bargain charge or with an arbitrator. Even with an arbitrator challenge, the arbitrator may opt to use the Board test, particularly if the case has been deferred to arbitration by the Board. The best procedure, then, would be to follow the Board's bargaining requirement prior to the implementation of a security program.

Returning to arbitration and the need for rules, while the "I didn't know about the rule" defense has to be overcome more often than not by the proven existence of a rule, there are circumstances, such as those alluded to in the *Green Co.* case, that do not require a rule. Theft is the best example. Theft is often mentioned in contracts as a reason for discharge but even if it is not, most arbitrators will sustain discharges based on theft because it is inherently wrong.[44] While it is understood that there cannot be a written rule for everything and some things are just plain common sense, it behooves management to insure that its employees are made aware of the rules of the workplace.

2. *Rules Based on Legitimate Interests of the Employer.* This is obviously the part of the balancing of rights process that requires management to explain how its rule is in the interest of running an efficient business and providing a safe workplace. The legitimacy of the specific rule is then usually measured against its incursion into privacy. Rules relative to searches and drug testing are constantly being weighed with this balance in mind.

Arbitrators have consistently held that the employer has a right to conduct a search of lunch boxes, lockers and persons and that refusal to permit a search may include discharge. These arbitrators have been attentive to the motivation for the search and the circumstances under which it was conducted, attempting to balance the legitimate interests of the employer and the personal dignity of the employee.[45]

These words set the tone and preceded the analysis of facts in a *Shell Oil Co.* case. The arbitrator went on to note that the company had "sufficient reason to be concerned, even alarmed at the reports C———was carrying a gun and drugs in his lunch box. The search was conducted by a professional with as much regard for personal privacy as the legitimate ends of the search permitted."

The search in question involved opening lunch boxes and disclosing their contents, loosening belts, shaking and raising pant legs, removing boots, opening lockers for inspection, and then allowing inspection of personal vehicles. The rule that was being followed not only set out the right to conduct reasonable searches but also the motivation for it: "To help insure a safe, healthy, and productive work environment." The arbitrator found the employer's search program in this case to be reasonable and the discharge for refusal to comply with the search request to be legitimate.

The purpose of a search rule was tested in *Chamberlain Mfg. Corp.*,[46] where the employer searched employees entering and leaving its place of business under well-publicized rules. The purpose of the entry search was to keep intoxicants out of the workplace. On entering, an employee refused a search of his lunch box and returned it to his truck on the parking lot. When he returned to reenter the plant without his lunch box, his entry was denied and he was terminated.

The union did not question the employer's search rule. It took the position that once the employee had returned the lunch box to the truck, the purpose of the rule had been met and he was now eligible to enter the workplace. In the arbitrator's judgment, the employee had acknowledged the legitimacy of the rule and had not challenged it. The company got what it wanted—an intoxicant-free workplace—and the employee should have been allowed to enter and should not have been discharged.

As work rules intrude more into employee privacy, their reasonableness or work-relatedness comes under closer scrutiny.[47] In *Vista Chemical Co.* arbitrator Duff was asked to decide whether the word "clothing" should be deleted from the company search policy. Duff commented that in his judgment,

To preclude the company from making searches of employees' clothing in all instances would create a sanctuary for contraband and emasculate most of its other efforts to police substance abuse altogether. To speak of conducting searches of employees' clothing as unreasonable per se and without reference to particular prevailing factual contexts ignores the realities of industrial life.[48]

Duff went on to say that the fact that searches are undisputably grievable provides a viable safeguard against insensitive, unnecessarily invasive or abusive clothing searches.

In *Aldens Inc.*[49] a female employee leaving a plant was asked to pull up her pant leg to uncover a bulge a guard had noticed on her leg. She refused and was discharged. In the arbitrator's judgment, "there is no need [to] authorize a personal search of an employee who patently has something unusual carried in an unusual place. It is not customary for people to have square bulges under their pant leg and it would be a clear dereliction of duty for a guard to observe such a condition and do nothing about it."[50]

The concern over legitimate employee interests is set out in numerous other cases. In a *Pepsi Cola Bottling Co.* case the arbitrator stated:

Employee drug and alcohol abuse is without question one of the most serious and difficult problems faced by employers today. It is of particular concern to those employers, like Pepsi Cola, whose business activities can be dangerous if performed by employees whose normal skills, judgment, and perceptions have been impaired. The hazards presented by drivers who operate large vehicles on public streets and roadways while under the influence of alcohol or controlled substances require no elaboration. . . . The grievance in this case squarely presents the conflict which is typical and fundamental in these disputes: that between the employee's right and expectation of personal privacy and the employer's need to detect and control drug and alcohol use which impairs the employee's ability to perform his job.[51]

An arbitrator was asked in a *Texas Utilities Electric Co.* case[52] to determine, among other things, whether a "snitching" provision was reasonable. The provision was related to a drug program and provided confidentiality for the informant. The arbitrator noted that both parties wholeheartedly agreed that they wanted a safe and efficient workplace free from drugs. He reasoned that to promote that end, the more information sources management could utilize, the more likely a drug-free environment could be realized. He concluded, "Hence, that asking hourly workers to cooperate with management in ferreting out those who would violate the drug rules was rational and reasonable. This conclusion was reached despite the fact social customs dictate that one should not be a rat or a snitch."[53]

In essence, then, employer rules should be based on some legitimate business needs and be viewed by the average person to be reasonable.

3. *Fair Procedures*. For success to be achieved by employers in a security-related case it is critical that employers follow their own rules. *Kerr-McKee Chemical Corp.*[54] is a case in point. The case involved the drug search of an employee's van on a company parking lot and whether or not the employer had reasonable cause for the search. The arbitrator framed it this way:

I have no question that the Company had a legitimate concern about the use of and sale of drugs at its Henderson facility.

I have no question that the Union . . . acknowledged the legitimacy of the Company's concern and the appropriateness of random testing of employees for drugs.

I have no question that the drug investigator hired by the Company . . . is well qualified to do any testing and any searching.

I have no serious question that the Company established . . . the required chain-of-custody of the substance found in the van. . . .

I am inclined to conclude that [items found in the van] were drug paraphernalia.

One would think at this point that the employer had run a perfect case, but this was not so.

The arbitrator could not sustain the discharge because, in his mind, the employer had failed to follow its own rules in handling the search. Two rules were involved. In one, the employer retained the right to search vehicles in the parking lot belonging to employees "who are suspected as 'pushers.'" In the other rule, employees were warned that "when warranted" an employee's vehicle can be searched for prohibited items and substances. As far as the arbitrator was concerned, unverifiable information that the grievant was involved in drugs on company property was not enough to trigger the search under the requirements of the policy.

If an employer finds its work rules overly restricting its own activities, the employer can change them and notify employees accordingly. Circumvention of one's own rules asks for trouble.

4. *Union Representation.* Arbitrators have found in numerous cases that failure to include union representatives in security-related interviews constituted a violation of due process. Generally these cases do not involve the application of *Weingarten* but the application of contract provisions. In *General Dynamics Corvair Division*[55] the arbitrator considered a situation in which the employer got an anonymous tip that an employee was bringing drugs onto plant property. An investigator with a companion interviewed the employee for several hours but never told her about marijuana seeds observed in her car or her right to have a union steward present. Again, this was not a *Weingarten* case but one in which the contract provided that if an employee is called in for a drug-related interview, a union representative would be given an opportunity to be present.

Following the interview, the investigators took her to her car where they were joined by a union steward. Nothing was said to the steward about the seeds. The employee was ordered to allow a search of the car and when she refused she was fired.

The arbitrator found that although the marijuana seeds in the employee's car gave the employer reasonable cause to believe that she had brought illegal drugs onto company property, the failure to call a union steward at the beginning of the interview was a serious deviation from the drug policy agreement. The arbitrator also stated that the employer had erred by not telling the employee or later the steward about the observation of the seeds in the car. The discharge was set aside.

In a like vein, the arbitrator in *Kraft Inc.*[56] considered the employer's failure to meet its contract obligation relative to union representation at interviews to be an impediment to sustaining a discharge. These employees were found by a guard squeezing themselves between pallets in a secluded area of a warehouse. An odor of marijuana smoke was also detected and ashes and charred paper were found on the floor. There was a work rule prohibiting the possession and use of drugs in the workplace. The employees were asked to submit to a search and were advised that if they did not consent they would be suspended for insubordination. They did not consent and they were suspended and later discharged.

The arbitrator found that the company's request was reasonable and the employees knew the consequences of not complying. In his judgment the employees were insubordinate, but the penalty was not appropriate because the employees were not permitted to have union representation. Much of the investigative discussion had taken place in the company office, and attempts by a steward to get into the office were thwarted. Further, supervisors had denied the employees an opportunity to meet with the steward prior to the interviews. The steward did have some time with the employees but the meeting was cut short when he was directed to leave.

As far as the arbitrator was concerned, "Equity requires that the Company not be permitted to fully enforce its contractual rights to discharge employees without first complying with the contractual due process requirements regarding representation."[57] The discharges were turned into suspensions.

5. *Constitutional Protections*. There has been some discussion of the application of criminal law standards in the prior section on evidence, but further exploration of the subject is valuable, as it is raised as a defense in numerous arbitration situations. These comments on burdens on private security people should be contrasted with the burdens placed on law enforcement officers as discussed in chapter 1. The arbitration cases to be covered preceded *New Jersey v. TLO*, *O'Conner v. Ortega*, and *Schowengert v. General Dynamics*, but they all seem to hammer at the same thing: the employers involved were not enforcing the criminal law.

The arbitrator in a *Dow Chemical Co.* case[58] was concerned over the possibility of a violation of the fourth amendment in a search matter. He noted that while constitutional limitations on unlawful searches are normally construed as restraints on government authorities and are not usually applicable to contractual disputes between private parties,

nevertheless the rights to privacy and personal dignity are so fundamentally a part of the American tradition that they should at least be given consideration by a labor arbitrator in passing on search problems in plants. This is because plant rules and their application must meet the test of fundamental fairness if they are to be sustained.[59]

It appears that this arbitrator was searching for some kind of benchmark for measuring the fairness of employer conduct, and while he was fairly sure the Fourth Amendment was not it, he was not quite sure what was. For example, he quoted from *Aldens Inc.*, in which the arbitrator said:

While everyone has a right to all constitutional protections, he does not have a right to a particular job. There are circumstances where an employee cannot contemporaneously fully enjoy all of his constitutional rights, and full freedom from Company discipline. The contract for wages carries with it the restrictions, and even complete suspension of many individual rights during working hours.[60]

This tendency to drift toward the constitution and peace officer analogies but not actually apply constitutional restrictions is evident in other cases. In a *Champion Spark Plug Co.* case the arbitrator stated:

It is quite inappropriate to attempt to establish an exact parallel between rights of citizens on the street and employees in the plant. When employees take on employment, they do so subject to normal restrictions inherent in a crowded industrial setting. The right of Management to fairly operate its business without undue impediments must be balanced against the right of the employees to continue to enjoy their civil rights to the fullest. However, the two will clash and in the factual setting of this case, it is not inappropriate to treat a supervisor by analogy to a peace officer in the plant setting.[61]

In this case, the arbitrator determined that a supervisor's request to an employee to unbutton his sweater with the steward present was appropriate considering the potential for a violation of a plant rule on possession of alcohol.[62] The analogy to peace officers, though, can cause the use of a legal standard that is not appropriate.

In a fifth amendment case, *Simoniz Co.*,[63] the arbitrator discussed the applicability of that amendment to criminal cases. In the case at hand, the employee had been called as a witness in the trial of a fellow employee involving plant thefts and had exercised his fifth amendment right against self-incrimination. The arbitrator was asked to include this refusal to testify as evidence of refusal to cooperate in the plant investigation. Other elements of lack of cooperation were also introduced.

As far as the arbitrator was concerned, a person invoking the fifth amendment has a right to this advantage in a criminal proceeding but does not also have the right to completely avoid any financial, social, or other possible losses that he might incur as a result of exercising his constitutional right. The arbitrator concluded that the grievant had a right to make himself 200 percent secure against criminal involvement, but he could not at the same time protect his rights to future employment when his action frustrated the rights and interests of the company.

This does not put the issue at rest, though, because some arbitrators will carry the constitution into the workplace. In a *King Company* case, arbitrator Bard concluded that an employee ought not be punished by his employer for failing to cooperate in an investigation which could lead to his incarceration.[64] In this arbitrator's judgment, "There can be no doubt whatsoever that to use the threat of termination or suspension to seek a confession of criminal conduct clearly impinges upon the Fifth Amendment rights of the grievants."[65] The arbitrator also brought the *Miranda* rule into the case and contended that under *Miranda* the Fifth Amendment creates a privilege against self incrimination which is available outside of the criminal proceedings and serves to protect persons in all settings in which their freedom of action is curtailed to incriminate themselves.

This approach seems to not only constitute a misinterpretation of *Miranda*, but also evidences a misunderstanding of the balance that arbitrators should attempt to maintain.

The differences between criminal proceedings and labor arbitration proceedings, as already mentioned, are critical in preventing loose borrowing that distorts the decision-making process.[66] If arbitrators feel that the employer has been unfair in its treatment of an employee or unreasonable in the application of its rules, they have recourse to the laws of industrial due process set out in considerable number of arbitration cases to draw from without trying to buttress their decisions by accessing an area of the law that is trying to solve another range of problems. In the *King Company* case, it would appear the employee was insulated from legitimate employer inquiry because of pending criminal action. A similarly situated employee without the criminal action hanging over his head would be obligated to cooperate with an employer investigation or suffer the consequences. Something seems to be out of balance; the one facing criminal action should not be placed in a better position.

6. *Application of Discipline*. Arbitrators will give considerable sympathy to employees with long unblemished service records in reaching their decisions in discharge cases. They will also look to see if employers have regularly enforced the work rules that are at issue and they will consider whether violations of the rules have been treated unequally.

The arbitrator in *Lakeside Jubilee Foods*[67] decided that the discharge of a twenty-two-year service employee with a good work record for off-site shoplifting was too severe a penalty. The employee, an assistant manager in a supermarket operation, had pleaded guilty to two counts of shoplifting at another store but recognized he had a problem and immediately went into counseling. The arbitrator returned the employee to work with no back pay with the understanding that he continue treatment and furnish his employer with regular reports. This lessening of the penalty was based on length of service, good work record, off-site activity, no actual financial loss to the employer, and no expressed reluctance on the part of fellow employees to work with him.

The phrase "double jeopardy" sometimes comes into the penalty end of arbitration cases but it should not be concluded that this means another sojourn into criminal law. "In industrial relations the doctrine of double jeopardy means that if an employee is punished for a specific act, he is entitled to regard such punishment as final for that particular misconduct."[68]

A good case for pulling a number of these elements together is *Georgia Power Co.*[69] The issues included whether a drug detection search was proper, whether a dog search provided reasonable cause to conduct a search of the grievant's vehicle, whether there was reasonable or probable cause to require the grievant to take a drug test when no drugs were found in his car, and whether the discharge was for sufficient and reasonable cause.

Arbitrator Holley had no problem in finding that the implementation of the dog search was proper and cited numerous precedents. He noted that the company had a problem, established a policy, effectively communicated it, demonstrated the use of the dogs to employees, and placed signs around advising of possible searches on the parking lot. Step 1, the established policy step, was completed. Holley next found that a dog search conducted on the day in question was a reasonable application of the policy. A supervisor had picked up a rumor that there might be a drug problem in a certain area. In Holley's judgment, then, the search was reasonable and not arbitrary and capricious. Step 2 was completed.

As to whether or not the two dogs alerting on the vehicle gave reasonable cause to search the car, Holley noted that the first checkpoint is on the dogs. Were they properly trained and certified? In this case they were. Then, was the dog search conducted with appropriate rest periods for the dogs? Okay, again. As far as Holley was concerned, Step 3 had been passed.

The dogs alerted on grievant's car but did this trigger a legitimate request to take a drug test? The battle then took place over whether the measure was going to be probable cause or reasonable cause. Keep in mind discussions in chapter 1 on the test approved by the federal courts in non–law enforcement government workplace searches. Those courts opted for a reasonableness test. Holley discussed prior arbitration decisions on the same subject at length and then decided that while the fourth amendment was not applicable, there must be a strong connection between the evidence and the employee before testing of the employ can be justified. Holley concluded

that in this case involving an employee in a safety-sensitive position, that two drug detection dog alerts coupled with the grievant's testimony providing additional support for the possibility of a drug presence, provided the requisite linkage between the evidence and the grievant in this case to require the grievant to take the drug test. But such linkage does not require the show of 'probable cause' under the Fourth Amendment standard.[70]

Step 4 was cleared. By the way, grievant tested positive for marijuana.

The arbitrator concluded that the grievant had violated the drug policy and was appropriately discharged.

FINALITY OF ARBITRATION

Benefits of arbitration include the relative speed and low cost of the process as compared to litigation. Another critical element in favor of arbitration is its finality. Most employers and unions are interested in resolving a problem and moving on with the business. Naturally, a number of arbitration decisions seem off-the-wall to one of the parties concerned, and a real question developed as to whether the interest in finality exceeds the interest in challenging a perceived miscarriage of justice.

The *United Paperworkers International Union v. Misco, Inc.* case[71] put the issue to rest. An employee was arrested by police in the back seat of someone else's car in Misco's parking lot with marijuana smoke in the air and a lighted marijuana cigarette in a front seat ashtray. Seeds were found by the police in a search of the employee's car. This information was passed on to Misco, which in turn discharged the employee for violation of a workplace rule against possession and use of controlled substances on company property.

The matter was arbitrated and the arbitrator ordered the employee returned to work because there was insufficient proof of use or possession. The normal challenge of arbitration decisions is via Section 301 of the Labor Management Relations Act and the challenge takes place in federal district court. In this case both the district court and the court of appeals found for the employer, ruling that reinstatement would violate public policy against the operation of dangerous machinery by persons under the influence of drugs.

The Supreme Court decided that absent fraud by the parties or dishonesty by the arbitrator, reviewing courts in arbitration cases are not authorized to reconsider the merits of an award. In the Court's judgment, to do so would undermine the federal policy of privately settling labor disputes by arbitration without governmental intervention. When the parties have agreed to submit all questions of contract interpretation to the arbitrator, the reviewing court is confined to ascertaining whether the award draws its essence from the contract and does not simply reflect the arbitrator's own notion of industrial justice. As long as the arbitrator is even arguably construing or applying the scope of his authority, the court cannot overturn his decision simply because it disagrees with his factual findings, contract interpretations, or choice of remedies.

As to the public policy issue, the court commented that it was only interested in some explicit public policy that is "well defined and dominant and is to be ascertained by reference to the laws and legal precedents and not from general considerations of supposed public interests."[72] In the court's judgment, the formulation of a policy against the operation of dangerous machinery under the influence of drugs did not meet the test.

The message of the case is that there is a very high degree of finality in arbitration matters and the best means of preventing bizarre decisions is to choose reasonable and balanced arbitrators.

PREEMPTION

The balance has been struck between the employer and the group as represented by a union. An employee's individual rights might have to take a less important position to those of the group and the employer. But what happens if the employee does not like that less important role and takes his grievance to a state court in the form of a civil action?

To answer the question it is necessary, again, to review congressional concerns in labor matters. Since the 1930s, federal legislation has evidenced a primary congressional interest in maintaining labor peace. As noted in chapter 4, the Supreme Court decided in *San Diego Building Trades Council v. Garmon*[73] that the National Labor Relations Act preempted state labor interests in matters that arguably were in violation of that statute. The idea was that it would be very difficult to maintain labor peace if management and labor had to contend with forty or fifty different sets of state rules. As discussed in chapters 2, 3, and 4, the Board's focus has been on maintaining a balance between employers and groups of employees. Preserving labor peace meant that the individual was placed in a less important role.

This congressional interest has carried over into the arbitration area. The NLRA provides the protection for the process of peaceful bargaining and arbitration provides the means for peacefully resolving conflicts that arise out of the product of the bargaining process—the labor contract. If numerous state laws could frustrate bargaining obligations, wouldn't the same or similar state laws confuse the interpretation of the labor contract? Federal courts have thought so, and a series of Supreme Court cases interprets Section 301 of the Labor Management Relations Act.

Section 301 was enacted in 1947 when Congress passed the Taft-Hartley Act. It provided in part that "suits for violation of contracts between an employer and a labor organization . . . may be brought in any district court of the United States." In a stream of cases since its enactment, the Supreme Court has emphasized the key role of arbitration as a means for providing industrial peace and the importance of developing a uniform body of law relating to contract interpretation.[74] The basic rule was that any incompatible state laws had to give way to the federal interest of creating uniform labor contract laws.

Of course, federal preemption is not automatic. For example, in *Allis-Chalmers Corp. v. Lueck*[75] the Supreme Court noted that preemption would take place only if the "resolution of a state law claim is substantially dependent upon analysis of the terms of an agreement made between the parties in a labor contract." In *Lingle v. Norge Division of Magic Chef, Inc.*,[76] the Court ruled that the discharge of an employee covered by a labor contract was not preempted, because it involved an action allegedly taken for filing a workers' compensation claim—a violation of state law. As far as the Court was concerned, the state could resolve the issue without recourse to the labor contract.

The preemption issue for security-related interests was best framed in a 1990 Ninth Circuit case, *Stikes v. Chevron*.[77] Stikes, a Chevron employee covered by a labor contract, was terminated for refusing to permit his employer to search his car. The car was parked in a company lot. At this point it sounds like a number of cases we have already considered in this chapter.

However, Stikes filed a suit in a California state court alleging that Chevron's actions were a violation of his right to privacy under the California constitution and amounted to wrongful discharge in violation of public policy as well as intentional infliction of emotional distress. Would the case stay in the state court or would it be preempted?

This was not this court's first confrontation with the issue, and it discussed two earlier cases of a similar nature.[78] Both cases involved challenges to an employer's drug and alcohol testing programs. In one of these cases, the employee refused to submit to a urine test and was suspended. He thereupon filed a state action contending that his suspension violated his California constitutional right to privacy. The Ninth Circuit opted for preemption even though the program was not specifically addressed in the labor contract. As far as the court was concerned, it was a legitimate working condition and fair game for the arbitration process.

In the other case, the court considered whether the California constitutional provision on privacy was a non-negotiable right that could not be lost in the bargaining process. The court concluded that while there might be some rights that are non-negotiable, this was not one of them and the employer's decision to institute a drug-testing program was a proper subject for collective bargaining. The court added a comment from Lingle that noted that even if non-negotiable rights were involved, if they turned on the interpretation of a collective bargaining agreement for its application, such a remedy would be preempted by Section 301.

The court decided that Stikes's privacy claim was completely preempted and properly dismissed by the lower court.

OBSERVATIONS

Security people at organized sites cannot perform their jobs effectively without having a feel for the common law of the workplace and the specific agreements, policies, and practices that govern their locations. Arbitration is a playing field on which the employer's need to run an efficient and safe business gets significant recognition, but a failure by security to recognize the other interests involved, the groups and the individuals, can lead to bad decision-making. Carrying out necessary bargaining and observing one's own rules are not unusually difficult burdens and go a long way toward performing a successful operation.

NOTES

1. *Lincoln Mills*, 352 U.S. 448 (1957); *Lucas Flower*, 369 U.S. 564 (1962); *United Steelworkers v. Warrior & Gulf Navigation* 363 U.S. 574 (1960); *United Steelworkers v. Enterprise Wheel & Car Corp.*, 363 U.S. 593 (1960).

2. *Meyers Industries, Inc.*, 281 N.L.R.B. 882 (1986).

3. Fairweather, *Practice and Procedure in Labor Arbitration* 313 (1983).

4. Comment, *Industrial Due Process and Just Cause for Discipline: A Comparative Analysis of Arbitral and Judicial Decisional Processes*, 6 UCLA L. Rev. 603 at 644, 645 (1959).

5. F. Elkouri & E. Elkouri, *How Arbitration Works* 298 (4th ed. 1985).

6. 86 LA 1 (1985).

7. *Kroger Co.*, 25 LA 906, 908 (1955).

8. 81 LA 974 (1983).

9. 81 LA 974 at 980.

10. Elkouri & Elkouri, *How Arbitration Works* 692–707.

11. *W. E. Caldwell Co.*, 28 LA 434 (1957).

12. 60 LA 613 (1973).

13. 60 LA 613 at 617.

14. 60 LA 613 at 618.

15. 60 LA 613 at 618.

16. 93 LA 1210 (1989).

17. 93 LA 1210 at 1213.

18. 93 LA 1210 at 1213.

19. 88 LA 425 (1987).

20. 81 LA 695 (1983).

21. 81 LA 695 at 699.

22. *Johnson & Johnson Patient Care*, 95 LA 409 (1990); *West Monona Community School District*, 93 LA 414 (1989); *Union Oil of California*, 89 LA 1 (1987).

23. *Simoniz Co.*, 44 LA 658, 661 (1964).

24. *Simoniz Co.*, 44 LA at 663; Flannery, *Termination of Employment for Refusal to Submit to a Drug Test*, 1989 Lab. L.J. 293, 295–301 (May 1989).

25. Elkouri & Elkouri, *How Arbitration Works* 298.

26. E.A. Jones, "Truth," *When the Polygraph Operator Sits as Arbitrator (or Judge)*, Proceedings of the 31st Annual Meeting of National Academy of Arbitrators, 75, 151 (1984); *see also* Elkouri & Elkouri, *How Arbitration Works* 315.

27. Comment, *Industrial Due Process*.

28. Fairweather O., *Practice and Procedure in Labor Arbitration* 314.

29. *United States Steel Corp.*, 49 LA 101 (1967).

30. 44 LA 711, 713 (1964).

31. 51 LA 469 (1968).

32. 51 LA 469, 470.

33. 90 LA 189 (1987).

34. 88 LA 208 (1987).

35. 85 LA 407, 409 (1985).

36. 85 LA 214 (1986).

37. 65 LA 1233, 1236 (1975).

38. *Abex Corp.*, 64 LA 721 (1975).
39. *Oil Center Tool Division, FMC Corporation*, 73–72 Arb. 1, 8335.
40. *Sahara Coal Co.*, 89 LA 1257 (1987).
41. 295 N.L.R.B. 180 (1989).
42. F. Elkouri & E. Elkouri, *How Arbitration Works*, Chapter 13, Management Rights.
43. 94 LA 37 (1989).
44. T. Bornstein & A. Gosline, *Labor and Employment Arbitration* Sec. 24:02 (1991).
45. *Shell Oil Co.*, 81 LA 1205, 1208 (1983).
46. 61 LA 159 (1973).
47. C. Craver, *The Inquisitorial Process in Private Employment*, 63 Cornell L. Rev. 1 (1977).
48. *Vista Chemical Co.*, 92 LA 329, 332 (1989).
49. 73 LA 396 (1979).
50. 73 LA 396 at 398.
51. *Pepsi Cola Bottling Co.*, 93 LA 520, 524 (1989).
52. 90 LA 625 (1988).
53. 90 LA 625, 632.
54. 90 LA 56 (1988).
55. 95 LA 500 (1990).
56. 82 LA 360 (1984).
57. 82 LA 360 at 366.
58. 65 LA 1295 (1976).
59. 65 LA 1295 at 1298.
60. *Aldens Inc.*, 58 LA 1213 1215.
61. 68 LA 702 (1977).
62. 68 LA 702 at 705.
63. 44 LA 658 (1964).
64. 89 LA 681 (1987).
65. 89 LA 681 at 685.
66. Comment, *Industrial Due Process*, 607–612.
67. 95 LA 358 (1990).
68. *City of Kenosha, Wisconsin*, 76 LA 758 (1981); *see also, Transit Mgt. of Southeast Louisiana*, 95 LA 74 (1990).
69. 93 LA 846 (1989).
70. 93 LA 846 at 855.
71. 484 U.S. 29 (1987).
72. 484 U.S. 29 at 43.
73. 353 U.S. 26 (1957).
74. *Textile Workers v. Lincoln Mills*, 353 U.S. 448 (1957); *Teamsters Local v. Lucas Flower*, 369 U.S. 95 (1962); *United Steelworkers v. American Mfg. Co.*, 363 U.S. 564 (1960); *United Steelworkers v. Warrior & Gulf Navigation Co.*, 363 U.S. 574 (1960); *United Steelworkers v. Enterprise Wheel & Car Corp.*, 363 U.S. 593 (1960).
75. 471 U.S. 202, 220 (1985).
76. 486 U.S. 399 (1988).
77. 914 F.2d 1265 (9th Cir. 1990), *cert. denied*, 111 S. Ct. 2015 (1991).
78. *Laws v. Calmat*, 852 F.2d 430 (9th Cir. 1988); *Utility Workers of America v. Southern California Edison Co.*, 852 F.2d 1083 (9th Cir. 1988), *cert. denied* 109 S. Ct. 1530 (1959).

6

The Employment World Outside of the National Labor Relations Act and Arbitration

Congress and the courts fostered collective bargaining and arbitration in order to protect the general public from labor unrest. In attempting to reach this objective it was deemed necessary to put management and labor on equal footing. By doing so, the individual employee in the organized sector was assigned a subordinate role.

This arrangement worked well until changes started to take place in the early 1970s. Individuals became increasingly more interested in their own rights and less interested in protecting them through collective action. The subsequent slowdown in union organizing activity did not mean that employees were more satisfied with employers; it only meant that they as individuals were finding new means to solve their personal employment problems.

To a great extent this search for alternative legal means had to take place outside the areas preempted by the National Labor Relations Act and arbitration. Two non-preempted areas offered rich grounds for challenge: one, applications for jobs, either organized or unorganized; and two, the whole unorganized private sector. As mentioned previously, applicants are not covered by the National Labor Relations Act. The subject matters to be legally tested in connection with job applicants cover a wide range but generally are related to privacy. Again, privacy issues are considered in both NLRB and arbitration cases but do not get high priorities because these two areas have a heavy focus on balancing management and group rights. With the growing interest in personal rights, there almost necessarily had to be an increased tension around privacy because privacy had not been a significant factor in the workplace. One's workplace was not one's castle. Further, employers, because of workplace problems, were becoming more interested in giving less privacy than more. The dynamics of these conflicts and their impact on the law will be pursued in both the hiring process and the unorganized workplace.

HIRING

One way some employers found to avoid problems with Title VII of the Civil Rights Act of 1964 and defamation suits was to make only very innocuous inquiries of employees and do almost no checks of references and prior employers, or other background investigations. The idea seemed to be, what you don't know won't be used to hurt you. The problem was, the head-in-the-sand approach did not work. The combination of applicants exaggerating their credentials or hiding weak spots in their own self-interest and an employer's reluctance to test their validity provided an opportunity for a number of unqualified people to be hired. Further, employers were becoming more and more exposed to new legal liabilities.

Negligent Hiring

In another era, unqualified and incompetent employees could have been weeded out over time or buried in the system, but now there was another dynamic at work: negligent hiring. For years, under the civil law, if an employee injured a customer, tenant, or other third party, the inquiry was whether or not the employee was acting within the scope of his or her employment. If the answer was "yes," the employer was liable; if the answer was "no," the employer was off the hook. This left the injured party with only the employee's resources to tap and, of course, in many situations these resources did not provide adequate coverage. Was there any way to reach the employer in order to furnish the needed compensation for the injuries suffered?

The thinking process has been explored in chapter 2 but is worth repeating. It is to businesses' benefit to have customers, visitors and tenants, on their property, so isn't it reasonable to require the employers to provide employees that do not injure them? After all, if the employee that caused the injury had done something of a similar nature while employed elsewhere, shouldn't this employer have known about it? If it did, maybe this innocent person would not now be injured. This kind of thinking appealed to the courts' sense of justice and got around the scope of employment problems.

The *Welch Mfg. v. Pinkerton's Inc.* case[1] sets out a Rhode Island court's approach to the problem. Pinkerton's, pursuant to a contract, supplied a guard to Welch for the purpose of protecting sizeable quantities of gold. The guard subsequently was involved as a co-conspirator in the theft of about $200,000 in gold. Welch sued Pinkerton's for the losses sustained on the theory that Pinkerton's had been negligent in hiring, training, supervising, and assigning the guard.

The court first found that Pinkerton's owed a duty, pursuant to the contract with Welch, to exercise reasonable care in selecting an employee who, as far as could be reasonably known, was competent and fit for the task. How, then, is the necessary degree of reasonable care going to be measured? According to the court it is a sliding scale—the greater the risk of harm, the higher the degree of care required. In the court's judgment, Pinkerton's was obligated to exercise a high degree of care because it was providing a service that definitely required honest, trustworthy, and reliable personnel.

The court framed the pre-employment task this way:

We believe a reasonable investigation would call for affirmative statements attesting to an applicant's honesty, trustworthiness, and reliability and perhaps also require the disclosure of the basis upon which the recommending person has relied. Realizing that job applicants generally provide references who are certain to produce favorable reports, we think that background checks in these circumstances should seek relevant information that might not otherwise be uncovered. When an employee is being hired for a sensitive occupation, mere lack of negative evidence may not be sufficient to discharge the obligation of reasonable care.[2]

Although Pinkerton's had made a number of pre-employment inquiries, these were not enough to meet the court's benchmarks. Even so, there still would be no liability unless the information the employer should have been aware of had some causal relationship to the injury. As noted in chapter 2, the mere fact that a bus company did not know that a bus driver did not make alimony payments would not have any connection with a bus accident. If the driver had a drinking problem and the employer did not know about it, that would be another thing. In the *Welch* case, the court concluded that the guard's succumbing to temptation and his participation in the criminal thefts could have been a reasonably foreseeable result of Pinkerton's negligence in not taking reasonable steps to assure its employee's honesty, trustworthiness, and reliability.

Of course, negligent hiring theories do not mean that in all instances employers have to conduct full field investigations. Not surprisingly, there is no fixed formula as to how much of an investigation has to be done. The theme seems to be that the scope of the pre-hire inquiries increases in relation to the nature and extent of the contact the employee will have with customers, visitors, the public, or other vulnerable people.[3]

It is assumed that the negligent hiring concern is coupled with an overall interest in hiring competent, reliable, and honest employees. The concern about defending against an allegation of negligent hiring provides only narrow motivation to do something, but the interest in creating a more efficient, profitable business provides a broader interest in screening potential employees.

Once it is decided to do some kind of pre-employment screening, thoughts necessarily turn to the tools that can be used, such as credit and character investigations, reference checks, review of arrest and conviction records, polygraph exams, honesty tests, and drug tests. How can these types of screening take place without the business backing into some other kind of legal problem? What are the potential legal obstacles? First, is there any law that covers the whole subject? The Privacy Act of 1974 seems to have the right name, but it is only applicable to restricting the employment information practices of federal agencies so it is not applicable to the private sector.[4] But there are a number of specific statutes, state and federal, as well as separate legal actions to consider.

Credit and Character Investigations

Fair Credit Reporting Act[5]

This act was passed in 1971 to better regulate the conflicts that were taking place between credit reporting and privacy. The focus of the legislation is on consumer reporting agencies and this means any person or firm that, for monetary fees, dues, or on a cooperative non-profit basis, regularly engages in whole or in part in the practice of assembling or evaluating consumer credit information for the purpose of furnishing consumer reports to third parties, and uses any means or facility of interstate commerce for the purpose of preparing or furnishing consumer reports.[6] This definition would not cover an industrial or retail employer that was doing its own investigations.

These consumer reporting agencies generate two kinds of reports: consumer reports and investigative consumer reports. Information in the consumer reports is gathered from two sources: customers of the credit agencies, banks, stores, insurance companies, and other businesses; and the public record on liens, judgments, bankruptcies, and the like. This information can be used to establish credit, receive insurance, and make employment judgments. The investigative consumer report covers information on a customer's character, general reputation, and personal characteristics or mode of living, and is obtained through personal interviews with neighbors, friends, associates, or others.[7]

The Fair Credit Reporting Act sets out guidelines on who may receive these reports. Both kinds of reports may be used for employment purposes. If only a regular credit check is desired, the interested employer is required to notify the applicant and give him or her the name and address of the supplying agency only if the applicant does not get the job. If the more complete investigative report is desired, the potential employer is required to first inform the applicant in writing that such a general report is being requested.

The scope of the phrase "employment purposes" was considered by a federal circuit court in *Zamora v. Valley Federal Savings and Loan.*[8] According to the court, these reports are to be used only to evaluate the person to be employed and may not obtained on others, for example, a spouse. Further, employment means only hiring, promotion, reassignment, or retention. The court went on to add that if a user requests information for a purpose not permitted by Section 1681(b) of the act, such as a report on a spouse, while representing to the reporting agency that the report will be used for a permissible purpose, the user may be subject to criminal liability for obtaining information under false pretenses. Civil liability may also be involved.

This, then, is the balance struck on a federal level between receiving employment decision–related information from credit agencies and protecting the privacy of the person involved. States may regulate in the same area and these statutes are not preempted by the federal law if they are broader or do not conflict with it.

Title VII of Civil Rights Act of 1964

While on the subject of credit checks, it should be mentioned that civil rights legislation touches on the same subject. This overlap of laws is another example of the danger of looking at laws in isolation. Statistics indicate that the percentage of minorities with poor credit ratings is significantly higher than that of non-minorities. As a consequence, the EEOC has taken a position that an employment policy of screening job applicants based on their credit records has a foreseeably disproportionate impact on minorities and will be considered to be a violation of Title VII unless an employer can demonstrate that the inquiry is based on a business necessity. Jobs in the banking industry where there is continual access to money would meet the business necessity test.[9] If good or bad credit has no bearing on the job in question, why bother getting the credit check?

Reference and Past Employment Checks

The interest in some kind of background investigation was stimulated by a desire to create a competent workforce and prevent negligent hiring suits. Emphasis has been placed upon some of the legal exposures of the new employer in conducting preemployment inquiries, but what concerns should the old employer have, particularly when inquiries are made about the applicant's work history? What kinds of potential legal exposures does the old employer face?

Defamation

Since defamation covers a number of other areas of interest to private security, it is appropriate now to give it a rather broad treatment in order to avoid undue repetition each time the subject is raised.

For most people, one of their most cherished possessions is their good reputation. The law has long recognized this and provides a defamation action in the interest of protecting reputations. Definitions of defamation vary slightly from state to state, but there are basically two types—libel, which is defamation by writing, and slander, which is defamation by speech.

Defamation generally is considered to be the communication of false information to a third party that injures a person's reputation.[10] In the employment arena, injury to reputation will be presumed if the false information involves allegations of criminal behavior punishable by imprisonment or crimes involving moral turpitude, such as theft. Injury will also be presumed if the communication negatively reflects on one's fitness to conduct one's business or profession.[11] In a real sense, most adverse employment-related communications fall into the presumptively defamatory category. The possibility of defamation hovers over responding to requests for references, performance evaluations, discharge communications, and even turning matters over to law enforcement.[12]

Anxiety over protecting reputations has to be balanced so that legitimate communications will not be smothered by fear of legal action. Employers and businesses generally have several defenses to defamation including truth and privilege, as well as contentions that the person gave consent. As to the truth defense, if a security person yells "Stop, thief" and the person he yells at is found with unauthorized or unpaid-for company property, there would be little grounds to contend that a good reputation had been falsely injured.

The privilege defense warrants some special attention because it is the one most often used. This defense developed out of the concern that if all negative statements had to be proven to be true, a lot of people with important information just would not take the chance of communicating it. Privileges were developed for certain types of statements so that truth was not a necessity if other tests were met. Absolute privileges providing total freedom from liability were extended to judicial and legislative proceedings. Qualified or conditional privileges were provided "whenever it is reasonably necessary for the protection of one's own interests, the interests of third persons, or certain interests of the public."[13] This includes communications in the workplace.

In analyzing the communication of potentially defamatory information, private security people should make a two-step inquiry, first deciding whether or not a privilege will apply and then determining whether the privilege will be abused by the method, nature, or scope of the communication.[14]

The qualified privilege will apply and the employer or business will be protected, even if it communicates false information, if it made the statement in good faith, for a business interest, on a proper occasion, and only to proper parties.[15] The privilege can be abused and lost if the employer or business acts with malice or ill will, or negligently, or for any purpose other than for protecting the particular interest for which the privilege is given. It also can be abused by communicating or publishing beyond the scope of its legitimate interests.[16]

A person's consent to the communication of defamatory information is sometimes a defense. For example, some courts will construe an agreement for a reference check to constitute a waiver of any subsequent tort claims if derogatory information is discussed.[17] Other courts find a release in the application process to contact references not to be a waiver of any rights to subsequent legal action.[18]

A review of a case might help understand the parameters of the qualified or conditional privilege in the hiring process. In *Zuscheck v. Whitmoyer Laboratories, Inc.*,[19] the plaintiff, Zuscheck, contended he was defamed by his former employer's responses to inquiries from a potential new employer. The former employer had said that Zuscheck as a manager was very dictatorial, quite devious, often demoralizing, and that he was "poor" in regard to his honesty, integrity, personality, and moral character. The court found that a conditional or qualified privilege was established and then focused on the possibility of abuse. The court pointed out that the former employer answered questions on a form supplied by the prospective employer and only responded per this inquiry. The court analyzed all the evidence and found that the privilege had not been abused.

A new development in the defamation area is called "compelled self-publication." As noted, one of the elements in defamation is communication to a third party. In some circumstances employees in filling out applications for employment are required to note the reason for leaving their former employer and put down the reason their former employer gave them. Even though the former employer does not communicate with the new employer, it can be held liable for the applicant's disclosure of derogatory information. The theory is that the former employer should have foreseen that its terminated employee would be placed in this predicament. This, of course, only satisfies the communication or publication element of defamation and the former employer still has access to the qualified privilege defense.[20]

Intentional Interference with Prospective Contracts

In the usual tort case there is a combination of legal theories generated by one set of facts. The combination of claims adds a certain psychological weight, provides alternatives in the event of weaknesses in one or several claims, and maximizes the potential for monetary recovery. It is sometimes amazing how different tort theories seem to have nothing in common until a particular set of facts drives them together.

As noted, defamation focuses on reputation and as evident in the name, interference with contracts or prospective contracts centers on contracts or at least property rights. Yet these two distinct torts can be pulled together in one action. As an example in a hiring situation, a Pennsylvania court considered a case in which an individual filed an application for a job as a security officer with Sears, Roebuck, and Co.[21] Sears checked back with prior employers and was advised by one that the applicant had a drinking problem and had been fired for failure to obey orders. Comments were also made by the former employer about turning over information to the government for possible charges on theft by forgery. The applicant contended that he resigned because of continuing personality conflicts with his employer. He was not hired, and litigation followed on both defamation and interference theories.

On the issue of intentional interference with prospective contractual relations, the court considered the privilege aspect for that tort. The privilege offers protection if the defendant gave a third person truthful information or honest advice within the scope of a request for that advice. The court noted that "there was sufficient evidence for the jury to find that many of Steinbronn's (the former employer) statements were not true and they were not made with a reasonable belief that they were true. Indeed there is evidence to support a finding that Steinbronn knew some of them were false."[22] The court did not disturb the jury's finding of liability for either defamation or interference with a prospective contract. The same facts were used for both findings.

There is not much question that fear of litigation has caused many former employers or references to go into a shell and only give very limited data when asked for information on prior employment. The consequence is that unreliable, dishonest, unqualified people are relatively unrestricted in seeking employment opportunities.

A prospective employer has a need to know what kind of employee it is hiring and an employee has a right not to be unfairly stigmatized by a former employer. The qualified privileges extended to former employers in both defamation and interference with contract actions, if properly used as in the *Zuscheck* defamation case, can facilitate the hiring process and minimize legal liabilities.

Arrest and Conviction Records

Two issues are presented in this discussion. First, the kinds of records that can be used in making a hiring decision and, second, the problems that are presented in trying to get those records. As to the first issue, the concern is one of potential discrimination under Title VII. The lead case relative to arrests is *Gregory v. Litton Systems, Inc.*, in which the court concluded that "the policy of excluding from employment persons who have suffered a number of arrests without any convictions, is unlawful under Title VII. It is unlawful because it has the foreseeable effect of denying black applicants an equal opportunity for employment."[23] This conclusion was based on the observation that blacks were arrested more often than whites and arrests were not proof of any wrongdoing.

The second aspect of the discrimination issue is conviction records, and the courts have a different view of their use. Courts recognize that persons convicted of serious crimes will have a higher incidence of future crime than those who were never convicted. At the same time, the courts are interested in some kind of job relatedness. In *Richardson v. Hotel Corporation of America*[24] a hotel discharged a black bellman after learning that the bellman had been convicted for theft and receipt of stolen goods. The court believed that since the bellman had access to hotel guests' luggage and their rooms, the position of bellman was properly treated as "security sensitive" and the requirement that such an employee be reasonably free from such convictions was lawful. While this was a discharge case the same approach is appropriate in hiring situations. Clearly the greater possibility of theft or injury to others justifies the use of a conviction record in making an employment decision. By the same token, rejection of a black applicant for a mechanics job because he had been convicted of a minor gambling charge is not sufficiently job related to be justified.[25]

Assume that the job an individual is to be hired for involves considerable contact with the public and access to cash or valuable materials. A conviction record check is justified in order to prevent a possible negligent hiring charge and it will not create a problem under Title VII. But will the government conduct the requested record check?

Privacy interests now resurface as a concern despite the Supreme Court's decision in *Paul v. Davis*,[26] wherein it concluded that the right of privacy does not extend to the disclosure of criminal records. But while it said there was no federal constitutional requirement to prohibit the disclosure of such records, it did not say that state governments could not legislate to restrict disclosure. And some have.

Usually such statutes provide an exemption from open record or public disclosure requirements "for police records in general, or for certain types of police records, usually those compiled for investigative purposes."[27] In the book *Thieves at Work*, the authors discuss the variations in statutes and local ordinances from jurisdiction to jurisdiction and set out a chart capturing the essence of the provisions in the different states.[28] They wisely counsel that because of rapid changes in the laws their research should only be used as a guide.

An examination of a few state statutes will help make the point that it is difficult to make generalities and that the laws of each state and local jurisdiction should be examined in detail:

- Revised Statutes of Nebraska Sec. 29-3520
  Complete criminal history record information maintained by a criminal justice agency should be a public record open to inspection and copying by any person during normal business hours and at such times as may be established by the agency maintaining the record.
- Code of Georgia Sec. 35-3-34

  (a) The center shall be authorized to:

    (1) Make criminal history records maintained by the center available to private persons and business under the following conditions.

        (A) Private individuals and businesses requesting criminal history records shall, at the time of the request, provide the fingerprints of the person whose records are requested or provide a signed and notarized consent of the person whose records are requested on a form prescribed by the center which shall include such person's full name, address, social security number, and date of birth and

        (B) The center may not provide records of arrests, charges, and sentences for crimes relating to first offenders pursuant to Article 3 of Chapter 8 of Title 42 in cases where offenders have been exonerated and discharged without court adjudications of guilt, except as specifically authorized by law. . . .

  (b) In the event the employment decision is made adverse to a person whose record was obtained pursuant to this Code section, the person will be informed by the business or person making the adverse employment decision of all information pertinent to that decision. This disclosure shall include information that a record was obtained from the center, the specific contents of the record, and the effect the record had upon the decision. Failure to provide all such information to the person subject to the adverse decision shall be a misdemeanor. . . .

  (d) Local criminal justice agencies may disseminate criminal history records without fingerprint comparison or prior contact with the center, to private individuals and businesses under the same conditions as set forth in paragraph (1) of subsection (a) of this Code section.

Other jurisdictions have varying degrees of limitations and complexities in obtaining records. For example, a Maryland court in 1985 had before it a case in which a tenant of a housing project was raped by an employee of a county housing commission.[29] The specific issue was whether evidence of ready availability of record information was admissible to help prove negligent hiring. The lower court took the position that the employer was not required to look at criminal records and it did not make any difference how easy it would have been to get them.

The appeals court did not agree and said that the relative ease in getting criminal records was a factor the jury could consider in determining whether the employer had made a reasonable inquiry. The court noted that federal and state statutes and regulations enacted since 1975 have limited to some extent the availability of criminal record information. It went on to say that private employers (except banks) generally cannot obtain federal criminal history information. At the Maryland state level, private employers ordinarily cannot obtain criminal arrest information, but can obtain criminal conviction information upon petition to the Secretary of Public Safety and Correctional Services showing a particular need. The state is prohibited from dissemination of criminal conviction information to a private employer unless the employer demonstrates to the Secretary that the activities or duties of the prospective employee would bring the employee

into such close and sensitive contact with the public that the use of the information in hiring, transfer, or promotion of the employee would serve to protect the safety or be in the best interest of the general public or bring the prospective employee or employees into such close and sensitive contact with the employer's enterprise as to endanger the goodwill or fiscal well-being of the enterprise.[30]

The court went on to say:

Clearly there exists a tension between competing interests. On the one hand, there is the individual's right to privacy, the desire of the previously convicted individual to secure employment in any area for which the person is suited, and the societal interest in rehabilitation of offenders. On the other hand, there is a significant need to protect society from the enhanced risk of careless employment practices.[31]

The court added that where the balance has been struck by the state and it is found that dissemination of criminal records is not warranted, the employer cannot be faulted for not obtaining it.

Pre-Employment Testing

Polygraph

Discussion in chapter 2 covers the essentials of this subject. The Employee Polygraph Protection Act of 1988 to a great extent prohibits the use of the polygraph for private sector employment screening except for:

1. prospective employees of security services, including uniformed or plainclothes security personnel, armored car personnel, and designers and maintainers of security alarm systems;

2. prospective employees of manufacturers of controlled substances who would
have direct access to such controlled substances.

Paper-and-Pencil Honesty Tests

Applicant testing certainly is not anything new in the process of screening applicants, but one phase of it, honesty testing, has received a lot of
recent attention. The premise of these tests is that dishonest people can
be identified and screened out of the workplace before they even enter
it. These tests are less offensive and intrusive than the polygraph, and
the Joint Congressional Committee in explaining the coverage of the Employee Polygraph Protection Act excluded written or oral tests commonly
referred to as honesty or paper-and-pencil tests. On the state level, a
Minnesota court found that these kinds of tests were not covered by the
state polygraph law.[32] However, the General Laws of Rhode Island provide that written exams may be used but the results must not form the
primary basis for an employment decision.[33] According to one article,[34]
Massachusetts employers use a derivative of honesty tests known as
dependability tests to avoid possible conflict with the state anti-polygraph
law. This article goes on to say that dependability tests do not seem to
be as strong a predictor of employee theft as overt honesty tests. The
authors of *Workplace Privacy*[35] comment that in Alaska, California, Delaware, Maryland, Wisconsin, and Washington plaintiffs could contend
that broad anti-polygraph statutes extend to written honesty tests. For
example, a Delaware statute (19 Del. Code Sec. 704) limiting the use of
polygraph examinations in employment situations includes a lie detector
"or similar test or examination." What "similar test or examination"
means has not been fully explored through any legal challenge.

Separate and apart from any statutory limitations there still is the potential for tort actions based upon invasion of privacy. This, again, means
that the factors in the balance will be the invasiveness of the activity
weighed against the needs of the employer. In reviewing tort cases, it
should be kept in mind that all employment tests are not honesty or
integrity tests. Different tests measure different things and are used for
different employment purposes. A test not related to honesty but more
in the area of dependability is illustrative of the kinds of questions that
should not be asked in any test unless there is some real evidence of job
relatedness. In *Cort v. Bristol Meyers Co.*, a Massachusetts court stated
that "in the area of private employment there may be inquiries of a
personal nature that are unreasonably intrusive and no business of the
employer. . . .[36] *Cort* is discussed in more detail under discipline and discharge in this chapter.

In October 1991, a California court found that an employer, Target
Stores, violated the state constitution's privacy provision by requiring an
applicant for a store detective job to take a psychological test that included

questions relating to religious beliefs and sexual orientation.[37] The court found that the questions did not further the employer's interest in employing emotionally stable persons. The court decided that employers must restrict pre-employment tests to job-related questions and must show a compelling interest for requiring applicants to take such tests. This is a higher standard than a reasonableness test that an earlier California court had set in a drug-testing case.[38] The point to remember is that these two apparently contradictory cases involve the interpretation of a state constitution and have to be looked at in that narrow context.

Applicant testing of any kind necessarily triggers an interest in how the Equal Employment Opportunity Commission (EEOC) and EEOC-type state agencies view them, and this is true of paper-and-pencil honesty testing. Their interest is not in invasion of privacy; it is in finding out whether the tests cause an employer to hire a disproportionate number of non-protected applicants. If there is a disparate impact on racial minorities or females, the employer assumes a burden of showing that the tests were job related or required by business necessity, and in some situations that alternative selection procedures of lesser adverse impact were unavailable.[39] To date, no honesty tests have been challenged on a disparate impact theory.[40]

Drug Testing

This issue has generated more legal heat and confusion in the private employment sector than any other in the past twenty years. It is an ideal example of the danger of making plans and decisions based on one case read in isolation. Further, it highlights the necessity of reading cases with a number of questions in mind, such as:

- What kind of law is involved—federal, state, local, criminal, or civil; and if civil, is it unjust termination, defamation, invasion of privacy, or another tort?
- Who is involved? If it an applicant for a job, what kind of job is he or she applying for? If it is an employee, what kind of a job is the employee performing or going to perform?
- Who is conducting the test—a government agency, law enforcement, a private company, or a person, and what is the nature of their business?
- What kind of test is involved and what is its purpose—is it simple, sophisticated, or intrusive? Is it given to all or some applicants, all or some employees, on a random basis, for cause, or in rehabilitation situations?
- What is the legal challenge—is it the whole concept of drug testing, the nature of the particular test, or a flaw within the procedure such as the chain of custody?

State Legislation Applicable to Drug Testing. Although difficult to do, this section will be limited to applicant testing in the private sector. On the federal level, there has been considerable discussion on providing a drug-free workplace but little specific direction on how that is to be accomplished. Since the mid-1980s, at least thirteen states and three major cities have passed statutes or ordinances that to one degree or another regulate workplace drug testing. As can be imagined, they range from very restrictive to very permissive positions.

In Iowa, employers may give applicants a test as part of a pre-employment physical so long as they are informed in any notice, advertisement, or application that a drug test will be required, and also are personally informed at the first interview.[41] The confidentiality of the results has to be protected and violations of the statute can be pursued by an injured party through a civil action and considered a misdemeanor as well.

Connecticut law provides that applicants are to be informed in writing at the time of application of the employer's intent to test and they are to be given a copy of any positive results.[42] The law also provides for a second confirmatory test and then a third examination. It appears that all three tests would be from the same specimen. A 1987 Minnesota statute[43] provides that an applicant may be tested if a job offer has been made. If the job offer is withdrawn, the employer must notify the employee of the reason. Montana prohibits any employer from requiring any applicant to submit to a blood or urine test, except for employment in hazardous work environments, or in jobs in which the primary responsibility is security, public safety, or fiduciary.[44]

Some jurisdictions such as San Francisco and Rhode Island have provisions that deal with testing employees but not applicants. Others, such as Maryland, avoid covering who or under what circumstances people might be tested, but target the testing procedure and require that the specimen be tested in a laboratory that holds a permit or is certified.

Handicap Legislation. While these state and local laws directly impact on drug testing programs for applicants, other federal and state statutes may have an indirect effect. Under the Federal Rehabilitation Act of 1973, handicapped individuals are protected from discrimination. People who are recovering from alcohol or drug abuse problems and who are not currently using alcohol or drugs are protected. In the language of the Rehabilitation Act, the exclusion from protection includes:

Any individual who is an alcoholic or drug abuser whose current use of alcohol or drugs prevents such individual from performing the duties of the job in question or whose employment, by reason of such current alcohol or drug abuse, would constitute a direct threat to property or the safety of others.[45]

While the federal Rehabilitation Act might not apply to all private employers since it is limited to federal contractors and recipients of federal financial assistance, there is still the possibility that a state handicap law might be applicable—forty-five states plus the District of Columbia have legislated in this area.[46] In addition, the Americans With Disabilities Act of 1990 (42 U.S.C. Sec. 12101) has extended the basic protections of the Rehabilitation Act to a much wider range of employees.

Anti-Discrimination Legislation. As with honesty or paper-and-pencil tests, the key element of interest is disparate impact on a protected group. This area seems to have little likelihood for legal applicability, as the drug problem crosses all socioeconomic lines and there is a general understanding that substance abuse is significantly related to job performance.

National Labor Relations Act and Arbitration. As discussed in chapter 5, the National Labor Relations Board is primarily interested in employees, not applicants, but some information related to substance screening of applicants may be appropriately requested by a union. Arbitration deals with interpreting and violations of collective bargaining contracts and only in certain industries becomes involved in the hiring process. For example, the organized construction industry commonly uses hiring halls for referral to job sites and applicants are sent to the jobs where they might be tested before being accepted for employment. Since the hiring system is incorporated into the collective bargaining contracts, applicants might receive contract protection similar to employees.

Observations on Hiring

There is a significant concern that a discussion of all the legal pitfalls created by doing different kinds of screening in the hiring process will lead to only one conclusion: Don't do any. Such a decision could be a bad mistake. Common sense and good business judgment should cause one to look at each job or group of jobs and measure them with some of the following questions in mind: What is the exact nature of the job, and what is the exact nature of the business? What exposures will the job holder have to the public and other employees? What exposures will he or she have to monies, financial instruments, controlled substances, or other "temptations"? What would the consequences to safety or the financial well-being of the company be if the job holder made an error in judgment?

It does not make sense to put a forty dollar saddle on a ten dollar horse but it does make sense to implement screening practices that can help insure a safe and efficient business. It is a bonus, then, that these positively motivated practices will help in the defense of any subsequent legal action. If the screening practices make sense to the business and the average person on the street, they should seem reasonable to any court.

DISCIPLINE AND DISCHARGE

Once an employee has been hired by an unorganized, private sector employer after clearing whatever screens were deemed appropriate, what laws are applicable to his or her discipline or continued employment? As explained in chapter 2, at one time such employees were terminable at will. There was little legal protection for the unorganized employee in terms of discipline and discharge. But times have changed, for better or worse. Many employers with unrepresented employees are not sure of what is developing in the legal arena and as a consequence feel very uncertain of their positions. These employers should first understand that the law has not heaped duties on them alone, and not on employees. For example, it is still a basic principle that employees, even the unrepresented, have an obligation to follow reasonable orders.[47]

Because of the wide variety of actions that are potentially applicable in this setting—unjust termination, defamation, invasion of privacy, false arrest, violation of statutes, and others—an attempt will be made to explain these various actions by considering the kinds of security-related activities that trigger them. Defamation following a discharge action was covered to a limited extent in chapter 2 because of its interrelationship with Title VII of the Civil Rights Act. It was considered in detail under hiring of employees in this chapter because of its use as a response to an unfavorable reference from a former employer. As noted in one hiring case, defamation can be coupled with a claim of intentional interference with a contract. Because of the potential for multiple exposures, broad thinking patterns in making decisions are necessary. In short, it might not just be a potential defamation situation but one that also would lead to a violation of a state statute, invasion of privacy, false arrest, or other potential liability.

The security-related problems that can trigger these legal challenges include use of questionnaires, interviews, searches, substance testing, fingerprinting, surveillance, use of cameras, electronic listening devices, and circulation of reports.

Questionnaires and Requests for Information

As mentioned under the hiring section, the theory in honesty testing is that there are certain predictors of honesty that can be professionally incorporated into paper-and-pencil test form that will tell an employer who should or should not be hired. As already noted, such honesty tests are considered illegal in Massachusetts under the anti-polygraph law. But this is not to say that even in Massachusetts all inquiries into what appears to be one's private life are prohibited. In *Cort v. Bristol Meyers Company*[48] a Massachusetts court considered a case in which several salesmen, when asked to fill out questionnaires relative to family life, home ownership, finances, and drinking and smoking habits, refused to do so or responded facetiously. Following their termination, they filed an invasion of privacy action and contended they were terminated in bad faith.

The court made short work of the invasion of privacy contention, noting that since the employees had refused to answer the questions there was no invasion and not even a beachhead was established. As to the terminations for incompleteness of responses, the court could not find any violation of public policy after first observing that there were state laws restricting employers from searching for certain information such as arrest records but that the information requested in the questionnaires did not fall into that category. The court then considered the application of the facts to a state statute (G.L.C. 214, §1B) to see if the inquiries constituted an "unreasonableness, substantial or serious interference with his privacy."

The court stated:

We would not go so far to say that an employer would always be liable for discharging an employee for his refusal to answer questions not relevant to his business purposes. In public policy terms, it is the degree of intrusion on the rights of the employee which is most important. In measuring the nature of the intrusion, at least as to its reasonableness (but perhaps as well as to its substantiality and seriousness) the nature of the employee's job is of some significance. The information that a high level or confidential employee should reasonably be expected to disclose is broader than that which should be expected from an employee who mows grass or empties waste baskets. A salesman, responsible for the sale of drug products to hospitals, doctors, and pharmacists falls in the middle of this range, but toward its upper side. The temperament and dedication of a salesman are important factors in his effectiveness and questions bearing on those subjects are certainly reasonable and should be expected.[49]

The court went on to say that most of the questions asked were relevant to the employees' job qualifications and represented no invasion of privacy. Those that may have been invasive were unanswered. As to the discharge, the court concluded that no public policy considerations protected an at-will-employee under such circumstances.

Perhaps this court did not initially give adequate weight to the employer's right to run an effective, profitable business and gave too much emphasis to the employees' right of privacy, but as the actual weighing process took place, the employer's needs were given consideration. The end point was that minor intrusions would not limit an employer's right to expect an employee to carry out reasonable orders.

Interviews for Work Rule Violations

A legal interest can start on the way to an interview for a work rule violation. A nurse at a nursing home in Maryland contended that she was defamed by her former employer by escorting her to her locker and then to her car after she had been discharged.[50] The focus of the court's inquiry was publication or communication; as noted in the earlier discussion in this chapter on defamation, there cannot be any defamation without it. In 1976 a Maryland court decided that publication could be implied through conduct.[51] In that case four security guards had forcibly detained an employee suspected of stealing and questioned him in a glass-enclosed guard shack that was in full view of the workforce. It was an unusual incident that caused the workforce to slow down as it went by. Publication was established by conduct.

In this case, there was nothing unusual in the escorting of the nurse. The court concluded that simply escorting an employee from the building after termination of employment, without more, did not constitute a defamatory publication.

Once in the room in which the interview takes place, those conducting the interview should not believe that since they are not law enforcement agents or the employee is not represented by a union, there are no legal concerns. The first imperative is that appropriate and proper decorum should be maintained in the interview. For example, an Arkansas court in 1984 considered an outrageous conduct case.[52] The court first noted that this was a new tort and it did not want to open the door of the courts to every slight which one must endure in life but it was still going to determine whether the alleged conduct was so outrageous or extreme in degree, as to be beyond all possible bounds of decency, and to be regarded as atrocious and utterly intolerable in a civilized society.

In that case, a Radio Shack store manager was suspected of stealing and was subsequently interviewed by security people. The manager contended that he was interrogated most of the day at thirty-minute intervals without a break for lunch and he was denied his medication when he was obviously under emotional distress and threatened with arrest. The court only had a problem with the alleged refusal to allow the manager to take his medication and felt that under the circumstances there would be substantial evidence upon which a jury could find liability for outrageous conduct.

The potential for a false imprisonment charge also might arise. If an employee gets up to leave during the course of the interview, can the interviewer tell the employee that if he leaves the room he will be fired? In considering such a situation in *Foley v. Polaroid Corporation*,[53] a Massachusetts court decided that if an employee is given a free choice—stay or leave employment—the employee is not falsely imprisoned. The court stated that it knew of no case that held that a threat of discharge from employment-at-will could effect imprisonment for tort purposes. It then quoted the Reporter's Note to Restatement (Second) of Torts, Section 92B (1982 App.), which states that threats of discharge from employment are not sufficient to constitute imprisonment. Again, the key is having a voluntary option and the threat of job loss does not make the choice to stay involuntary.

In these kinds of situations it is important to understand that employees have an obligation to be reasonably cooperative in investigations, and refusal to cooperate can result in discharge. It is control over the employment status that provides the pressure needed to insure the continued presence of the employee at the interview. If the employer attempts to maintain the presence of an employee through lengthy, intimidating interrogations that include threats to go to law enforcement, courts may construe the employer's actions as constituting false imprisonment.[54] The court's objective in these cases is to measure the detaining force used by the employer.

False imprisonment and false arrest are discussed at length in chapter 8 relative to thefts by non-employees. That chapter's narrow focus on detention includes the development of shoplifting laws. In some situations, as will be discussed, employee detention for theft might be covered under a shoplifting statute.

Searches

The subject of searches was discussed at some length in chapter 1, particularly as it related to criminal law and the role of law enforcement versus the role of private security. It was also discussed in chapter 3 relative to bargaining obligations on search policies, and in chapter 5 on arbitrators' attitudes toward the subject. In the chapter 5 discussion, it was made evident that most arbitrators do not look to the criminal law as a guideline for searches. They look toward the reasonableness of the search activity. Reasonableness was also the watch word in recent Supreme Court cases discussed in chapter 1 involving non–law enforcement searches carried out in the public sector. But how does the tort law and more particularly invasion of privacy address the matter? Will the courts hearing these cases give proper weight to the need of employers to run an efficient, profitable business?

Considering the peculiarities of the various state laws, no single case can answer these questions, but a 1984 Texas court makes a reasonable try. *K-Mart Corporation v. Trotti*[55] involved a situation in which store management opened the locked locker of an employee and the employee sued for invasion of privacy. The employee, with the employer's knowledge, had obtained her own combination lock, placed it on the locker, and did not advise the store of the combination. This was not contrary to any instructions or directions. In her absence, store management opened her locker and went through the contents because security believed an unidentified person, not this employee, had stolen a watch. They were also looking for price-marking guns. The manager said that all prospective employees received verbal notification that store policy included conducting ingress-egress searches of employees and also conducting unannounced searches of lockers. Two administrators denied that employees ever received this notification.

The court divided the tort of invasion of privacy into two segments. It said that there had to be an unjustified intrusion into the person's solitude or seclusion and this intrusion had to be of such a magnitude that it would cause an ordinary individual to feel severely offended, humiliated, or outraged.

In analyzing the unjustified intrusion aspects, the court noted that in situations in which an employee used a lock provided by the employer it could be inferred that the employer

manifested an interest both in maintaining control over the locker and in conducting legitimate reasonable searches. Where, as in the instant case, however, the employee purchases and uses his own lock on the lockers, with the employer's knowledge, the fact finder is justified in concluding that the employee manifested, and the employer recognized an expectation that the locker and its contents would be free from intrusion and interference.[56]

Expectancy of privacy prevailed and the intrusion was found to be unjustified.

But that is only half the story, because in this court's view the intrusion also had to be highly offensive to a reasonable person. The lower court had not instructed the jury on this point and the appeals court pointed out that its exclusion in the decision-making process

would result in fundamentally unfair assessments against defendants who offended unreasonably sensitive plaintiffs but whose transgressions would not realistically fill either an ordinary person or the general society with any sense of outrage.[57]

The appeals court held that the element of a highly offensive intrusion is a fundamental part of the definition of invasion of privacy and the case was remanded for a new trial because of the lower court's failure to properly define the tort in its instructions to the jury.

References to invasion of privacy allegations will be made at a number of points and while there are variables, the courts will generally look for highly offensive intrusions and not give much consideration to slight incursions into privacy. However, the final decisions on the facts are often made by juries and it is very difficult to predict the outcomes. Keep in mind that if the employer is organized, the decision will be made by an arbitrator in accordance with workplace practices and the common law of the workplace. Whether courts will weigh all the factors considered by arbitrators is an open question.

Surveillance

This investigative technique has never been high on the intrusiveness scale. In a Michigan 1989 invasion of privacy case, the court was presented with a situation in which an employee had been injured but the company believed she was malingering.[58] A private investigating firm was hired and subsequently investigators talked to sanitation workers who picked up the employee's trash, walked by his house, observed him through windows, telephoned him to see whether he was home, and followed him when he went to doctor appointments. More to the employee's displeasure, though, they observed his home continuously from a car parked down the street and observed him from the car in his house through a window with a high-powered camera lens, and one investigator entered his house posing as a process server.

In balancing the various interests, the court considered that some of the activity, particularly the use of the high-powered camera, might be objectionable to a reasonable person but the company had rights, too; in this case the right was to investigate a work-related matter and "also to investigate matters that are potential sources of legal liability." The court found no invasion of privacy. At what point is the balance tipped? It is hard to say, but in one case in which an employer put a motion detector on an employee's door at home, the court found a violation.[59]

Substance Testing

If surveillance is low on the intrusiveness scale, substance testing is well up there—not anywhere near as high as use of polygraphs or electronic monitoring, but it is considered highly intrusive. As a consequence, there has been a blizzard of litigation as employers have attempted to implement programs to keep drugs and alcohol out of the workplace. Testing of applicants and employees in the organized sector has been discussed previously, and now attention will be given to unrepresented private employees.

Because of the overwhelming number of cases, it is critical to sort out the cases in some organized way. Are the cases being reviewed federal, state, or local administrative agency cases that are implementing agency regulations? Do they involve constitutional law questions that might apply in the private sector because of government regulation? Or are they wrongful discharge cases, or cases that cover the traditional tort areas of defamation, invasion of privacy, false imprisonment, outrageous conduct, infliction of emotional distress, and similar causes of action? Understanding what law is involved in a case is a necessary element in establishing how it impacts on any employer plan of action. What might be an appropriate substance test for the New York City Transit Authority or in the state of Rhode Island, might not be appropriate for a private employer in Delaware.

Much of the early litigation on substance testing involved federal constitutional questions. The fourth amendment was being tested in *Skinner v. Railway Labor Executives' Assn.*[60] over a federal regulation requiring post-accident testing of train crews. *National Treasury Employees Union v. Von Raab*[61] involved drug testing of Customs Service employees who carried firearms or had access to classified materials. The court was searching for guidelines in deciding what kinds of employees the government could require to be tested. The point here is that while the thinking in these and similar government cases might well foreshadow what will happen in the private sector, they have no direct application to private, non-government-regulated activities. Government-regulated aspects of private employment will be considered in chapter 10.

State Laws

As noted with applicants, state laws applying to private employers are numerous and confusing. Rhode Island's law, for example, does not cover applicants but as to employees, it provides that no employer may require any employee to submit to a body fluid test as a condition of employment.[62] However, a specific employee may be required to submit to testing if:

- the employer has reasonable grounds to believe, based on specific objective facts, that the employee's use of controlled substances is impairing his ability to perform his job,
- the employee provides the test sample in private, outside the presence of any person, and
- the testing is conducted in conjunction with a bona fide rehabilitation program.

As part of the same provision, the employer must provide the employee, at its expense, the opportunity to have the sample tested or evaluated by an independent testing facility and provide the employee an opportunity to rebut or explain the results. Criminal penalties also are provided for.

The Rhode Island statute is discussed only as an example of the uniqueness of some state laws and the difficulty in making generalities as to what the states and cities provide. Some jurisdictions, such as Berkeley, California have an absolute ban on testing; others such as Vermont and Iowa provide a probable cause test and Vermont prohibits random testing; some, Rhode Island included, use a reasonable cause standard; Minnesota limits random testing to employees in safety-sensitive positions; and as noted under testing of applicants, some, such as Maryland, focus on using certified or licensed laboratories.

It is critical, then, to know the details of the applicable state laws, if any, that pertain to substance testing before any testing program is implemented.[63]

Knowing the pertinent state laws is only part of the battle. For example, employers in trucking and maritime activities also have to be aware of the drug testing regulations instituted by such agencies as the Department of Transportation and Coast Guard.[64] As noted, the government regulated area will be covered in more detail in chapter 10. Apart from complying with applicable laws and regulations, there is the possibility of some kind of tort action based either on the test itself or the manner in which the test was conducted. As already discussed, the challenge may involve an alleged violation of a state constitution privacy requirement, an implied contract to discharge only for cause, a discharge in violation of state policy, an invasion of privacy, assault, false imprisonment, defamation, or any combination of the above.

Testing Procedures

In one case, a discharged employee, Kelley, filed an action against his former employer, Schlumberger Technology Corp., contending that Schlumberger's drug-testing program invaded his privacy under the Louisiana constitution, tortiously invaded his privacy, inflicted emotional distress, defamed him, and brought about his wrongful discharge.[65] Kelley was a barge engineer on a drilling rig operating sixty miles off the coast of Louisiana. He was discharged after two urinalysis tests allegedly showed positive results for marijuana. The state jury found for Kelley on the two invasion of privacy charges and on the emotional distress charge. On appeal, the First Circuit was asked to consider the instructions given to the jury on the emotional distress count.

Kelley's chief objection to the test was that it required him to be personally observed while urinating. The state court had instructed the jury that in Louisiana a plaintiff may recover for negligently inflicted emotional injuries even in the absence of any accompanying physical injury. Liability is limited to these emotional injuries that were foreseeable or that could have been anticipated to result from the negligent act. Further, the mental suffering must be more than the minimal worry and inconvenience over the consequence of the damage. The reviewing court found no error in the way the lower court had instructed the jury on the law. In this case, the jury decided that personal observation met the test and awarded Kelley $125,000 on the emotional distress claim. Although finding there had been an invasion of privacy, it only awarded him $1 on that cause of action. One lesson in this case is that even if you know what the law is you can never be sure how a jury will weigh the facts. Even though the outcome was somewhat strange, it does highlight the need to explore the various elements of a drug testing procedure to see that they are reasonable and have legitimate business justification.

Discharge for Refusal to Take a Test

In discussing the organized sector, attention was given to the long-standing principle that employees should follow orders and grieve later. Mention was also made in this chapter about the principle that, in general, private sector employees have an obligation to follow reasonable orders. Remember, the *Cort v. Bristol Meyers* questionnaires case concluded that it was permissible for employers to discharge employees who had not complied with a reasonable request to supply certain information even though there was some incursion into their privacy. And the *Foley v. Polaroid Corp.* court found that there was no false imprisonment when an employer told an employee to stay in the room during an interview or be fired. What can an employer do, though, if an employee refuses to take a drug test that is not in violation of any state law that regulates such tests?

The tort challenges in most jurisdictions cover a number of elements as in the *Kelley v. Schlumberger* case, but two discharge cases in California and Alaska are worth some attention because of the involvement of the state constitutions.

In the California case, *Semore v. Pool*,[66] Semore, a Kerr-McGee employee, refused to consent to a pupillary reaction eye test under the company's random testing program and was discharged. He subsequently filed a wrongful termination case, contending that the right to privacy guaranteed in the state constitution prohibits such testing. Accordingly, his position was that his termination was in violation of the state's public policy. The three concepts—violation of state constitutional protection of privacy, violation of state public policy, and wrongful discharge—were linked together.

Kerr-McGee responded that state action was required to trigger the constitutional privacy protection provision but the court concluded, "We have no doubt that at least some types of non-governmental conduct can interfere with the right granted by the constitutional provision." Next, Kerr-McGee contended that there was no violation of state public policy because the exception to the employment-at-will doctrine did not cover situations in which only one employee benefitted—it had to benefit the public at large. The court responded by saying that

The employee's right not to submit to the drug test is a right he shares with all other employees . . . and . . . in asserting the right, he gives it life. . . . The assertion of the right establishes it and benefits all Californians in the same way that an assertion of a free speech right benefits us all.[67]

The court then made the linkage between the state constitution, the public policy theory, and the wrongful discharge contention and remanded the case to the lower court for trial. It would be the job of the lower court to weigh and balance the degree of intrusiveness and the employee's needs to provide a drug-free workplace. At that point, evidence concerning the nature of the test, the equipment used, the manner of administration, its reliability, and the handling of results would be considered.

The point of this case is that before the court gets to the facts, it has to determine what, if any, laws or rights might have been violated, assuming the facts alleged by the plaintiff are true. Remember, this case did not involve a California statute that regulates drug tests—it was initially a state constitutional privacy issue. In employment-at-will jurisdictions that do not regulate drug testing, the case would not get to the jury because there would be no legal cause of action. This, of course, would not eliminate the potential in any jurisdiction for a tort action such as defamation or infliction of emotional distress, but it would eliminate the wrongful discharge action that drives many of these actions.

In *Luedtke v. Nabors Alaska Drilling, Inc.*,[68] an Alaska court wrestled with the same issue of whether the state constitution extended to private sector activity. After stating that the state constitutions did not create a direct right of private action, it went on to find that Alaska recognized that public policy supported the protection of employee privacy. The focus shifted from the constitution to the employment relationship. The court then took on the job of balancing the right of privacy against the public policy of supporting workplace health and safety. The court relied heavily on the developing federal constitutional law on drug testing and ultimately decided that since this employer was involved in the hazardous oil drilling business, the balance should be struck in the employer's favor. However, certain restrictions were placed on the employer as to the timing of the tests after appropriate notice.

As an overall observation on substance testing, it should be remembered that the more intrusive a test gets, the more potential there is for employee challenge. Tests that are administered at random or have other onerous aspects should not be implemented unless there is a justifiable need, and before any tests are implemented there should be a review of statutory and tort law in the jurisdictions involved.

Regulated Investigative Techniques Common to Both the Organized and Unorganized Sector

Fingerprinting

The specialized nature of many state and local statutes and ordinances makes it difficult to generalize about aspects of the law that relate to security. For example, in 1937 New York State passed a law that states, "Except as otherwise provided by law, no person as a condition of securing employment or of continuing employment shall be required to be fingerprinted."[69] The purpose of the law was to prevent private employers from using fingerprinting as a means for blacklisting union leaders and members. However, numerous exceptions have been made in order to better regulate certain industries. These exceptions include auctioneers, employment agencies, cabarets, sightseer guides, locksmiths, second-hand dealers, security firms, explosive handlers, and others.[70]

A California statute makes it a misdemeanor for an employer to require an employee, as a condition of securing or retaining employment, to be photographed or fingerprinted for the purpose of conveying the photograph or fingerprints to another employer or third person, if that conveyance could be used to the detriment of the employee.[71] No other state regulates in this area.

Electronic Surveillance, Particularly Telephone Intercepts

For the purpose of refocusing on the laws involved, it should be remembered that federal constitutional rights do not extend to private sector activity even if it involves telephone monitoring. State constitutional rights of privacy actions and traditional invasion of privacy tort cases are not the usual vehicles for testing electronic surveillance including telephone intercept issues.[72] As pointed out in chapter 2, most litigation in this arena involves the interpretation of the Omnibus Crime Control and Safe Streets Act and state statutes regulating similar activity.

There are two exceptions to the federal prohibition against the electronic interception of communications. One is prior consent and the other is the business extension exception. Section 2511 (2)(d) of Title III of the act sets out the prior consent exception, and courts have limited the meaning in the interest of protecting privacy. For example, as set forth in *Watkins v. L. M. Berry & Co.*,[73] in a telephone intercept call, consent will not be implied merely because the employee has knowledge that his or her employer has the capability of monitoring telephone calls. If an employee knows that a telephone line is regularly monitored, then consent to intercept may be implied, particularly if another line has been provided for personal use or the employee has been warned not to use the business line.[74]

The business extension exception is a separate issue. As explained by the *Watkins* court, "Consent may be obtained for any interceptions and the business or personal nature of the call is entirely irrelevant. Conversely, the business extension exception operates without regard to consent."[75] If an employee has not given consent and no consent can be implied by the circumstances, the court will then shift its attention to the business extension exception.

Under this exception, intercepts are legitimate if they are made in the ordinary course of business. The *Watkins* court pointed out that the phrase "in the ordinary course of business" does not extend to everything that interests the company. The court stated, "We hold that a personal call may not be intercepted in the ordinary course of business under the exemption in Section 2510(5)(a)(i) except to the extent necessary to guard against unauthorized use of the telephone or to determine whether a call is personal or not."[76]

In *Briggs v. American Filter Co., Inc.*[77] the Fifth Circuit discussed the elements of the business exemption at length. Roby, an employee of American Filter, had a friendship with Briggs, a former employee who was now a competitor of American Filter. American Filter believed Roby was providing confidential information to Briggs and warned Roby not to discuss business with Briggs. An American Filter supervisor listened to and taped a telephone conversation between Roby and Briggs that concerned an Air Filter project. No consent had been given and Air Filter was sued by both Briggs and Roby for invasion of privacy and violation of Title III. The court stated:

When an employee's supervisor has particular suspicions about confidential information being disclosed to a business competitor, has warned the employee not to disclose such information, has reason to believe that the employee is continuing to disclose the information and knows that a particular phone call is with an agent of a competitor, it is within the ordinary course of business to listen in on an extension phone for at least so long as the call involves the type of information he fears is being disclosed.[78]

Attention also has to be given to state statutes and regulations in this area. While many statutes track the federal statute, others do not. Some states require that all parties subject to electronic eavesdropping give consent. These include Pennsylvania, Maryland, and Michigan.[79] Maryland, however, does provide a business extension exception.

As already noted, electronic monitoring in the workplace beyond telephone monitoring has generated considerable controversy at both the federal and state levels. Interest in passing some form of legislation is continuing and growing. A number of articles have dealt with this very sensitive subject.[80]

Polygraphs, Deceptographs, and Voice Stress Analyzers

The Employee Polygraph Protection Act of 1988 was discussed in some detail in chapter 2 and more specific legal questions related to these devices can best be resolved by referring to the Act itself. Suffice it to say that state and federal legislation has severely restricted the use of these devices in private employment–related matters.

Disclosure of Personal Information

It is the nature of a security function to have within its control sensitive employee information during and after an investigation. Real questions exist as to what can be done with this type of data. Can it only be provided on a need-to-know basis? Can it be circulated to all management? Can it be circulated to all employees as an example of what can happen if plant rules are violated?

The legal issues raised by these questions are normally invasion of privacy and defamation. As to privacy, the issue is not the truth or falsity of the information, it is whether or not the employer by its circulation of personal information invaded the employee's privacy. Although not security-related, the *Bratt v. IBM*[81] case is a good example of what factors are considered by a court in making these kinds of decisions. This case had been up and down in several courts before the federal circuit court set about to find whether a lower court had been correct in determining that Bratt's privacy issues did not warrant going to a jury and accordingly could be managed by summary judgment. Bratt, an IBM employee, had contended his employer had breached his privacy by disclosure of his use of a confidential grievance procedure and information about his medical problems.

The test in Massachusetts as to whether a privacy violation had taken place required the balancing of the employer's real business interest in obtaining and publishing the information against the degree of impact of the intrusion on the employee's privacy. Using this balancing framework, the lower court found that there was no evidence in the record that this information was published other than to managerial employees who had a reasonable interest in the information because of its bearing on Bratt's work assignments. As to the medical information, it had apparently been disclosed to only two managerial employees and they both had a need to know.

The circuit court agreed that there was no evidence that his privacy had been invaded because of circulation of information relative to the use of the confidential grievance procedure because, first, it was not very personally intrusive information anyway and, second, it only went to managers who had legitimate business in knowing. As to the medical information, the court noted that it certainly was more personal that the grievance procedure information and necessarily the degree of disclosure deserved more attention. An examination of the limited disclosure and the legitimate business need of those few people who got the reports convinced the court that there was insufficient evidence to justify sending that issue to a jury.

A sticking point, however, was the discussion of Bratt's medical problem with his managers without Bratt's permission. In this case, the discussion violated IBM's own rules. As the court saw it:

The existence of company regulations protecting the confidentiality of medical information serves to enhance an already existing expectancy of privacy concerning information of this kind. The substantiality of an invasion upon privacy is thereby increased where a company violates such internal regulations. In addition, where a company has established certain information as private, and has set up strict rules for the publication and use of such information internally, the company has imposed on itself a heavy burden of showing that its business interest in obtaining the information warrants a violation of its own rules.[82]

In the court's judgment, this is the kind of situation that should have been presented to a jury.

The points to remember are these: minor personal intrusions and intrusions that result in limited disclosure only on a need-to-know basis do not create liabilities. However, if an employer has established rules to protect employees from disclosure, the employer should follow its own rules or have a very good reason for not doing so.

The second potential employee challenge of unwarranted disclosures of information is through a defamation action. The elements of defamation were covered earlier in this chapter relative to reference checks. Defamation was also discussed to a limited extent in chapter 2 to show the interrelationship of several areas of the law. In the *Graziano v. E. I. Du Pont de Nemours & Co.* case,[83] the court recognized the company's concerns about meeting its obligation under Title VII and properly advising employees' supervisors about sexual harassment matters. Publication of the sexual harassment policy was one thing but attention had to be given to limiting termination details to those who had a need to know.

In the earlier discussion of defamation in this chapter, comment was made about certain communications being privileged and others being qualifiedly privileged. While the emphasis there was on qualified privileges, it should be noted that communications in a judicial proceeding are absolutely privileged and the checkpoints listed for the qualified privilege do not have to be tested. The Colorado Supreme Court held in October 1990 that collective bargaining grievance procedures are not judicial proceedings triggering the total privilege.[84] A former employee had contended that he was defamed by disciplinary notices contending that he had been involved in, among other things, sexual harassment and falsification of a time card. While this is an organized sector case, it does make it clear that there is a continuing concern with the disclosure of disciplinary-related data.

The employer had argued that refusal to recognize an absolute privilege would "interfere with the discipline grievance and arbitration process contrary to federal labor policy arising under Section 301 of the LMRA." The court did not agree and distinguished cases to the contrary.[85] The point to remember is that employers cannot count on absolute privilege in grievance communications but can still rely on the qualified privilege discussed earlier in connection with reference checks. In the employment setting, the qualified privilege is good until it is abused.

This does not end the concern about the potential for defamation actions in the termination process. Assume that an employee was involved in the theft of company property and in addition to discharging the person, the employer decided to pursue some kind of criminal action. What are the legal exposures? Again, the subject for discussion is privilege, absolute or qualified.

The purpose of the absolute privilege is to provide freedom of access to the courts without fear of triggering a defamation action. The question raised is when do legal or court proceedings start. The Colorado court felt that a quasi-legal proceeding, a grievance procedure, did not meet that test, and other courts have found that taking a matter to the police did not start the necessary legal proceedings for absolute privilege coverage.[86] The most the complaining party gets in those circumstances is a qualified privilege.[87]

The qualified privilege certainly does not give the employer all the protection it would like but it still allows the employer to get the job done, even though the issue can be placed before a jury. In short, the employer should still be reasonably comfortable if it did not act out of malice or ill will, believed the truth of the statements, felt the statements were based on facts, and limited the publication of the information to only those who needed it.

OBSERVATIONS

It has always been in the best interest of society as a whole and business as part of that society for business to hire capable, stable, and efficient employees and treat them fairly. As part of this equation, it has been of equal importance that employees provide a fair day's work for a fair day's pay. The problem is that the fine balance that is necessary to carry out these simple expectations can become distorted. The courts, in theory, understand the need for maintaining some kind of balance and most attempt to do so. Without question, though, there are bad cases and these sometimes frighten employers out of doing their jobs.

While there are numerous laws affecting employers and growing legal exposures, there is a common theme that keeps repeating itself. If an employer uses common sense and is up-front, straightforward, earnest, and reasonable, it can take steps to insure it is hiring good people and firing bad employees. If an employer does nothing out of fear of legal exposure, it will not be in the best interest of the business, good employees, or society as a whole.

NOTES

1. 474 A.2d 436 (1984).
2. 474 A.2d 436 at 441.
3. *C. K. Security Systems, Inc. v. Hartford Accident & Indemnity Co.*, 137 Ga. App. 159, 223 S.E.2d 453, 455 (1975).
4. 5 U.S.C. Sec. 552(a) (Supp. Feb. 1975).
5. 15 U.S.C. Sec. 1681 et seq.
6. 15 U.S.C. Sec. 1681 (a).
7. 15 U.S.C. Sec. 1681 (a).
8. 811 F.2d 1368 (10th Cir. 1987).
9. *EEOC v. United Virginia Bank*, 615 F.2d 147 (4th Cir. 1980); *EEOC v. American National Bank*, 652 F.2d 1176 (4th Cir. 1981).
10. *Restatement (Second) of Torts* Sec. 558, 559 (1977).
11. *Restatement (Second) of Torts* Sec. 571, 573 (1977).
12. R. Jacobs, *Defamation In the Workplace*, Lab. L.J. 567 (1989); *Dijkstra v. Westerenk*, 168 N.J. Super. 128 (1979), 401 A.2d, 1114 *cert. denied*, 81 N.J. 329 (1979) 407 A.2d 1202.
13. *Zuschek v. Whitmoyer Laboratories, Inc.*, 430 F. Supp. 1163 (E.D. Pa. 1977).
14. *Garziano v. E. I. du Pont de Nemours & Co.*, 818 F.2d 380 (5th Cir. 1987).
15. Shattuck, *The Tort of Negligent Hiring and the Use of Selection Devices*, 11 Indus. Rel. L.J. No.2, 14 (1989).
16. *Zuschek v. Whitmoyer Laboratories Inc.*, 430 F. Supp. 1163 (1977), *aff'd*, 571 F.2d 573 (3d Cir. 1978); *Beckman v. Dunn*, 276 Pa.S. 527, 419 A.2d 583 (Pa. Super. 1980); *Garziano v. du Pont*, 818 F.2d at 13.
17. *Turner v. Halleburton*, 722 P.2d 1106 (Kan. 1986).
18. *Kellums v. Freight Sales Centers*, 467 So. 2d 816 (Fla. 1985).
19. 430 F. Supp. 1163 (E.D. Pa. 1977), *aff'd*, 571 F.2d 573 (3d Cir. 1978).
20. *Lewis v. Equitable Life Assurance Soc.*, 389 N.W.2d 876 (Minn. 1986).
21. *Geger v. Steinbronn*, 351 Pa.S. 536, 506 A.2d 901 (Pa. Super. Ct. 1986).
22. 506 A.2d 901 at 910.
23. 316 F. Supp. 401, 403 (D.C. Cal. 1970) *aff'd as modified*, 472 F.2d 631 (9th Cir. 1972).
24. 332 F. Supp. 519 (D.C. La. 1971).
25. EEOC Decision #71 - 2682, June 28, 1971.
26. 424 U.S. 693 (1976).

27. Annot., 82 A.L.R. 3d 19, *Public Access to Police Records* (1978).

28. Shepard & Duston, *Thieves at Work: An Employer's Guide to Combating Workplace Dishonesty* appendix B (1988).

29. *Cramer v. Housing Opportunities Commission*, 304 Md. 705, 501 A.2d 35 (1985).

30. 501 A.2d 35 at 40.

31. 501 A.2d 35 at 41.

32. *Minnesota v. Century Camera, Inc.*, 309 N.W.2d 735 (Minn. 1981).

33. R.I. Gen. Laws Sec. 28-6.1-4 (1987).

34. P. Ash, J. Jones, and C. Soto, *Employment Privacy Rights and Pre-Employment Honesty Tests*, 15 Employee Rel. L. J. 561, 575 (Spring 1990).

35. Duston, and Russell Sheppard, *Workplace Privacy* 156, A BNA Special Report (1987).

36. *Cort v. Bristol Meyers Company*, 385 Mass. 300 431 N.E.2d 908, 912 (1982).

37. *Soroka v. Dayton Hudson Corp.*, 1 Cal. Rptr 2d 77,235 Cal App.3d.654 (1991).

38. *Wilkinson v. Times-Mirror*, 215 Cal. App.3d 1034 264 Cal. Rptr. 194 (1989).

39. Civil Rights Act of 1991, Sec. 105, Burden of Proof in Disparate Impact Cases 42 U.S.C. 1981.

40. G. Dodge, G.J. Tysse, *Winning the War on Drugs, The Role of Workplace Testing* (1989).

41. Iowa Code Sec. 730.5 (1987).

42. Conn. Gen. Stat. Ann. 31-51 V.3 (1987).

43. Minn. Stat. Sec. 181.950 et seq. (1988).

44. Mont. Code Ann. Sec. 39.2-304, 27-62-212 (1987).

45. 29 U.S.C. Sec. 706(8)B (1981).

46. T. Sager, H. Trigg, *A Legal Framework for Implementing and Enforcing a Comprehensive Substance Abuse Policy and Program*, Eastern Mineral Law Foundation Eighth Annual Institute (1988).

47. *Restatement (Second) of Agency* Sec. 385 (1958).

48. 385 Mass. 300, 431 N.E.2d 908 (1982).

49. 431 N.E.2d 908, 913.

50. *Gay v. William Hill Manor, Inc.*, 74 Md. App. 51, 536 A.2d 690 (1988).

51. *General Motors Corp. v. Piskor*, 277 Md. 165, 370 A.2d 767 (1976).

52. *Tandy Corp. v. Bone*, 678 S.W.2d 312 (Ark. 1984).

53. 400 Mass. 82, 508 N.E.2d 72 (Mass. 1987).

54. *DeAngelis v. Jamesway Dept. Store*, 205 N.J. Super. 519, 501 A.2d 561 (N.J. 1985); *C. F. Malanga v. Sears, Roebuck & Co.*, 109 A.D.2d 1054, 487 N.Y.S.2d 194 (1985).

55. 677 S.W.2d 632 (Texas App. 1 Dist. 1984).

56. 677 S.W.2d 632 at 637.

57. 677 S.W.2d 632 at 637.

58. *Saldana v. Kelsey-Hayes*, 4 IER Cases 1107, (Mich. Ct. App. 1989).

59. *Pemberton v. Bethlehem Steel Corp.*, 65 Md. App. 133, 502 A.2d 1101 (Md. App. 1985).

60. 489 U.S. 602 (1989).

61. 489 U.S. 656 (1989).

62. R.I. Gen. Laws Sec. 28-6.5 (1987).

63. See Dodge, *Winning the Drug War: The Role of Private Sector Workplace Testing* Chap. IV (1989) for details on jurisdictions.

64. See, e.g., Department of Transportation Procedures for Transportation Workplace Drug Testing Programs, 49 C.F.R. Part 40 (December 1, 1989).

65. *Kelley v. Schlumberger Technology Corp.*, 849 F.2d 41 (1st Cir. 1988).

66. 217 Cal. App.3d 1087, 266 Cal. Rptr. 280 (1990).

67. 266 Cal. Rptr. 280 at 285.

68. 768 P.2d 1123 (Alaska 1989)

69. N.Y. Lab. Law, § 201 (McKinney 1973).

70. *Friedman v. Valentine,* 291 N.Y.2d 836, 30 N.Y.S. 891 (1941).

71. Cal. Lab. Code Sec. 1051 (1987).

72. However, there are exceptions such as *LeCrone v. Ohio Bell Telephone Co.*, 201 N.E.2d 533 (Ohio App. 1963); *Barksdale v. IBM*, 620 F. Supp. 1380 (W.D.N.C. 1985).

73. *Watkins v. L. M. Berry & Co.*, 704 F.2d 577 (11th Cir. 1983).

74. *Jandak v. Village of Brookfield*, 520 F. Supp. 815 (N.D. Ill. 1981); *Simmons v. Southwestern Bell Telephone Co.*, 452 F. Supp. 392 (W.D. Ok. 1978), *aff'd*, 611 F.2d 342 (10th Cir. 1979).

75. 704 F.2d 577 at 581.

76. 704 F.2d 571 at 583.

77. 630 F.2d 414 (5th Cir. 1980).

78. 630 F.2d 414 at 420.

79. *Barr v. Arco Chemical Corp.*, 529 F. Supp. 1277 (1982); Md. Cts. & Jud. Proc. Code Ann. Sec. 10-402(C)(3); Mich. Comp. L. Ann. Sec. 750.539a(2) (1967).

80. *House Bill Would Curb Employee Monitoring, Individual Employment Rights*, I.E.R. BNA, May 9, 1989; *9–5 Report on Electronic Surveillance Details Stories of Monitored Workers*, Daily Labor Report, February 15, 1990, 4–12; *Industry Labor Clash Over Electronic Monitoring*, 135 Labor Relations Reporter 229, October 22, 1990; Senate Bill 2164, Privacy for Consumers and Workers Act, introduced by Sen. Paul Simon, February 22, 1990; Susser, *Electronic Monitoring in the Private Sector: How Closely Should Employers Supervise Their Workers*, 13 Employee Rel. L.J. 575 (1988).

81. 785 F.2d 352 (1st Cir. 1986).

82. 785 F.2d 352 at 360, 361.

83. 818 F.2d 380 (5th Cir. 1987).

84. *Thompson v. Public Service Co.*, 800 P.2d 1299 (Colo. 1990) October 22, 1990.

85. *General Motors Corp. v. Mendicki*, 367 F.2d 66 (10th Cir. 1966).

86. *Dijkstra v. Westerink*, 168 N.J. Super. 128, 401 A.2d 1114, 134 (App. Div.), *cert. denied*, 81 N.J. 329 (1979).

87. *Dairy Stores, Inc. v. Sentinel Publishing Co.*, 104 N.J. 125, 137 (1986).

7

Liability for Assaults

In chapter 2, while discussing the cross section of laws that pertain to private security, some attention was given to injuries caused by owners or users of property or caused by the criminal activity of third parties. It is the intent of this chapter to expand on that discussion and provide a better understanding of these aspects of the law, particularly as they apply to assaults. Attention will be focused on three areas: assaults on employees, assaults by employees or by the owner's agent, and assaults by strangers, visitors, or customers. Consideration will be given to the duty owed by the owner-occupier in each situation and how that duty is violated. Finally, some thought will be given to the legal parameters of the use of force in managing assault incidents.

ASSAULTS ON EMPLOYEES

Role of Workers' Compensation

Simply put, injuries to employees are covered by state workers' compensation laws. Of course, the problem with making such a general statement is that there are many exceptions. For example, seamen are covered under the Jones Act, railroad workers under the Federal Employer's Liability Act, and longshoremen under the Longshoremen's Act. But since the bulk of legal exposure is to the various state laws, they will be the focus of these comments.

To get a feel for how workers' compensation functions, it is necessary to understand its fundamental purpose and contrast it with torts. Workers' compensation is socially driven. Unlike torts, its intent is not to right a wrong but to see that the injured employee is not reduced to poverty and does not become a ward of the state. As a consequence, there is no need to find negligence by the employer or consider any contributory negligence on the part of the employee. If the employee is injured, he or she receives compensation according to a prescribed formula. The trade-off for not having the negligence factor in the equation is that the employee gives up any right to sue the employer for damages. Of course, the employee retains the right to sue a third party whose negligence caused the injury, and if monies are received through such an action, the employer usually is first reimbursed for any payments made under workers' compensation. This is because the employer's payments were for social needs and not to right a wrong; if these needs are satisfied by a separate negligence action, there is no reason for the employer to pay for them.[1]

Injuries Arising Out of and in the Course of Employment

The essence of workers' compensation is the requirement that the injury arise out of and be received in the course of employment. There are some variations among the states, but these two elements are critical parts of nearly all state statutes. The "arising out of" element is established in many courts by showing that the injury was caused by a risk of employment. An increasing number of states have established a "but for" test. Under this test, an injury is compensable if it would not have happened but for the fact that the conditions of employment put the employee in the position where he or she was injured.

In focusing on assault, most states—no matter what the sophistication of the standard for work-connectedness might be—at a minimum will find an injury compensable if the probability of assault was increased by the nature of the work or the environment in which the work was performed. By the same token, "assaults for private reasons do not arise out of the employment, unless, by facilitating an assault which would not otherwise be made, the employment becomes a contributing factor."[2]

A review of a few cases will help illustrate these points. In one case, a female employee, Giracelli, was working by herself in a cleaning establishment when she was attacked and raped by a customer.[3] In considering the "arising out of" requirement, the court concluded that the employee was exposed to a danger of attack and that the danger was a circumstance of the employment. The court favorably cited an earlier case in which the comment was made, "If the danger was one to which the employee was exposed because of the nature of the employment, the accident arose out of the employment."[4]

The *Giracelli* case involved a situation in which the employee was working at the kind of job that exposed her to the public in an unprotected, isolated setting. How about a situation in which the employee's job does not give her any unusual exposure and her injury takes place as she is coming to work? These are the kinds of facts a Georgia court considered in an attack and rape case that took place on a company parking lot.[5]

The Georgia court was considering a tort action in which an employee contended that her injuries suffered in an assault and rape were caused by the negligent failure of her employer to maintain a well-lighted and secure parking lot. The employer defended on the premise that the employee's only recourse was through workers' compensation.

The court first noted that a felonious assault does not prevent the resulting injury from being treated as an accident under the workers' compensation law if the act is not directed against the employee for reasons personal to the employee. In this case, the employee had arrived at the parking lot in the very early hours of the morning and was attacked by an employee who did not know her. She was not singled out and attacked because of who she was. For workers' compensation purposes, the attack was not "personal."

As to the "arising out of and in the course of" tests, the court observed that the woman had been injured on the employer's premises while going to work. In the court's judgment, "The early morning hour at which plaintiff was required to report to work and the location of the company parking lot in the vicinity of an area of known criminal activity provide the causal connection with her employment."[6] The court then concluded that "plaintiff's remedy, if any, lies exclusively under the provisions of the [workers' compensation] act and plaintiff may not maintain a common law tort action against her employer."[7]

The parking lot incident raises a question as to off-premises activity. Again as to parking lots, they will be considered part of the employer's premises if, although not owned by the employer, the employer exercises control over the lot by regular use.[8] But how about the normal coming to and going from work situations? The general rule is that an employee injured in such a situation is not entitled to compensation unless he or she is engaged in the service of the employer at the time. However, the employee is within workers' compensation protection during a reasonable period of time for purposes of ingress and egress.[9]

However, where an employer does furnish a safe means of ingress and egress and the employee, for his own convenience chooses not to use it but, instead selects a more hazardous means of leaving the premises, not customarily used by employees, he steps outside the scope of his employment and it cannot then be said that an injury which he sustains while so leaving the premises arises out of his employment.[10]

Returning to incidents within the workplace, what happens when an employee is injured as the result of a private quarrel? As stated in A.

Larson, *The Law of Workman's Compensation*, "When the animosity or dispute that culminates in an assault is imported into the employment from the claimant's domestic or private life, and is not exacerbated by the employment, the assault does not arise out of the employment under any test."[11]

In *Fair v. People's Savings Bank*,[12] a bank employee received harassing calls from her former boyfriend. The caller, Fair, subsequently arrived at the bank, threatened the employee, and was escorted from the bank by security personnel. The employee, fearing for her safety, decided to resign and was in the process of an exit interview when Fair reappeared in the bank and killed her. A workers' compensation claim was filed on behalf of the employee's infant son.

The court pointed out that even though the bank was aware of Fair's potential to injure the employee, the foreseeability of the crime did not supply the linkage to the need to prove the death arose out of the employment. Foreseeability is a factor in tort cases, but not in a non-fault system of liability. The court found no causal relationship between the employee's death and her employment. Since the death did not arise out of the employment, there was no requirement to make workers' compensation payments.

If the assault is carried out by a co-employee on the employer's premises, there is no obligation to pay if the assault was privately motivated.[13] Naturally, though, the decision will be to the contrary if there is some kind of work-related connection. In *Kerr-McGee Corp. v. Hutto*,[14] a Mississippi court considered a situation in which an employee was shot to death by a superior because of his alleged relationship with the superior's wife. Hutto, the employee, was requested by one of his superiors, a woman with whom he was living, to talk to another superior, her husband. The husband had directed her to do so and Hutto, on complying with the request, was shot by the superior-husband. The court labored over the "arising out of" issue but concluded that since Hutto appeared to be responding to a work-related order from a superior, the linkage was created and the test was passed. As the court stated, "Benefits will not be denied where it is reasonable to conclude that the deceased was acting under the instructions of a superior and that he was conducting the business of his employer."[15]

There are numerous aspects of workers' compensation law that warrant further attention, but for our purposes the essence is that if an employee is injured in an assault, the first legal arena to consider is workers' compensation. It should be kept in mind that even if the employer has an exemplary security and safety system and nonetheless the employee is injured, the employee will come under the coverage of the act even if he has done something stupid. By the same token, the validity of a weak security system will not be exposed to the tests typical of a tort action for damages where negligence is a critical element. This is the balance that has been struck.

ASSAULTS BY EMPLOYEES OR OWNER-OCCUPIERS' AGENTS

Chapter 2 dealt, in part, with the identification and classification of people who come onto property and the duties owed by owner-occupiers to those different classifications of people. According to the common law, people who come onto property are divided into three categories: trespassers, licensees, and invitees. A different level of duty is owed to each. Some repetition at this point might be of value.

Definition of Trespassers, Licensees, and Invitees

Trespassers come onto property without consent and the most owner-occupiers owe them is refraining from inflicting willful or wanton injury. Licensees are a cut above trespassers in that they have the consent of the owner-occupier but their visit is in their own self-interest. They must usually assume the risk of whatever they encounter and look out for themselves. Invitees stand at the top of the list in terms of duty owed, in that their presence is not only with consent but could be in the best business interest of the owner-occupier. This group includes customers and patrons. While the owner-occupier does not insure the safety of invitees, there is an obligation to exercise reasonable care for their protection. These generalities are subject to wide interpretation and in fact, in some jurisdictions, the owner-occupier owes the licensee the same duty of reasonable care as owed to the invitee.[16] However, the labels and distinctions in duty are often mentioned in case law and should be kept in mind. For our purposes, we can assume that there is an obligation to refrain from intentionally inflicting physical harm to all three categories.

Definition of Assault

The subject of assault has been treated in discussing injuries to employees. It is now proper to isolate assault as a subject for discussion and give it a definition, if one exists. First, an assault may either have criminal or civil aspects and oftentimes both.

Criminal assault has numerous slight variations from state to state, but it is usually defined as an unlawful attempt, coupled with a present ability, to commit a violent injury upon the person of another.[17] Violent injury does not necessarily mean bodily harm, as it includes any wrongful act committed by means of physical force against a person, even though only the feelings of the person are injured.[18] In most instances assault is coupled with battery, and battery usually is defined as an unlawful touching or striking of a person by the aggressor or by any substance put in motion by him.[19] In a nutshell, assault is the attempt by force to do violence to a person and battery is the application of the force and violence.

Now for the civil side. The Restatement of Torts provides that an act, other than the mere speaking of words, that directly or indirectly is a legal cause of putting another in apprehension of an immediate and harmful or offensive contact renders the actor civilly liable, if he intends thereby to inflict a harmful or offensive contact upon the other or a third person or to put the other or third person in apprehension thereof, and the act is not consented to by the other, and the act is not otherwise privileged.[20] As on the criminal side, battery constitutes the actual physical contact.

Civil and criminal cases are separate actions and guilt might be found in one and not the other. It seems that the criminal courts put greater emphasis on intent to do harm.[21]

Obviously an individual who commits an assault can be sued in a civil action for damages. But how does this impact an employer if the assault is carried out by an employee or a customer or visitor?

Assaults by Employees—Are Employers Responsible?

Of course, if an employer participates, orders, or ratifies an assault, then he or she may be liable for any resultant damages. This is only part of the answer, because the employer may also be liable for injuries inflicted by an employee in the scope or course of his or her employment. This doctrine, often referred to as respondiat superior, is another mechanism for involving employers in civil actions. The theory is that

every person shall so conduct his affairs as not to cause an injury to another, and if he undertakes to manage his affairs through others, he remains bound so to manage them that third persons are not injured by any breach of legal duty on the part of such others while they are engaged upon his business and within the scope of their authority.[22]

The scope of employment subject has a further refinement that is of interest. If an employee's duties involve the preservation of peace and order upon the premises, or the protection of the employer's property from theft or vandalism, an inference arises that force, to a reasonable extent, may or is expected to be used in the fulfillment of the duties of the employment, and hence, the use of such force is within the scope of the employment.[23]

This, of course, puts private security people and their employers in a particularly vulnerable position. A review of a few cases will help make the point. Most of these cases involving security people incorporate other charges such as false imprisonment, but for these purposes the focus will remain on assault. False imprisonment will be covered in chapters 6 and 8.

In *Sebastianelli v. Cleland Simpson Co.*,[24] a 1943 case, two store security people accosted two suspected shoplifters outside their store, seized and dragged one, and searched both against their will. No stolen goods were found. The store defended on the premise that the employees had operated outside the scope of their employment. The court concluded that the store was liable although its servants abused their authority and their acts went beyond the bounds of propriety. On reviewing a number of cases, the court concluded the rule is:

The master who puts the servant in a place of trust or responsibility or commits to him the management of his business or the care of his property, is justly held responsible when the servant, through lack of judgment or discretion, or from infirmity of temper, or under the influence of passion aroused by the circumstances and the occasion, goes beyond the strict line of duty or authority and inflicts an unjustifiable injury upon another.[25]

But does this mean everything a guard does will saddle his employer with liability? Is there an end point?

In *Rusnack v. Giant Food, Inc.*,[26] a chain food store security person, Davis, was shopping during his off-duty hours at a company store to which he was not assigned. An altercation took place in a checkout line between Davis and a customer over their relative positions in line. The fight concluded with Davis putting handcuffs on the customer. The customer sued the chain over the injuries he received.

The court, after analyzing the law on the subject, noted that:

Even if Davis were authorized to guard his employer's property and keep the peace while off-duty in a store to which he was not assigned to work . . . the evidence was not sufficient . . . to permit a jury to find that Davis' presence in the store and his acts with respect to Rusnack [the plaintiff] were in any way actuated by a purpose to serve his employer. . . . It cannot be fairly said that Davis was advancing Giant's interests in doing what he did at the time he did it.[27]

Giant was found not to be liable for Davis' conduct. While a security person's duties might extend the scope of employment into some wide-ranging activities, there is an end point and it appears to be situations, as in this case, where there is no color of gain that the employer gets out of the employee's conduct. Here Davis was acting in his own self-interest—not the employer's.

This is not the end, though, to the possible linkage of the assault by an employee to employer liability. It has been contended that some employers, because of the nature of their business, have an absolute duty to protect customers from injury. The hotel/motel business is the one in which the issue most often comes up. The concept of absolute liability was discussed in passing in chapter 2, but the essence of it is that common carriers and hotels take complete control over a traveler and in a sense cause the traveler to give up his or her normal defenses. The trade-off was that these businesses acquired an absolute duty to protect travelers against harm, a much higher standard than reasonable care.

There has been significant argument as to whether this strict duty of care still exists for hotels and motels. In *Tobin v. Stutsky*,[28] a federal court pondered New York law on the subject and at the same time discussed the state of the law on a nationwide basis. The court described considerable variations in interpretations from state to state but observed that the prevailing view seemed in accord with the duty of reasonable care position it had taken here, not absolute care.

The *Tobin* case shows an interesting twist to reasonable care standard: in New York hotel cases, reasonable care is commensurate with the quality of the accommodations offered. Some other states have a similar approach. In the case of a first-class family resort, reasonable care would mean a high degree of care. The federal court went on to say that its examination of the New York cases led it to believe that the hotel's duty of reasonable care had generally been interpreted to be quite strict. Even though faced with a heavy burden, a hotel is not automatically liable for injuries inflicted on a guest by an employee.

Assaults by Contractor Personnel—Who is Responsible?

To this point, the discussion on liability for assault has focused on acts committed by employees and the critical factors were the nature of the employee's job, the circumstances under which the assault was carried out, and the relationship, special or otherwise, between the employer and the person assaulted. Generally speaking, in establishing liability for injury, the inquiry requires an examination of the scope of employment of the employee and the duty owed to the injured person.

In today's world a lot of functions, security among them, are often carried out by contractors and contractor employees. What happens if an assault is carried out by one of the latter? Is the business that contracted out the function off the hook? The search for the balance of rights and duties will now center on control: Did the primary business maintain sufficient control over the day-to-day activities of the contractor or contractor's employees to warrant a finding that the primary business should be held liable?

In 1982, the District of Columbia Court of Appeals considered a *Safeway Stores* case in which a contractor's security guard was charged in a civil action with the assault and battery of a customer.[29] The security guard, employed by Seaboard Security Systems, while on duty at a Safeway store, in conjunction with a police officer, used force on a customer who, in the store's judgment, had been creating a problem. The customer sued the store for injuries received in the assault.

Safeway argued that it was not liable because the guard service company was an independent company and not a servant of Safeway. The court observed that in order to establish the relationship between the guard service and Safeway, it had to answer the critical question of whether the employer has the right to control and direct the guard in the performance of his work and the fashion in which the work was to be done. If there is control, there is liability.

With this as the benchmark, the court stated:

Although Seaboard hired the guards, Safeway had the right to discharge an individual guard, subject to Seaboard's approval. Safeway hired the guards to work on a continuous basis at several of its stores and paid for their services on a monthly basis in a lump sum payment to the agency. Most importantly, Safeway enjoyed the right to control the guards' conduct.... The store manager had operational control over the guards, who worked under his general direction.[30]

Numerous examples of this day-to-day control were listed, including instructions to lock the doors, keep juveniles out of the doorways, and watch for shoplifters. As the court summed it up, there was evidence upon which a reasonable jury could properly have found that the guard was a servant and not an independent contractor of Safeway and that, accordingly, Safeway was liable for the guard's allegedly tortious conduct. Of course, finding that Safeway had the right of control over the guard did not automatically mean Safeway was liable. As in the employer-employee cases, there had to be proof that the guard was acting in the interest of his employment. That was not an issue in this case—he was clearly acting in Safeway's interest.

Several jurisdictions consider that the duties owed to the public by one who is protecting his own property cannot be delegated to security personnel in a way that allows the primary—the owner or user—to avoid liability for assaults by contractor personnel. Under this approach, right of control is not the issue. For example, some courts have discussed the issue of whether the use of armed guards by contractors automatically links the principal to injuries inflicted by contractor employees. Generally courts will find that the use of firearms is not so inherently dangerous to third persons as to require a finding that the duties were non-delegable.[31]

ASSAULTS BY STRANGERS—WHO IS RESPONSIBLE?

Duty Owed

Injury caused by the criminal activity of a third party to a non-employee was discussed at some length in chapter 2 and is worth reviewing. The purpose at that point was to give some feel for the breadth of legal issues faced by private security people and the shifts in the balance of rights that take place as new parties and new theories of liability are introduced into the problems. It was noted that there has been a growing concern by commentators and the courts over an increase of assaults at quasi-public locations such as parking lots and shopping malls by strangers. Part of the concern is over who will pay for the injuries sustained. The victim often can't afford to pay for the injuries suffered and it is highly unlikely that the perpetrator of the assault can or will pay. The search for the payor then centers on the owner-occupier of the shopping mall or parking lot. However, owner-occupier liability should not be artificially created in order to find someone who can pay the bills. There has to be some logic to the conclusion. The logic has to make sense not only in relation to the duty owed to the person injured but also in relation to other legal theories that exist for compensating injured parties. For example, it would be strange if Giant Food were not liable for injuries to the customer caused by Davis, the security guard, and very strange indeed if Giant were to be found liable if a fight were carried out by a stranger. In the interest of finding some way to compensate an injured party, legitimate defenses such as scope of employment should not be undermined.[32] There should be some symmetry to the various elements of the law that have an impact on a matter and if there is not, there should be some explanation for it. Otherwise, the search for a balance of rights would be fruitless.

For many years it was understood that in most circumstances owner-occupiers were not responsible for injuries sustained on their property that were inflicted by strangers. The exceptions covered injuries to passengers in common carrier cases, guests at hotels and motels, and sometimes students at schools and patients in hospitals. The nature of these functions dictated that some kind of extra protection be provided. The reasons for the general rule of non-liability were that these kinds of assaults by strangers were really a police problem and it did not seem reasonable for businesses to be responsible for individuals over whom they had no control. After all, if a business was not responsible for an employee acting in his own self-interest, why should it be responsible for an individual who had no employment relationship at all?

The kinds of cases that caused a gradual change in thinking had certain common characteristics. For the most part they involved vicious attacks with death or serious injury as the end result, they took place on quasi-public business properties such as parking lots and shopping malls, and there was a concern about who was going to pay the bills. An analysis of a few cases will help explain how many courts got over the hurdle that no duty was owed by most businesses, and then once a duty was established, who actually owed the duty, and then how courts determined whether or not the duty was violated.

In 1981, an employee, Craig, on leaving work from a business located in a Delaware mall, was kidnapped from the mall parking lot and subsequently murdered by a stranger. The administrator of her estate brought a wrongful death action against TMA, the owner of the mall; AAR Realty Corp., the leasor and manager of the mall; and the merchants' association made up of various businesses on the mall. TMA filed a motion for summary judgment contending that as the non-possessing owners they had no duty of care to invitees such as Craig. AAR filed a similar motion contending that punitive damages were not a legitimate part of the suit.[33]

As to TMA's contention of non-liability, the court first quoted from *Prosser and Keeton on the Law of Torts* 358 (5th ed. 1984), in which it was stated:

As our ideas of human relations change the law as to duties changes with them. Various factors undoubtedly have been given conscious or unconscious weight including convenience of administration, capacity of the parties to bear the loss, a policy of preventing further injuries, the moral blame attached to the wrongdoer, and many others. Changing social conditions lead constantly to the recognition of new duties. No better general statement can be made than that the courts will find a duty where, in general, reasonable persons could recognize it and agree that it exists.

Continuing to build on the duty issue, the court quoted from the *Restatement (Second) of Torts*, Sec. 344:

[The possessor of land] may ... know or have reason to know, from past experience, that there is a likelihood of conduct on the part of third persons in general which is likely to endanger the safety of the visitor, even though he has no reason to expect it on the part of any particular individual. If the place or character of his business, or his past experience, is such that he should reasonably anticipate careless or criminal conduct on the part of third persons, either generally or at some particular time, he may be under a duty to take precautions against it, and to provide a reasonably sufficient number of servants to afford a reasonable protection.[34]

Bringing these comments more into focus, the court noted:

Predicated on principles of premises liability and coupled with a cost-benefit analysis, a number of courts have recognized that special conditions connected with the ownership and operation of a mall which lend themselves to criminal activity may require that a duty of care devolve upon the mall owner who is in the best position to take action and distribute the cost.[35]

After citing a number of cases in which other courts found a duty of care because criminal attacks in the lots or malls were reasonably foreseeable, the court took the next step and considered who was liable under this duty. The court observed that, "Balanced against the compelling policy reasons for establishing a duty upon the premise owner is the well established common law principle that a landlord who has neither possession nor control of the leased premises is not liable for injuries to third persons."[36]

The control issue keeps popping up. For example, in the contracting out of services discussion it was observed that the owner-user generally would only be liable for injuries inflicted by a contractor's employee if the owner-user had retained control over the contractor and its employee. Here again control plays a critical role. As the court pointed out in the AAR case, "The traditional test for the determining liability of a landowner/landlord to third party business-invitees is, therefore, whether the landowners/landlord had control of the premises."[37]

As far as this Delaware court was concerned, that meant actual control—that is, actual management of the leased premises. As an aside, some jurisdictions do not require actual control. Actual control usually is not necessary to prove in cases involving the contracting out of services. It is interesting that in the Safeway case regarding contracting of security services, the attempted linkage to the owner, Safeway, was via the master-servant theory and in the AAR case it was by means of a landlord-tenant relationship. Under both theories, control plays a critical role. The court went on to say:

While I am mindful that the modern shopping mall which attracts criminal activity may warrant the imposition of a duty upon the non-possessing mall owner who retains no control because such an owner is arguably in the best position to take preventive measures and, therefore, allocate the costs, the decision to change common law landlord-tenant principles rests with the legislature and not with the courts.[38]

After considering the facts set out in the pleadings, the court concluded that TMA, the owner, did not have actual control and, accordingly, had no duty to protect business invitees such as Craig from assault by strangers. But what about AAR, the mall manager? The court concluded that AAR not only could be held liable because of the foreseeability of the injury based upon prior criminal conduct at the mall but also could be subject to punitive damages because of facts in the pleadings evidencing "conscious indifference" to the rights of others. As the court stated it,

"AAR was reasonably on notice concerning crimes at the mall, the nature of which approach the magnitude of kidnap, rape, and murder. Indeed, I am satisfied that given the frequency and severity of reported crimes at the mall—a reasonable juror could conclude that a virtual crime wave existed."[39] The court was satisfied that jurors using the conscious indifference standard for punitive damages based upon AAR's statements in a deposition to the effect that the crime situation was a matter for the public security authorities and not for individual owners of real estate. As AAR saw it, their concern was with the well-being of tenants and the crime statistics would be left to the political authorities. This is an interesting reaction by the court to AAR's defense because for many years this defense was one of the accepted reasons for not making owner-occupiers liable for injuries inflicted by strangers on customers. It appears that what might be a reason to find punitive damages in one jurisdiction might be a good defense resulting in no liability at all in another. The motion for summary judgment on the punitive damages issue was not granted.

This *AAR* case is interesting because it evidences the development of a legal theory and shows how far some courts will go before they feel they are making changes that should properly be within the control of the legislature. In some jurisdictions, some legislatures do solve the problems by creating new law. For example, an Arizona court has determined that a state law imposes a duty on school boards to extend protection to school children.[40]

To understand shifts in the law, it is first necessary to understand the process by which the law develops. It starts off with the recognition of a societal need and then moves to the satisfaction of the need, either by imaginative court decisions or new legislation. As courts react to new problems, they generally resort to the thinking of the reasonable or prudent person. The court tries to adopt the position it believes would make sense to a reasonable person. Apparently, in a lot of situations, what a reasonable person would have thought twenty years ago is not the same thing he or she would think today. While there is nothing wrong with security people being advocates of a certain position, it is in their best interest to understand how courts operate and be objective observers of trends so that they do not get caught off base in their planning.[41]

Violation of Duty

To this point the focus has been on whether or not a duty exists. But once a legal duty has been established, the next question is whether that duty has been violated. While the new obligations of reasonable care are being expanded into stranger-inflicted injuries at shopping malls and in parking lots, it is of interest to explore this negligence area in two cases, one of which involves a motel. Even though hotels and motels are sometimes put on a higher level of care, the security elements juries look at will often be the same.

In *Orlando Executive Park, Inc. v. P.D.R.*,[42] a Florida appeals court considered a damages action involving a sexual assault by a stranger on motel property. The court first established that the hotel must provide security commensurate with the facts and circumstances that are or should be apparent to the ordinarily prudent person: "An innkeeper's standard of care in providing security will vary according to the particular circumstances and location of the hotel."[43]

Using this as a benchmark, the court listed a number of factors in deciding whether or not the hotel had exercised ordinary care in providing adequate security. These factors included:

industry standards, the community's crime rate, the extent of assaultive or criminal activity in the area or in similar business enterprises, the presence of suspicious persons, and the peculiar security problems posed by the hotel design. A hotel's liability depends upon the danger to be apprehended and the presence or absence of security measures designed to meet the danger. The particular circumstances may require one or more of the following safety measures: a security force, closed circuit television surveillance, deadbolt and chain locks on the individual rooms as well as security doors on hotel entranceways removed from the lobby area.[44]

A Minnesota court discussed a number of aspects of a sexual assault by a stranger in a commercial parking garage, including the circumstances to be considered in determining whether the owner-operator had been negligent in performing its duty of reasonable care.[45] Again, time was first spent in establishing whether or not there was a duty. The court followed the developing pattern of liability from its origin and commented that as to businesses generally, the law has been concerned about imposing a duty to protect. A simple merchant-customer relationship is not enough to impose a duty on the merchant to protect his customers. The court then went on to say, though, that it did not think the law should take a position that the operator of a parking garage owes no duty to protect its customers. Some duty is owed. In this court's judgment, the operator or owner of a parking garage had a duty to use reasonable care to prevent criminal activity on its property that might cause personal harm to customers. The degree of care to be provided was to be measured by what a reasonably prudent operator or owner would provide under the circumstances.

With the duty established, the court then considered the elements that would help determine whether the duty had been violated. These included "the location and construction of the ramp, the practical feasibility and cost of various security measures, and the risk of personal harm to customers that the owner or operator knows, or in the exercise of due care should know, presents a reasonable likelihood of happening."[46]

As in nearly all of these cases, the court added that the owner or operator is not an insurer of the safety of its property and cannot be expected to prevent all criminal activity. The fact that a criminal assault occurs on the property, by itself, is not proof that the duty to deter criminal acts has been breached.

Numerous assault cases have dealt with specific evidence of negligence such as lax control over pass keys, inadequate numbers of security people, failure to investigate or remove suspicious persons, poor lighting, and inadequate responses to request for assistance. There is no specific judgment as to where the tipping point is between negligence and no negligence. What might be adequate for a "mom and pop" business might not be adequate for a larger, more sophisticated operation. As the cases keep reiterating, the courts look at the totality of circumstances and are not interested in establishing set formulas.[47]

LEGAL PARAMETERS FOR RESPONSES TO ASSAULT

It is easy enough to talk about removing a suspicious person from the premises or adequately responding to a call for help, but how can this be done without the risk of the security person being held liable for assault? How much force can be used to get the job done? As already discussed, assault can either be criminal, civil, or both. Within the criminal area, assaults can be defined under the common law or more often under state statute. Defenses to both criminal and civil charges can be raised on the basis of self-defense, defense of others, and defense of property. Generally, criminal cases seem to focus on intent to do harm.[48] Since in most instances the distinctions between the elements that make up criminal and civil violations are minor, they do not warrant separate treatment. For these purposes, defenses to both kinds of charges will be treated together.

Self-Defense

As the term implies, a person has a right to protect himself from force and violence. The person resisting attack must believe that his or her injury can be prevented only by the immediate infliction of force on the other. Generally, only a present danger can be a legitimate justification for the use of force. However, the person resorting to self-defense does not have to show that he or she was in actual danger; apparent danger is sufficient. Thus, if a person honestly believes that he or she is in danger and in light of all the circumstances that belief seems reasonable, acquittal or a defense verdict is warranted. In short, the defender can be wrong and still be legally protected.

The degree of defense is measured against the degree of attack. One may not use a sledge hammer to get rid of a mosquito. The degree of response will also be measured by the relative strength of the parties. A two hundred pound, twenty-five year old athletic male security guard probably does not have to use much force to protect himself from a ninety-five pound, older female shopper or employee who kicks him in the ankle. By the same token, if the woman has a large knife and has slashed at the security officer, the degree of force obviously can be escalated. The person attacked does not have to retreat, as long as he or she uses only such force as is necessary to meet the attack, even though he or she might safely avoid the threat by retreating. The key is that the defender can use that force which he reasonably believes is necessary for his protection. The defender has to act as a reasonable person, one possessing ordinary courage and firmness.[49]

Defense of Others

States vary somewhat in their interpretation of the right to use force in defense of others. In most situations, though, the right to use force to protect a third person is geared to the right to protect oneself. Without getting into all the elements, a review of parts of one typical statute will be of value.

In Delaware, "The use of force upon or toward the person of another is justifiable to protect a third person when:

1. the defendant would have been justified in using such force to protect himself against the injury he believes to be threatened to the person whom he seeks to protect; and

2. under the circumstances as the defendant believes them to be, the person whom he seeks to protect would himself have been justified in using such protective force; and

3. the defendant believes that his intervention is necessary for the protection of the other person."[50]

Defense of Property

In situations where force is used in defense of property, care should be taken in identifying the kind of property involved—whether it is real property or personal property. Also, attention should be given to whether it involves protecting property in possession of the owner or recovering property that has been taken from the owner's possession. Further, it should be determined, if possible, whether the security person was trying to protect property or make an arrest. It should always be recognized that in the eyes of the law the preservation of human life and limb from grievous harm is of more importance to society than the protection of property.[51] Understanding the factors to be weighed by the courts helps toward understanding the end results.

Relative to trespassing, an owner or occupier can use such force as may be reasonably necessary to prevent an unlawful entry, or to remove trespassers. A request to leave and a reasonable time to respond are usually required. A person who is legitimately on property may lose that status and may be forced to leave after being given proper notice and reasonable time to leave. Reasonable force may be employed to remove patrons of a store or business establishment whose permission to enter has been withdrawn. This could be the case if a business invitee became disorderly.

In 1977 the New Mexico court of appeals considered an action brought against a store owner by a business invitee for damages incurred in an alleged assault by a store employee.[52] The business invitee, Griego, was in the store when he became angry, abusive, and profane, and used obscene gestures toward several employees, advancing on one of them. Wilson, the defendant, cautioned Griego to stop and, becoming apprehensive that Griego was provoking a disturbance, restrained him. The court stated:

We hold that the proprietor of a business has the right to expel or restrain a person who by virtue of abusive conduct refuses to leave or persists in his abusive conduct after being cautioned, though that person was initially on the premises by express or implied invitation, so long as the expulsion or restraint is by reasonable force.[53]

Under normal circumstances, the trespasser should be asked to leave before force is used.

The use of force in protecting personal property is a difficult area. An owner or an owner's agent may use force to prevent the tortious taking of such property provided he or she uses only such force as is reasonably necessary. "The taking or endangering of life is not justified, however, for the mere protection of personal property, unless in some jurisdictions, it should become necessary to prevent the commission of a felony."[54] Even in these situations, the felony to be prevented must usually be an atrocious crime such as murder, arson, burglary, rape, kidnapping, sodomy, or the like.

Courts regularly look to the *Restatement (Second) of Torts* for guidance, and it is of value to now consider the Restatement's position on recaption of chattels.[55] According to the Restatement, the use of force to retake personal property or chattels is privileged if:

• The chattel has been tortiously taken (Sec. 101).

• The actor is entitled to immediate possession (Sec. 102).

• The recaption is effected promptly after dispossession (Sec. 103).

• The actor first requests the other to return the chattel. This element is not applicable where the "actor correctly or reasonably believes a request to be useless, dangerous to himself or a third person, or likely to defeat the exercise of the privilege" (Sec. 104).

• The force is employed for the purpose of effecting the recaption (Sec. 105).

• The recaption is effected by the use of force which is no greater than is reasonable and is not intended or likely to cause serious bodily harm or death (Sec. 106).

One particular aspect of the Restatement's position warrants further attention. What happens if the person believed to have tortiously taken the property has not actually taken it? According to the Restatement, the actor's reasonable but mistaken belief does not create the privilege to use force unless the mistake was created by the other person. The Restatement goes on to contrast this to the use of force in self-defense, where the privilege is not lost because of mistake.[56] However, it should be noted that, apart from the Restatement, other commentators and some case law indicate that a property owner in possession has a privilege of using force even if a mistake has been made. "In possession" means that the owner still has physical control over the property. "Out of possession" would cover shoplifting situations where the shoplifter has actually taken physical possession.[57] The distinction between in possession and out of possession seems to be made on the premise that it is difficult to stretch the property owner's inherent right to protect property to situations where the owner is out of possession. The problem is that the chance for mistake is much more likely in out of possession incidents. This may be another reason why the privilege to use force has not been extended to out of possession mistakes.

USE OF FORCE IN MAKING AN ARREST OR PREVENTING THE COMMISSION OF A CRIME

These comments will be made without any real discussion at this time about the nature of arrests and the elements that are normally an integral part of them such as detentions and searches. Arrest is covered in detail in chapter 8. The arrest aspects are only covered now to complete the subject of the use of force in performing the security function.

As noted, the Restatement does not provide for the use of force that is intended or likely to cause death or serious bodily harm in the recovery of personal property. The Restatement, however, does state that there may be circumstances in which the person involved, the actor, is seeking not only to recover his chattel but also to prevent the commission of a crime or to arrest the criminal, "and in such cases he may be permitted to use for the other purposes a degree of force which he would not be privileged to use merely to recapture the chattel."[58]

The obvious question in some security-related cases where serious bodily harm was sustained is whether the security person was merely trying to recover property, or was he or she trying to prevent the commission of a crime or make an arrest? If the former, at least in many jurisdictions, there is liability; if the latter, there may be no liability. A review of a case or two will help make the point. Cases invariably involve multiple issues, but only those relevant to this inquiry will be explored.

In *Giant Food, Inc. v. Scherry,*[59] a Maryland court of appeals considered a case in which a security guard shot at a fleeing robber and put a bullet through the window of a house located near the store. The neighbor sued the store for negligence and the jury awarded her damages for mental and emotional distress.

Remember, under the recovery of property provision of the Restatement, the actor may not use deadly force but under the arrest provisions he may, under certain circumstances. The court addressed itself to the latter area and, after noting the elements of the Maryland statute on arrests by private parties, concluded that the security officer had probable cause to believe that the person he was pursuing had just committed an armed robbery, a felony, and he therefore had the right and authority to arrest him. That was an important finding because it moved the focus from recovering property to arrest, but it was still only step one. Keep in mind that if a felony has been committed, the citizen making the arrest needs reasonable or probable cause to think the arrested person did it. There is some room for making a mistake but, again, only if the felony has been committed.

As to the means used to accomplish his objective, the firing of the shots, the court first reviewed the standards set out in the Restatement. It then agreed that a person authorized to make an arrest may use reasonable or necessary force, but did not agree that the firing of the shot was justified.

As far as this court was concerned, the guard had a double responsibility—one to the prospective arrested person not to use unnecessary force against him, and one to the public at large to use reasonable force in a reasonable manner. The court commented:

These kinds of situations in which an innocent bystander is injured or killed in the course of an attempt to apprehend or defend an attack on one's person or property, arise in a variety of contexts—some more life threatening to the actor than others, some involving felons and felonies, others involving misdemeanants and misdemeanors. The context is important in determining the reasonableness of the action taken, but the basic standard remains the same. Where the evidence shows that the actor, whether a police officer or a private citizen, acted without due regard to the danger caused to innocent third parties, he (and his employer) have been held liable.[60]

This court framed the question as to whether it was reasonable for the security officer to have fired the shot. "Was there a prospect for injuring someone else?" In its review of the facts, the court noted that (1) the fleeing robber posed no imminent danger to the security person or anyone else; (2) the security person could have assisted in recovering his employer's property and effected the robber's arrest by noting his description and the license tag number of the getaway car and summoning the police; and (3) the security officer was literally shooting in the dark at a rapidly moving target. The court added that the security person should have been aware that he was shooting in the general direction of the apartment complex and that if the bullet missed its target, it might strike someone there. The court had no problem based upon all these factors in finding that a trier of facts could rationally conclude that the security person did not act reasonably.

An Oregon court came down the other way on not completely dissimilar facts, after a somewhat similar review of the law.[61] The point is that even within the same legal parameters one jury's idea of what is reasonable might not be the same as another's. Jury decision-making is not an exact science.

OBSERVATIONS

Assault seems to be an increasing phenomenon across society as a whole and there is a growing societal concern over who is going to pay for the increased medical costs of injuries. The traditional ways of handling the remedies for injuries sustained by employees while working and for injuries inflicted on invitees by owner's employees are relatively free of direct demand for change. The legal shift in response to injuries inflicted by strangers on invitees is a reaction to new societal demands. Shifts in the law will probably continue as long as assaults increase and extend into new business areas. Right now the new areas are parking lots and shopping malls, and it is difficult to say what the future might bring. Traditional, tightly controlled worksites might see little legal change, but they are being replaced by industrial parks that are visitor-friendly. As noted, changes in ways of doing business often create changes in laws.

In making security-related judgments, it has to be understood that society does not put the protection of property on the same level as the protection of people. Any decisions made relative to the use of force have to be based on this fundamental principle. Further, even within the area of protecting property there is a sliding scale for the use of force, and the right to use force changes, depending on the nature of the property, real or personal, and the circumstances under which its possession is being jeopardized.

There is no exact formula for establishing how much force can be used under given circumstances, and the only legitimate advice is to focus on three words: objective, reasonable, and prudent. If security people measure their activities by this standard, they should feel comfortable that a court will try to do the same. This, of course, does not guarantee favorable legal results but it's about as close as you can come.

NOTES

1. 1 Larson, *The Law of Workmen's Compensation*, Sec. 1:00–2:20 (1991).

2. 7 Larson, *The Law of Workmen's Compensation*, Sec. 6:00–6:50, 11:00–11:11(b).

3. *Giracelli v. Franklin Cleaners & Dyers*, 132 N.J.L. 590, 42 A.2d 3, (1945).

4. 42 A.2d 3 at 4.

5. *Helton v. Interstate Brands Corporation*, 155 Ga. 607, 271 S.E.2d 739 (Ga. App. 1980).

6. 271 S.E.2d 739 at 741.

7. 271 S.E.2d 739 at 741.

8. *Cox v. Quality Car Wash*, 449 A.2d 231 (Del. 1982).

9. *Goff v. Farmers Union Accounting Service*, 308 Minn. 440, 241 N.W.2d 315 (Minn. 1976).

10. *Corcoran v. Fitzgerald Brothers*, 239 Minn. 38, 58 N.W.2d 744, 746 of (Minn. 1953).

11. Vol. 1, Sec. 11:21 (a).

12. 207 Conn. 535, 542 A.2d 1118 (Conn. 1988).

13. *Devault v. General Motors Corp.*, 149 Mich. App. 765, 386 N.W.2d 671 (Mich. 1986).

14. 401 So. 2d 1277 (1981).

15. 401 So.2d 1277 at 1281.

16. *Mounsey v. Ellard*, 363 Mass. 693, 297 N.E.2d 43 (1973).

17. 6 Am. Jur. 2d *Assault and Battery* Sec. 3, 5, 7, 8, 9 (1963).

18. *People v. Whalen*, 124 Cal. App. 2d 713, 269 P.2d 181 (1954).

19. 6 Am. Jur. 2d *Assault and Battery* Sec. 5, 7, 8, 9 (1963).

20. *Restatement, (Second) of Torts* Sec. 21(1) (1965).

21. 6 Am. Jr. 2d *Assault and Battery* Sec. 109.

22. Annot., 34 A.L.R.2d 380–396, *Assault by Servant* (1963).

23. Annot., 34 A.L.R.2d 372, *Assault by Servant* Sec. 14.

24. 152 Pa.S.203, 31 A.2d 570 (1943).

25. 31 A.2d 570, 572.

26. 26 Md. App. 250, 337 A.2d 445 (Md. 1975).

27. 337 A.2d 445 at 454.

28. 506 F.2d 1097 (2d Cir. 1974).

29. *Safeway Stores, Inc. v. Kelly*, 448 A.2d 856 (D.C. 1982).

30. 448 A.2d 856 at 861.

31. Annot., 38 A.L.R. 3d 1332, *Liability of One Contracting for Private Police or Security Service for Acts of Personnel Acquired* Sec. 5, 9 (1971).

32. *Rusnack*, 26 Md. App. 250, 337 A.2d 445, (Md. 1975).

33. *Craig v. AAR Realty Corp.*, 576 A.2d 688 (Del. Super. 1989).

34. 576 A.2d 688 at 692.

35. 576 A.2d 688 at 693.

36. 576 A.2d 688 at 694.

37. 576 A.2d 688 at 695.

38. 576 A.2d 688 at 696.

39. 576 A.2d 688 at 698, 699.

40. *Chavez v. Tolleson Elementary School District*, 595 P.2d 1017 (1979).

41. Annot., 49 A.L.R. 4th 1257, *Parking Lot—Duty Owed to Patron* (1986); 34 A.L.R. 4th 1054, *Land Carriers Liability to Assault Victim* (1984).

42. 402 S.2d 442 (1981).

43. 402 S.2d 442 at 447.

44. 402 S.2d 442 at 447, 448.

45. *Erickson v. Curtis Investment Co.*, 447 N.W.2d 165 (1989).

46. 447 N.W.2d 165 at 170.

47. Annot., 28 A.L.R. 4th 80, *Hotel Liability—Third Party Assault* (1984).

48. 6 Am. Jur. 2d *Assault & Battery* Sec. 8 (1963).

49. 6 Am. Jur. 2d *Assault & Battery* Sec. 69, 80 (1963); *Restatement (Second) of Torts* Sec. 70 (1965).

50. Del. Code Ann., tit. 11, Sec. 465.

51. *Commonwealth v. Emmons*, 157 Pa. 495, 43 A.2d 568 (1945).

52. *Griego v. Wilson*, 91 N.M. 74 570 P.2d 612 (1977).

53. 570 P.2d 612 at 614.

54. 6A C.J.S. *Assault & Battery* Sec. 23 (1963); 6 Am. Jur. 2d *Assault & Battery* Sec. 88 (1963).

55. Sec. 100.

56. Sec. 106.

57. Comment, *Shoplifters Beware*, 11 Drake L. Rev. 31, 33–34 (1961); Comment, *The Protection and Recapture of Merchandise from Shoplifters*, 46 Ill. L.Rev. 887, 889–891 (1952); 32 Am. Jur. 2d *False Imprisonment* Sec. 91 (1982).

58. Sec. 106 (f).

59. 51 Md. 586, 444 A.2d 483 (1982).

60. 444 A.2d 483 at 487.

61. *Hatfield v. Gracen*, 279 Or. 303, 567 P.2d 546 (1977).

8

Individual Rights of Non-Employees and Protection of Property and Business Interests

DETAINING AND INVESTIGATING

As discussed above, the law provides that a certain amount of force can be used in protecting property without committing an assault and battery. A property owner does not commit an assault and battery by gently placing his hands on a customer who has been helping himself to goods for which he does not intend to pay and escorting that person out of his place of business.[1] But that is not the end of the property owner's legal concerns.

Trespassers can be escorted off the property and in some situations a thief might hand over property that has been taken. In such situations, a security officer can avoid the use of force in carrying out his or her job. But the job often cannot be completed successfully without detaining a suspected thief in order to carry out an investigation and recover any property involved. The detaining, though, can lead to such legal problems as charges of false arrest or false imprisonment.

False Arrest and False Imprisonment

The best way of getting at this issue is to first briefly discuss what arrest means before getting into the meaning of false arrest. There are numerous complex definitions of arrest, but one that seems to capture the essence of it is set out in the *Restatement (Second) of Torts* as the taking of another into custody for the actual or purported purpose of bringing him before a court, or otherwise securing the administration of the law.[2] Most states set out the definition of arrest in statutes, and while there are variances they are all quite similar. For example, Delaware defines arrest as "the taking of a person into custody in order that he may be forthcoming to answer for the commission of a crime."[3]

The power to make an arrest also varies from state to state but uniformly the power of a law enforcement or police officer embraces and exceeds that of a private citizen. For example, the common law, which has been incorporated into statutes in most states, provides that a private person may arrest without a warrant in a felony case if the felony has actually been committed and he has reasonable grounds for believing that the person arrested was the one who committed it. Under this rule, if no felony has in fact been committed, an arrest without a warrant by a private citizen will be illegal, although an officer would have been justified in arresting under the same circumstances.[4]

As to arrest by private citizens for misdemeanors, there is also a variance among the states but the common law and most states generally limit such arrests to breaches of the peace committed in the arresting person's presence.[5] Thefts of personal property, without more, are not normally considered to be breaches of the peace. Thus, the use of arrest by private security people as a tool in managing theft cases is in most cases limited to felonies, and then it better be an actual felony. The limitation on private citizens seems to be based on the premise that enforcing the criminal law is primarily a job for law enforcement officers.

With regard to false arrest or false imprisonment, again, there are variances among the states but more often than not these two tort actions are treated as one and the same. However, it is useful to explore the bases for the two actions. False imprisonment is usually considered to be a matter between two private parties when there is no intention of bringing the person detained before a court. Some courts take the position that "there can be no such thing as an action for false imprisonment where the plaintiff has not been arrested,"[6] but that fine-tuning of legal niceties is not engaged in by most courts. For the purposes of this discussion, the critical element in both tort actions is unlawful detention. Explaining what the term "unlawful detention" means requires some background.

As already noted in chapter 7, one in possession of property has a privilege to use reasonable force to prevent someone from taking that property. This privilege protects the possessor from assault and battery charges and charges of false imprisonment or false arrest if the owner has made a reasonable mistake. However, the law shifts once the owner loses possession and attempts to recover his or her property. In such a situation, the owner acts at his or her own peril in making a recovery, because any mistake, even a reasonable one, will not justify the use of force or detention.[7]

This presents a problem for any property owner, but consider the circumstances of a self-service store owner, who by the nature of the business allows customers to pick up and handle goods. If the customer appears to have taken possession of the goods without paying and is confronted by a store security officer, that security officer had better be right.

This is only part of the picture, in that it only covers the court's attitude toward recovering personal property. Many courts slide over the property aspects of the matter and look at it as a criminal action triggering an interest in the legality of the arrest or detention under the criminal law definitions of arrest. Often in these situations, the relatively small value of the property taken places the case in the misdemeanor category and the store is not in a position to make a legal citizen's arrest. If the property value places the activity in the felony area, there will still be a need to prove the theft has been committed in order to avoid liability.

Shoplifting Statutes

This balance between property rights and freedom of movement became distorted at about the time of World War II. Merchants were shifting toward a self-service way of doing business and more and more merchandise was being handled directly by customers outside the immediate presence of store personnel. With this change came a dramatic increase in shoplifting.

Some states adjusted to the change via case law and gave greater latitude to detention for probable cause.[8] Others adopted the *Restatement (Second) of Torts* position that carved out a qualified privilege for involuntary detention.[9] Generally, though, the problem was managed through the passage of shoplifting statutes. By 1971, forty-one states had statutes extending some kind of immunity to merchants who detained suspected shoplifters.[10] Legislators were responding to social changes by readjusting the balance between the owner's right to protect property and the individual's right to freedom of movement. In a way, merchants were being given the right to be wrong and not suffer the consequences.

The different shoplifting statutes have certain common features. They provide that merchants can detain any person they believe is removing goods from their stores without paying for them if they have probable cause or reasonable grounds and if the detention is for a reasonable time and is conducted in a reasonable manner.[11]

A review of a few cases will help clarify some common aspects of this qualified right of detention. In *Coblyn v. Kennedy's Inc.*,[12] a Massachusetts court considered an action for false imprisonment brought by a small, seventy year old man against a store owner and an employee. The man had gone into the store to buy a sport coat and while doing so took off an ascot he was wearing and put it in his pocket. Following the purchase the coat was left for alteration, and as he left the store he replaced the ascot around his neck.

At that point an employee confronted him, asked him where he got the ascot, grabbed him by the arm, and said, "You better go back and see the manager." Another employee was nearby, as well as eight or ten other people. The man agreed to go back into the store and after stopping several times for chest pains, found the salesman that sold him the coat. The shoplifting issue disintegrated quickly and the next problem was related to treating the elderly man's heart attack.

The first legal question was whether there had been sufficient restraint to constitute imprisonment. The court focused on two elements, one physical and the other psychological. First, the man had been grasped by the arm and told he had better go back and see the manager. "Considering the plaintiff's age and heart condition, it is hardly to be expected that with one employee in front of him firmly grasping his arm and another at his side the plaintiff could do other than comply with Goss's request."[13] The court added that the honesty and veracity of the plaintiff had been clearly challenged, because if he had not returned, onlookers would have interpreted his departure as an admission of guilt. The restraint or duress imposed by the mode of investigation was for the accomplishment of the store's purpose, even if no threats of public exposure or of arrest were made, and no physical restraint of the plaintiff was attempted. This all added up to imprisonment or detention.

Before moving off the restraint and detention issue, some parameters should be put on the definition. In a later Massachusetts case, *Foley v. Polaroid Corp.*, already covered at length in chapter 6, a court explained that, while *Coblyn* stated that a plaintiff who relinquishes his right to move about freely as the only available alternative to relinquishment of another right, such as the right to an unsullied reputation, is restrained or imprisoned, all types of restraint would not constitute imprisonment. The *Foley* case was discussed in chapter 6 because it dealt with detention of an employee for interview purposes. Although this was not a shoplifting case, it does give an added feel for the meaning of detention. Keep in mind that the applications of false imprisonment are broader in scope than just shoplifting matters. The court said that an at-will employee who relinquishes his right to move about in return for continued employment, to which he is not entitled, is not imprisoned. He has a free choice— comply with the employer's request for an interview or lose his job. Fear of losing one's job, although a powerful incentive, does not render involuntary the behavior induced.[14]

The message is that a security person can create an imprisonment by words and actions that question a person's honesty in front of a group of people, leaving the person no alternative but to comply with the property owner's request. This definition might be too broad for some jurisdictions but it does give a feel for the subject.

Assuming that there is a detention, the next question is whether there was probable cause for the detention. First, the *Coblyn* court found that "probable cause" and "reasonable grounds" in these shoplifting statutes are concepts having virtually the same meaning. As a consequence, the terms generally are used interchangeably. Once again the reasonably prudent person test comes into play. Would the facts available to the store employee who confronted Mr. Coblyn convince a person of reasonable caution that the action taken was appropriate? Remember, the store employee's subjective state of mind is not what is important. What he or she actually thought does not count; what is at issue is what a reasonably prudent person would have thought. In this case, as far as the court was concerned, a reasonably prudent person would not have grabbed a customer and confronted him in front of a group because he took an ascot out of his pocket and put it around his neck.

Many courts as part of their search for reasonable grounds will look to see if a reasonable investigation was conducted prior to the detention. If a security person quickly checked a clothes rack or asked pertinent questions of a sales clerk prior to detaining a customer, the courts would be more inclined to find probable cause.[15] However, even if there is probable cause, the investigation has to cross two more hurdles before it can be considered legitimate. It has to be conducted in a reasonable manner and for a reasonable length of time.

The qualified right of detention is given to merchants to prevent the immediate theft of their property. It does not extend to investigations of old cases or completing the niceties of a current investigation such as getting a confession from or fingerprinting or photographing the person caught taking goods.[16] Neither will the privilege cover incidents involving excessive force or needless rudeness.[17] Again, the purpose of the shoplifting statutes is to give merchants an opportunity to detain people who are believed to be stealing from their businesses. As long as owners stay within the bounds of reasonableness as to cause, manner, and duration they will be protected, even if the person detained was not actually stealing.[18]

The focus to this point has been on the commonality of features in the various statutes but there are, of course, numerous differences among the statutes, as well. Some states are quite exact in limiting the privilege to theft of merchandise from stores and not extending it, for example, into the industrial or other non-store settings.[19] Iowa extends the coverage to library materials and Wisconsin includes innkeepers, motelkeepers, and hotelkeepers.[20]

States vary, too, in establishing the permissible purposes of the detention. Some say detention can only be used for investigation, but do not set out just what might properly be done during an investigation. Others are more specific. Oklahoma provides that an investigation can include a reasonable interrogation, notification of police, and a reasonable search.[21] On the other hand, the Wisconsin statute states the person involved "shall not be interrogated or searched against his will before the arrival of a peace officer who may conduct a lawful interrogation of the accused person."[22]

Some states also set out in some detail just what reasonable time and reasonable manner mean. In West Virginia, a detention cannot exceed thirty minutes, and in Louisiana it cannot exceed an hour unless it is reasonable under the circumstances to extend that period.[23] Wisconsin provides that the detained person "must be promptly informed of the purpose for detention and be permitted to make phone calls."[24] As to the probable cause or reasonableness factor in causing the detention in the first place, Louisiana provides that that burden is satisfied if a signal from an electronic device alerts the owner that specially marked merchandise is being removed. The statute provides, however, that sufficient notice first has to be posted to advise patrons of its use.[25]

In exploring the shadings and variations in the three reasonableness requirements—cause, time, and manner—in the different states it becomes evident that some states focus on criminal activity and the loosening up of arrest standards. For example, West Virginia has decided that shoplifting constitutes a breach of peace and uses this as a mechanism for expanding a merchant's right to detain.[26] Others provide that no search may be conducted other than by someone acting under the direction of a peace officer or when the person to be searched has given permission.[27] On the other hand, some states seem to recognize that all shoplifting detentions are not arrest or criminal law–related. Keep in mind, most business owners are primarily interested in retrieving their property and then only secondarily, if circumstances warrant it, consider involvement of law enforcement. Oklahoma seems to recognize this distinction and provides several alternatives an owner might follow including the use of the detention to recover goods by themselves or inform the police.[28] Under this approach owners seem less likely to become agents of law enforcement and assume the entangling aspects of Section 1983, *Miranda*, and other legal problems described in chapter 1.

Over all, though, the point is that social circumstances have changed the law. The dramatic increase in shoplifting that followed the change in merchandizing style caused state legislatures and courts to carve out privileged areas in which owners have a greater opportunity to protect their goods. This privilege is not wholesale in scope, however, and courts continue to be concerned with protecting individuals' freedom of movement. The factors in the balance of rights have shifted, but not precipitously—just enough, theoretically, to help merchants cope with shoplifting problems.

Defamation

Assault and detention do not stand by themselves as tools used in defending property. They are part of a sequence of events that almost necessarily includes some kind of communication. This communication can often take place in a confrontational situation and what hangs in the balance is the protection of property and a person's reputation. In short, there is a great likelihood that allegations of assault and false imprisonment will be coupled with charges of defamation.

Defamation was discussed at length in chapter 6 relative to the employment setting. It was established that because of the need to run a sound business, an employer is given certain latitude in the kinds of things it can say or write about present or former employees. Even if these statements are false, the employer is protected from liability by a qualified privilege if it acted in good faith, without malice, and did not communicate the message to anyone who did not have a real interest.

The first question here is whether a business has the same kind of qualified privilege if it communicates something of a defamatory nature about a non-employee. Can it be protected even if it is wrong? The approach is the same as in the employment setting: the focus is on determining whether the passage of true information is reasonably necessary for the protection of one's own interest, the interests of third persons, or certain interests of the public. If the information is necessary to protect these interests, then the qualified privilege is triggered as it is in the employment setting.

In *Ling v. Whittemore*,[29] a Colorado court considered a car repossession case in which the owner of an automobile, Ling, was searching for an automobile taken by a former employee, Whittemore. In conducting his search, Ling talked to Whittemore's landlady and told her that Whittemore had stolen a car from his lot. This was defamation on its face but the real question was whether or not Ling had any protection in making the statement. Was it privileged?

Following a detailed analysis, the court concluded that one has a privilege to communicate, in good faith, to another even though it is defamatory where the publisher is promoting a legitimate interest such as the recovery of stolen goods. But the receiver of the communication must have a sufficient corresponding interest to warrant the communication to him or her; this is often the sticking point.

The court commented that Ling was not talking to a disinterested stranger, but to one who could be expected to know something on the subject and who, as his landlady, had an interest in the character and activities of her tenant and could be expected to render assistance if she knew Whittemore was acting contrary to law. A privilege had been established and the burden now shifted to the former employee to show that Ling had abused the privilege. The case was remanded for a new trial.

So, a privilege will attach in a protection of property case if the communication takes place between interested parties. But not everyone is an interested party. In *Bennett v. Norban*,[30] a Pennsylvania court found that a store manager engaged in defamatory action when he followed a woman to a parking lot, blocked her path, put his hand on her shoulder, ordered her to take off her coat, said "What about your pockets?" and looked into and took things out of her purse. Passersby stopped to watch, and no stolen property was found.

Maybe there were no defamatory words but in the court's judgment there was sufficient conduct to get across the defamatory message. The conduct included the direction to remove her coat, the questions about her pockets, the action of feeling in them, and then searching her purse. As the court phrased it, "these events formed a dramatic pantomime suggesting to the assembled crowd that appellant was a thief."[31] Of course these passersby were not interested parties within the meaning of the privilege and the manager's conduct, accordingly, was not protected.

Certainly not all security-related conduct sends a message that the subject of an inquiry is a thief. In *Burron v. K-Mart Corp.*,[32] a store had posted a sign that read, "We deserve the right to inspect all packages." In addition, the store routinely used an employee to inspect packages, as indicated by the sign. At the time of the questioned incident, the store employee told a customer, "I'm going to check your boxes, it's my job." As far as the court was concerned, these circumstances did not imply that the customer was engaged in a theft, and, accordingly, no defamation was found. However, if there is defamatory activity, and the message only goes to interested parties and the privilege attached, it does not mean the business is home free, because the privilege can be lost through abuse. The elements that make up abuse were discussed in chapter 6; fundamentally, the court will look to see if the statements or conduct were carried out with malice or in bad faith.

Invasion of Privacy

With increasing frequency the tort of invasion of privacy has become a part of the legal response to security activity involving non-employees as well as employees. Employee privacy has been covered in some detail in chapters 2, 5, and 6. In many non-employee security-related cases, invasion of privacy is joined with assault, false arrest, and defamation, depending on the facts. At this point, it makes sense to set out a general outline of the tort of invasion of privacy. It is generally accepted that it can be divided into four different wrongs:

1. the intrusion upon an individual's solitude or seclusion;
2. publicity that violates the ordinary decencies;
3. putting the individual in a false but not necessarily defamatory position in the public eye; and
4. the appropriation of some element of the individual's personality for a commercial use.[33]

Any one or a combination of the first three types of invasion of privacy might arise in security-related cases. The first of the three, intrusion, does not require any communication or publication to third parties but the other two do. Thus, it is possible that an individual's privacy might be violated in the gathering of information or in the dissemination of information.

Intrusion activity must involve a person's private affairs and be conducted in a manner highly offensive to a reasonable person,[34] and the individual has to have a reasonable expectation of privacy in the subject matter of the inquiry. These are the factors that must be balanced to determine whether the person causing the intrusion was acting reasonably.

As discussed in chapters 2, 5, and 6, workplace privacy recently has generated a considerable amount of interest. Balancing the rights of employers and employees requires an insight into the factors at play in the National Labor Relations Act, arbitration, and tort actions. At least in the former two areas, weight is given to the employer's right to run a profitable business and to the collective rights of the group as well as to the rights of individual employees. An employee's right to privacy is qualified by work rules and the common law of the workplace—such as the "comply now and grieve later" rule. But what happens in non-employee privacy cases?

Non-work-related privacy cases continue to be of significant concern to private security. Often these issues surface in searches, surveillances, investigations, and in the dissemination of information. The common thread in all privacy cases, criminal, tort, or employee-related, is expectancy of privacy. Does an employee in a workplace have as much expectancy of privacy as a customer in a store? How far can an owner go in protecting his property without violating an individual's right to privacy?

Searches

Invasion of privacy allegations are often included with charges of assault, false imprisonment, and defamation in shoplifting cases. A review of a 1982 North Carolina case, *Morrow v. King's Department Stores, Inc.*[35] will give some perspective to the development of this legal theory. A customer was stopped by a security person on leaving a store and the security person looked through her shopping bag and removed a shirt. The charges against the store included, as one might expect, assault and battery, defamation (slander), intentional infliction of mental suffering, and invasion of privacy.

As to the invasion of privacy aspects, the court first noted that North Carolina had recognized, as most states, a cause of action for an invasion of an individual's right of privacy. It went on to note that the question of the existence of this right is a relatively new field in legal jurisprudence. In respect to it, the "courts are plowing new ground and before the field is fully developed unquestionably perplexing and harassing stumps and runners will be encountered."[36]

With that uncertainty established, the court added that while some states have recognized an action for invasion of privacy based on an illegal search by a private individual, North Carolina has not. The court cited the Pennsylvania case of *Bennett v. Norban*[37] as a case in point. *Bennett* was discussed earlier in discussions under defamation. Focusing on the search issue, the court divided it into two areas: did the tort of invasion of privacy apply to searches and if it did, did the shoplifting statute absolve the defendant from liability for the searches? After framing the issue, the court avoided resolving it by finding a flaw in the pleadings, but the point raised is still a valuable one—shoplifting statutes might provide protection against invasion of privacy or other actions beyond false imprisonment.

Two aspects of these shoplifting statutes warrant attention. First, does the statute specifically refer to searches or can the right to search be inferred from other language such as the right to conduct an investigation? This latter element can best be established by reviewing case law on the subject. Second, does the statute specifically refer to invasion of privacy or does it encompass all civil actions? Most seem to fall in the latter category. It should be remembered that the protections carved out for errors made in detention cases have been limited, for the most part, to merchants.

As earlier described in the discussion of the *Bennett v. Norban* case, the court made a finding on defamation and then went on to make a similar finding on invasion of privacy. Remember, among other things, the store manager had reached into the customer's pockets, took her handbag, emptied the contents, and examined them before a crowd. The court noted that "passers-by stopped to watch to appellant's great distress and humiliation." After referring to the *Restatement of Torts* Vol. A Sec. 867 and focusing on such words as "unreasonably" and "intrusion has gone beyond the limits of decency," the court concluded, "The angry performance of defendant's agent was an unreasonable and serious interference with appellant's desire for anonymity and an intrusion beyond the limits of decency."[38]

For situations not covered by shoplifting statutes, it should be remembered that the invasion of privacy tort is much wider than shoplifting situations and its primary application is in redressing unreasonable interference with a person's interest in not having his or her affairs known to others. Liability only exists if the intrusion has gone beyond the limits of decency. If there is justification for the intrusion and the intrusion is reasonably carried out, there should be no liability.

In the non-merchant, non-employee setting, a right to search is often made a condition of doing business at the business site. This is particularly true in industrial settings where usually owners insist on a right to search contractor employees and equipment in order to place contractors on an equal footing with the owner's employees. To do otherwise would be to say that it is only employees that steal. After all, a reasonable rule should be applicable to all. There should be a clear understanding on the part of contractors or visitors that the owner's right to search is a condition of entering the private premises.

Surveillances on Property

Retail stores, again, seem to be the center of many of these kinds of privacy actions and more often than not the problems arise in dressing or fitting rooms. Legal analysis usually starts with a consideration of expectancy of privacy, and although it is a suppression of evidence case, a California court did a good job in setting down some fundamentals that should also be applicable in a tort action.[39] It is unusual to use a criminal case to help understand a civil action, but since it is only for the purpose of exploring a thread common to both legal actions it is of value.

In this case a store security guard observed a woman with a large bag take several items off a rack and go into a fitting room. From the security guard's position in the aisle, she saw the woman in the fitting room place the bag on the floor and put the items from the rack into the bag. These observations were possible because of the relatively small size of the door to the fitting room. The woman was detained by the guard as she left the store. Subsequent litigation involved the legitimacy of the surveillance and the woman's expectancy of privacy.

The court commented that what constitutes a reasonable expectation of privacy depends on the circumstances and is measured by common habits in the use of domestic and business proprieties. The court went on to say that retailers face a shoplifting epidemic and fitting rooms are particularly suited to the concealment of stolen property. So much for the justification; now how about the manner in which the intrusion was carried out—did it go beyond the limits of decency?

In answering the question, the court stated that one way to fight the problem is to provide facilities that shield intimate body parts but do not hide the entire room area. To hide the entire area from view, in the court's view, would not comport with either general practice nor sound policy. The court then applied this standard to the facts and concluded that the occupant of the fitting room had no expectancy of privacy when she placed her purse or bag on the floor where it was in full view of any passing customer, salesclerk, or security guard. The owner had properly maintained the balance between its right to protect its property and the customer's right to privacy.

Investigations

This discussion will focus on unreasonably intrusive investigations. In the 1963 case *Pinkerton National Detective Agency, Inc. v. Stevens*,[40] a Georgia court considered a situation in which private detectives surveilled a person relative to an insurance claim. The court pointed out that a right of privacy may be waived by one who files a tort action to the extent that they must expect the other party to conduct its own investigation. But that right to investigate does not give the party the right to use unreasonably intrusive means. The case included pretense appearances at the door and, in the court's words, peeping, snooping, and eavesdropping. The detectives apparently ran a continuous and very close surveillance, to the point that one night the subject was so closely followed on the way home that she ran into the house in panic, hit a piece of furniture, and knocked herself unconscious.

The court noted that, "The conduct of the defendants in shadowing, snooping, spying, and eavesdropping upon plaintiff was done in a vicious and malicious manner not reasonably limited and designed to obtain information needed for the defense of plaintiff's lawsuit against Bell but deliberately in a way calculated to frighten and torment her."[41] Further, the investigation was conducted in such a conspicuous manner that it excited speculation among neighbors. This was enough to override the justification for the activity as the intrusion into privacy was more than needed to do the job.

For contrast, compare this case to *Saldana v. Kelsey-Hayes*, discussed in chapter 6.[42] The *Saldana* court first agreed that there was intrusion because the employer's agents entered the employee's home under false pretenses and observed the employee through the window of his home with a powerful camera lens. However, the court added that even if there had been intrusion it was not into areas in which he had a right to keep private. As far as the court was concerned, "Plaintiff's privacy was subject to the legitimate interest of his employer in investigating suspicions that plaintiff's work-related disability was a pretext."[43] Further, the employer had a right to investigate matters that possibly could create legal liability. The court saw no reason to go any further in the inquiry to test the reasonableness of the means used to gain the information.

The minority of the court had a problem. In dissent, it agreed that the employee's right of privacy was subject to limitations derived from the employer's legitimate interests in investigating the alleged work-related injury, but felt that this did not end the case. The minority pointed out that some means of investigation are so objectionable that they can violate the right of privacy even if there was a legitimate purpose for the investigation. It felt that the pervasive nature of the surveillance, particularly the use of the camera, warranted sending the case to the jury. Whether the majority would have reached the same decision if it had been a non-employee case and based solely on a waiver of rights following the filing of a legal action is hard to say. At least, though, as far as this one case is concerned, an employer has something more in the balance of rights than an ordinary business person defending a legal action.

Not all cases evidence an understandable business interest on the part of the company conducting an investigation. Even so, the plaintiff has to show that there first was a significant intrusion into privacy.

In *Nader v. General Motors Corporation*,[44] a New York court tried its hand at drawing parameters around this difficult right of privacy. Nader, a non-employee, had alleged that in retaliation for his criticism of General Motors, the company

1. questioned acquaintances about his political, social, racial, and religious views and his integrity, sexual proclivities, and personal habits;
2. kept him under surveillance;
3. caused him to be accosted by girls for the purpose of entrapping him into illicit relationships;
4. made threatening, harassing, and obnoxious telephone calls to him;
5. tapped his telephone and electronically eavesdropped on his private conversations; and
6. conducted a continuing harassing investigation of him.

The court first noted that it was going to interpret the law of the District of Columbia and that that jurisdiction defined privacy as the right to protect oneself from having one's private affairs known to others and to keep secret or intimate facts about oneself from the prying eyes or ears of others. In the court's judgment, privacy was invaded only if the information sought was of a confidential nature and the defendant's conduct was unreasonably intrusive. As far as this court was concerned, Nader had to show that General Motors' conduct was really intrusive and that it was intended to gather information that would not be available through the usual methods of conducting investigations.

In further setting the scene, the court noted that "some intrusions into one's private sphere are inevitable concomitants of life in an industrial and densely populated society, which the law does not seek to proscribe even if it were possible to do so."[45] The law does not provide a remedy for every annoyance that occurs in everyday life.

In discussing the interviewing allegations, the court said, "Although those inquiries may have uncovered information of a personal nature, it is difficult to see how they may be said to have invaded the plaintiff's privacy. Information about the plaintiff which was already known to others could hardly be regarded as private to the plaintiff."[46]

The court found that there was no invasion of privacy in the accosting by girls and telephone harassment allegations because neither of these activities involved intrusion for the purposes of gathering information of a private and confidential nature.

However, the court believed that the phone-tapping and mechanical eavesdropping allegations were in the invasion of privacy arena. As to the physical surveillance, the court stated that "it is manifest that the mere observation of the plaintiff in a public place does not amount to an invasion of his privacy. But, under certain circumstances, surveillance may be so 'overzealous' as to render it actionable." The court went on to say:

a person does not automatically make public everything he does merely by being in a public place, and the mere fact Nader was in a bank did not give anyone the right to try to discover the amount of money he was withdrawing. On the other hand, if the plaintiff acted in such a way as to reveal that fact to any casual observer, then, it may not be said that the appellant intruded into his private sphere.[47]

It has to be understood that this was not simply a privacy case and even though several elements did not measure up to the court's test for invasions of privacy, the same actions might support a case for intentional infliction of emotional distress. As pointed out several times, merely because a fact situation can make out a case under one area of the law, does not mean it will not run into problems in another.

Dissemination of Information

The privacy cases analyzed to this point have concerned the methods used in gathering information—searches, surveillance, and investigations. In some situations the methods were so obvious that they also constituted publication, in that customers or neighbors were attracted to the activity. But there are situations in which the information, even though legally gathered, may, if communicated, either violate common decency or put the person in a false light. These are two areas of invasion of privacy that can trigger liability.

While *Porten v. University of San Francisco*[48] is not a security case, it still helps make the publication or communication point. A student complained that the university tortiously disclosed grades he had earned at another university to the state scholarship and loan commission. According to the student, he had received assurances that these grades would only be used to evaluate his application for admission and they would not be used for other purposes without his authorization.

As the court saw it, the essence of the complaint was the unwarranted publication of intimate details of the plaintiff's private life. Public disclosure of private facts, however, requires disclosure to the public in general or to a large number of persons as distinguished from disclosure to one individual or a few people. In the court's judgment, disclosure to the commission did not meet that test. So much for the privacy tort theory. But, the case went on to consider a privacy provision of the California state constitution, which applied to private persons as well as to the government. The consideration now shifted from the factors that make up the privacy tort action, and the court agreed that the constitutional provision applied to the "improper use of information properly obtained for a specific purpose, for example, the use of it for another purpose or the disclosure of it to some third party." Under this state constitutional provision there was a color of legal right and the case could go to a jury to evaluate the facts relative to a violation of the state constitution.

The *La Fontaine v. Family Drug Stores, Inc.* case[49] stays with the communication or publication factor. A Connecticut pharmacist became suspicious that a prescription involving a controlled substance had been altered, and after checking with a doctor called the police. The customer was arrested by police leaving the store and after the charges were dismissed, the customer filed the suit.

The court stated that for the plaintiff to recover she had to establish that the pharmacist either publicly disclosed a private embarrassing fact about her or created publicity that placed her in a false light. The court then distinguished these facts from those in *Bennett v. Norban*, noting that the pharmacist's two calls were not made in a loud or public manner whereas the manager in the *Bennett* case had ostentatiously searched the customer in a public street outside the store in front of a group of passersby.

The telephone call remained private even though it did lead to the arrest. The court pointed out that it was the arrest that created the publicity and even though the pharmacist might have foreseen that the media would pick up the story, the court would not hold him responsible for it. The court added that once the arrest occurred, the facts related to it were no longer private and they became part of the public record. Once a person is charged with a violation of the law that person loses his or her right of privacy regarding the subject matter of the charge.

The pharmacist was off the hook for invasion of privacy, but what would have happened if this had been a defamation action? Remember, invasion of privacy can involve any one of four different wrongs but they are keyed to one's right to be left alone. Publication is a necessary part of several of these wrongs, but this kind of publication involves the public and not just a very few. The heart of a defamation action is the publication of false information and the size of the audience is not critical; the deciding factor in defamation is whether those receiving the communication had an interest.

In the *La Fontaine* case, the pharmacist and the police had an interest as it involved a possible criminal action. The communication was not absolutely protected but still it was qualifiedly privileged. The next question is whether the pharmacist lost the privilege through abuse. This involves looking at the facts to determine whether or not the call was made out of malice or in bad faith. Since that issue was not before the court, all the facts leading to such a judgment were not placed in evidence. But on the face of it, it looks like the call was made in good faith and, accordingly, there would be no defamation.

What would have happened in the *Bennett v. Norban* case if there had been no passersby, no audience. Since there would have been no publication there would have been no defamation. But remember, there still might have been an invasion of privacy based on intrusion into solitude or seclusion, because publication is not a necessary element. That aspect of the case was not explored, because the presence of the audience opened up the publication-oriented wrongs for discussion.

Intentional Infliction of Emotional Distress or Outrageous Conduct

As noted in the *Nader v. General Motors* case, although the facts might not support a finding of a privacy violation, they might amount to intentional infliction of emotional distress. However, this tort, by whatever name, is only found "where the conduct has been so outrageous in character, and so extreme in degree, as to go beyond all possible bounds of decency, and to be regarded as atrocious, and utterly intolerable in a civilized community."[50] Generally, to prevail in this type of action the case must be one in which the recitation of the facts to an average member of the community would arouse resentment against the actor, leading him to exclaim "outrageous." Insults, indignities, inconsiderations, or petty oppressions do not rise to the level of conduct needed to sustain a finding of violation.[51]

NON-WORK-RELATED DEMONSTRATIONS ON
PRIVATE PROPERTY

Much of what has been said relates to the interface between a business person and an individual. However, this is an era of mass activity including demonstrations on private property, and this phenomenon warrants some attention.

Considerable attention was given in chapter 4 to employee- and union-related activity on and around employer property. In *Jean Country* the NLRB balanced the rights of employers and the Section 7 rights of employees, and employees were allowed to make incursions onto their employer's property depending upon the use the employer made of the property, the manner in which the employees acted, and the potential for alternative means of carrying out employee activity. Much of the new case law focused on shopping centers and the quasi-public nature of those centers.[52]

The Supreme Court in *Sears Roebuck & Co. v. San Diego County District Council of Carpentry*[53] balanced the state's inherent interest in such issues as trespass and the NLRB's interest in protecting the rights of employees to engage in protected concerted activity. These and numerous other cases considered in chapter 4 dealt with employee-related issues. But what about situations in which a property owner is faced with a demonstration, handbilling, or soliciting on its property but employees or workplace issues are not involved? What rights are now in issue, how are they balanced, and what are the factors considered in balancing them?

A good case to start off answering these questions is *Lloyd Corporation, Ltd. v. Tanner*.[54] This 1972 Supreme Court case concerned the right of a privately owned shopping center to prohibit the distribution of handbills on its property. Anti–Vietnam War protestors were passing out handbills on the mall until they were told by security guards that they were trespassing and would be arrested unless they stopped the distribution. The protestors continued the distribution outside the mall on public property.

Subsequent litigation centered on whether the mall violated the distributors' first amendment rights. As the Supreme Court framed it,

The basic issue in this case is whether respondents, in the exercise of asserted First Amendment rights, may distribute handbills on Lloyd's private property contrary to its wishes and contrary to a policy enforced against all handbilling. In addressing this issue, it must be remembered that the First and Fourteenth Amendments safeguard the rights of free speech and assembly by limitations on *state* actions, not on action by the owner of private property used nondiscriminatorily for private purposes only.[55]

This is nothing new or startling, as a number of cases covered in chapter 1 drew the same conclusion. If the law is that clear, why focus on this case? Because in an earlier case, *Marsh v. Alabama*,[56] the Supreme Court had extended first amendment rights to a company-owned town. The court now distinguished *Marsh* by noting that that case

involved the assumption by a private enterprise of all the attributes of a state-created municipality and the exercise by that enterprise of semi-official municipal functions as a delegate of the state. In effect, the owner of the company town was performing the full spectrum of municipal powers and stood in the shoes of the state.[57]

In the *Lloyd* case it was determined that the shopping mall, while open to the public, did not step into the shoes of the state. The court noted that the essentially private character of a store does not change by virtue of being large or clustered with other stores in a modern shopping center. In the court's judgment there had been no dedication of Lloyd's privately owned and operated shopping center to public use so as to entitle the protestors the protection of the first amendment. This point was further explained by the court in *Hudgens v. NLRB*[58] and the point is the same— the first amendment is not applicable.

But as noted in chapters 1 and 6, some states have constitutional provisions that extend individual rights beyond those of the federal constitution. In 1980 the Supreme Court considered another shopping mall case, *Prune Yard Shopping Center v. Robbins*,[59] in which a California constitutional provision was at issue. A group of high school students were soliciting signatures to a petition opposing a United Nations resolution against Zionism. The soliciting took place on mall property and they were told to leave because they were violating the shopping center's regulation prohibiting visitors or tenants from any publicly expressive activity not directly related to the center's commercial purpose. This phraseology is similar to that used by the Supreme Court in its *Lloyd* case. However, this time the federal first amendment was not at issue, it was the California constitutional provision that extended free speech rights into the private sector.

The Supreme Court, when presented with the case, acknowledged its position in *Lloyd* but stated that this does not limit a state's authority to exercise its police power or its sovereign right to adopt in its own constitution individual liberties more expansive than those conferred by the federal constitution. According to the Supreme Court, a state may adopt reasonable restrictions on private property so long as the restrictions do not amount to a taking without just compensation or contravene any other federal constitutional provision.

So the question was whether the California constitution conflicted with the federal. The owner contended that a right to exclude others underlies both the fifth amendment guarantee against the taking of property without just compensation and the fourteenth amendment guarantee against the deprivation of property without due process of law. The court's response was that while the right to exclude others was part of the bundle of property rights that required protection, not every destruction or injury constituted a taking of property. Property rights are not absolute.

In analyzing the factors in the balance, the court considered the character of the government's action, its economic impact, and its interference with reasonable investment-backed expectations. As far as the court was concerned, there was no evidence that California's limitation of Prune Yard's property right unreasonably impaired the value of their use of the property. In this conflict of rights the protestors soliciting signatures prevailed.

Predictably, after *Lloyd* and *Prune Yard* the battles over incursions onto private property were fought primarily in state courts. Shopping malls and private college campuses are often scenes for this activity. A Pennsylvania court in *Western Pa. Socialist Workers v. Conn. Gen.*[60] gives a good outline of the development of the law in this area. The court first noted that the results have not been uniform in sister states in the application of state constitutions in cases like *Prune Yard*. The Pennsylvania court, like the federal court, searched for some kind of equivalent to state action and did not find it. It commented that, "We cannot in common sense and good reason extend constitutionally protected free speech to privately owned stores and shopping centers merely because the public is invited to enter for purposes of doing business."[61]

The court went on to note that it had no problem with an earlier Pennsylvania case, *Commonwealth v. Tate*,[62] in which protestors who had entered a private college campus were found not to be criminal trespassers. In the *Tate* case, an educational institution, Muhlenberg College, had held itself out to the public as a community resource and cultural center, had allowed members of the public to enter its campus, and had permitted community use of its facilities as a public forum for public officials of national prominence, including the Director of the FBI. As far as the court was concerned, these were sufficient trappings of public function to make the necessary nexus to state action.

In a 1989 article in the *Industrial Relations Law Journal*, the author noted that outside of California, the highest courts of only a few states have created limited state constitutional rights of access to shopping malls or university campuses or other quasi-public locations for purposes of speech or petitioning.[63] The *Tate* case is one of these. The author went on to say that such rights of access have been denied by the highest courts of five states—Connecticut, Michigan, New York, North Carolina, and Wisconsin. In the author's judgment most courts have given a high priority to owners' property rights in these kinds of cases.

In resolving cases involving access to property, it is of critical importance to determine who is involved, what rights are being balanced, and in what forum they will be considered. Employees engaging in protected concerted activity on their employer's property are going to have more rights than non-employee activist groups.

REMOVING DEMONSTRATORS FROM PRIVATE PROPERTY AND CONTROLLING ACTIVITY AT ENTRANCES

Traditional Methods

If demonstrators are on private property and they have no right to be there, how are they to be removed? The traditional legal methods are arrest for criminal trespass and injunctive relief for civil trespass. In the *Commonwealth v. Hood* case, a Massachusetts court in 1983 considered a situation in which nuclear arms protestors were arrested for refusing to leave a private technological laboratory.[64] The court first cited *Lloyd Corp. v. Tanner* and *Hudgens v. NLRB* and noted that a business does not have to wall itself in in order to maintain non-public status. The fact that the business allowed pedestrians and cars to pass through its property did not alter its private status. Neither did the fact that it was working on a government contract. Thus, neither federal nor state constitutional protections were appropriate and the issue was reduced to whether or not they were trespassers.

The demonstrators contended that they were not trespassers but had an implied right to enter the premises. The court questioned this position but added that at best it only protected them until a security officer asked them to leave. Even if they had an implied right to enter, they had no right to remain after they were asked to leave. In this case the security officer had followed up his statement requesting the demonstrators to leave with a call to the local police who made the subsequent arrest after the demonstrators refused to comply with a similar request.

Courts will follow the appropriate state criminal statutes and make decisions accordingly. For example, in Minnesota it is necessary for the state to prove that the alleged criminal trespasser had no claim of right to be on the property. This element is not looked upon as a defense but a basic element in the state's case that the state needs to prove.[65] Some jurisdictions will consider defenses related to necessity or justification for being on private property but nearly all courts have found them to fail.[66]

Courts will invariably look for no trespassing signs, warnings, and requests to leave in these kinds of cases.

Civil actions relative to trespassing, including requests for injunctions,
are premised on the owner's right to be protected in its business and
property from tortious activity. Even in jurisdictions accommodating the
need to extend statutory or constitutional protections into the quasi-public
area, the right to property protection is still recognized and injunctive
relief is granted accordingly.[67] These injunctions normally cover not only
the actual trespassing but also interference with ingress and egress. They
are based on a showing of irreparable harm, which includes such things
as spoilage of product, freezing up of the production process, loss of
business contracts, and pollution problems if waste is not removed. Injunctions are an interim measure and the restraints are finalized following
a hearing on the facts or an agreement of the parties.

Once the demonstrators are back on public property, constitutional
protections reenter the balance of rights; it becomes the government versus individuals. In *Davis v. Francois*[68] a federal circuit court in 1968
addressed the legitimacy of a local ordinance that provided for public
sector picketing under limited circumstances. Peaceful civil rights pickets
were arrested for violating the ordinance and they, in turn, contended
that the ordinance violated the first and fourteenth amendments and that,
accordingly, the arrests were illegal.

The court reflected on the pervasiveness of demonstrations and protests
in society at that time, 1968, and noted, "The issues posed by these
movements are controversial and demand that courts strike an accommodation between liberty and order by reconciling the interest of allowing
free expression of ideas in public places with the protection of the public
peace and use of public facilities by others."[69] The court went on to point
out the importance for affording a public forum for peaceful protests but
added that no matter now laudatory, protests have often created problems
such as riots, disorder, interference with traffic, blockage of sidewalks or
entrances to buildings, and disruption of the normal functions of public
facilities.

The court stated that

these rights to picket and to march and to assemble are not to be abridged by
arrest or other interferences so long as asserted with the limits of not unreasonably
interfering with the rights of others to use the sidewalks and streets, to have
access to store entrances and where conducted in such a manner as not to deprive
the public of police and fire protection.[70]

It is in this area that government entities in passing ordinances have the
difficult job of maintaining the balance between the two conflicting interests.

In this *Davis* case, the court found that the ordinance that was being enforced was too restrictive in that it limited demonstrating activity to two people regardless of time, place, and other circumstances. It unjustly infringed on protected freedoms and accordingly was found unconstitutional. The message, though, is still clear: The courts, while protective of first amendment rights, still will not tolerate violence or disruption of public roads and right of ways.[71]

Property owners can also seek injunctive relief and file for damages in civil actions in situations where entrances and exits are blocked. Again, as in the arrest cases, the courts will be concerned about balancing rights. While demonstrators standing on public property and interfering with ingress and egress might not literally be trespassing on private property, their activity can be enjoined on the premise that they are tortiously interfering with the use of private property. Such civil challenges normally incorporate counts for trespass, interference with contractual relationships, and such torts.

Demonstrations—Use of the Civil Rights Statutes

In chapter 2 there was some discussion on the Civil Rights Act of 1871 and more particularly Section 1985(C) of that act. It was mentioned that this federal statute focuses on conspiracies intended to deny certain classes of people equal protection or equal privileges or immunities. In many Section 1985 situations there is a need for state action before the federal government will intervene, but in some limited cases state action is not needed. The general right to travel falls into this latter category. So how does this fit into managing a demonstration?

Clinics in the Northern Virginia areas that provided abortion-related services had their entrances and exits blocked by an anti-abortion group, Operation Rescue, and sought relief under Section 1985 in federal court.[72] In 1990, the Fourth Circuit decided that women, the users of the service, were qualified as a protected class under Section 1985. Further, many of these women were traveling interstate in search of these services and Operation Rescue was interfering with this right to travel.

The only question left was the scope of the relief and the court then weighed the women's travel rights against the anti-abortion group's free speech rights. The court limited the injunction to blocking of ingress and egress to facilities in Northern Virginia and did not include activities that tend to "intimidate, harass, or disturb patients or potential patients because to do so would risk enjoining activities clearly protected by the First Amendment."[73]

Thus, while Section 1985 has some use in managing demonstrators, its use is presently limited to situations in which there is both a need to protect a class of people probably based on race, sex, or national origin and a recognized interference with interstate travel. The scope of this section has not yet been fully explored by the Supreme Court.

Use of RICO in Controlling Demonstrations

One of the most recent developments in controlling demonstrations is the use of the Racketeer Influenced and Corrupt Organization Act (RICO).[74] RICO is discussed in considerable detail in chapter 9 and it will receive only enough coverage here to explain its use in dealing with demonstrations.

RICO has application on both the criminal and civil sides of the law. On the civil side it has the potential, as a federal statute, of reaching multi-state activity and it has the added punch of treble damages. RICO is geared to impeding certain repetitive criminal activity, but it does not create any new substantive criminal law. To make use of RICO it is necessary to have what are generally referred to as predicate acts. That is, there must be violations of certain state or federal criminal laws. For purposes of controlling demonstrations, the predicate acts of interest are violations of the Hobbs Act, 18 U.S.C. Sec. 1951.

As is the case with RICO, the Hobbs Act is discussed in some detail in chapter 9. In a nutshell, Hobbs covers situations in which property is extorted through force, violence, or fear. But what does this have to do with demonstrations? A review of *Northeast Women's Center, Inc. v. McGonagle*[75] supplies the answer.

On several different occasions in 1985 and 1986 anti-abortion demonstrators entered the Northeast Women's Center's Pennsylvania facilities, blocked access to rooms, threw medical supplies on the floor, knocked down employees blocking their way, and interfered with ingress and egress to the center and its parking lot. Arrests were made, and in addition, the center sought civil RICO relief in federal district court. The RICO action was coupled with a request for relief under state tort charges of trespass and intentional interference with contractual relationships.

There could not be a RICO case unless there were predicate acts; in this case the predicate acts were alleged violations of the Hobbs Act by the use of force and violence to extort property. How did the demonstration activity translate into extortion? The court looked at it this way. The center had a property right in its business of performing abortions and the demonstrators were trying to make the center give up that business through force and violence. This constituted extortion. In the court's judgment, the demonstrators did not have to succeed in their attempt, the attempt itself was sufficient. Further, the court was not interested in a justification defense. As far as the court was concerned, the demonstrators could not decide to violate the law and expect to be absolved of punishment for disobedience. Since there were multiple violations of the Hobbs

Act and since the center had been injured in its business, the court found a violation of RICO.

Interference with Railroads

Since some demonstrator activity has involved disrupting train transportation, some thought has been given to a federal train-wrecking statute.[76] This statute provides that anyone willfully derailing, disabling, or wrecking a train or making tracks, signals, and such unusable "shall be fined not more than $10,000 or imprisoned not more than twenty years, or both." Despite the common use of the term "train-wrecking statute," it also covers any conduct which could substantially interfere with an interstate rail system.[77]

OBSERVATIONS

An owner's right to protect his or her property has to be balanced against an individual's freedom of movement, preservation of a good reputation, protection of the private aspects of his or her life and, on public property, the right to engage in free speech. In some areas of change, such as the growth of the self-service retail business and more aggressive activity by demonstrators, the law has adjusted by giving merchants more legal latitude in detaining customers and giving owners access to relief via such statutes as RICO.

While the courts recognize many owner needs, they normally give only qualified rights in order to maintain a balance. The question asked in most cases relative to owner activity is, "Was the conduct reasonable in light of all the circumstances?" Business invitees and certainly trespassers do not have all the rights of an employee, or the responsibilities either, and this is reflected in the balances that the courts try to maintain. In order to understand legal developments it is critical to understand the rights of the parties involved. What was good law ten years ago won't necessarily be good law today.

NOTES

1. *Raefeldt v. Koenig*, 152 Wis. 459, 140 N.W. 56 (1913).

2. *Restatement (Second) of Torts* Sec. 112 (1965).

3. Del. Code Ann. tit.11, Sec. 1902 (1935).

4. 5 Am. Jur. 2d *Arrest* Sec. 36 (1962).

5. 5 Am. Jur. 2d *Arrest* Sec. 35.

6. *Tumbarella v. Kroger Co.*, 85 Mich. App. 482, 271 N.W.2d 284 (Mich. 1978); *Hill v. Taylor*, 50 Mich. 549, 15 N.W. 899 (Mich. 1883).

7. Comment, *Shoplifters Beware?*, 11 Drake L. Rev. 31, 33–34 (1961); Comment,

The Protection and Recapture of Merchandise from Shoplifters, 47 Nw. U.L. Rev. 82 (1952); 32 Am. Jur. 2d *False Imprisonment* Sec. 91 (1982).

8. Comment, *Detaining Shoplifters*, 50 N.C.L. Rev. 188 (1971); *Collyer v. S.H. Kress & Co.*, 5 Cal. 2d 175, 54 P.2d 20 (Calif. 1936).

9. Sec. 120A.

10. Comment, *Detaining Shoplifters* 194.

11. Annot., 47 A.L.R. 3d 998, *False Imprisonment—Shoplifters*; 32 Am. Jur. 2d *False Imprisonment* Sec. 92–94 (1982).

12. 359 Mass. 319, 268 N.E.2d 860 (1971).

13. 268 N.E.2d 860 at 861.

14. See also *Malanga v. Sears Roebuck & Co.*, 487 N.Y.S.2d 194 (1985) *aff'd*, 494 N.Y.2d 302 484 N.E.2d 665 (1985).

15. *J. S. Dillon & Sons Stores Co. v. Carrington*, 169 Colo.242, 455 P.2d 201 (1969).

16. *Johnson v. Bloomingdales*, 94 misc.2d 208, 404 N.Y.S.2d 267 (1978), *aff'd*, 101 misc. 2d 49, 420 N.Y.S.2d 840 (1979), 79 A.D.2d 850, *rev'd* 434 N.Y.S.2d 351 (1980).

17. *Adams v. Zayre Corp.*, 499 N.E.2d 678 (Ill. 1986).

18. *Tota v. Alexanders*, 314 N.Y.S.2d 93 (1968).

19. *General Motors Corp. v. Piskor*, 27 Md. App. 95, 340 A.2d 767, 791–793 (1975); *Washington County Kennel Club v. Edge*, 216 So. 2d 512 Fla. App. (1968).

20. Iowa Code Ann. Sec. 808.12 (West 1980); Wisconsin Criminal Code, Sec. 943.50.

21. Okla. Stat. Ann. tit. 22, Sec. 1343 (West 1967).

22. Wisconsin Criminal Code Sec. 943.50(3) (1988).

23. W. Va. Code Sec. 61-3A-4 (1981), La. Code Crim. Proc. Ann. art. 215 (West 1987).

24. Wisconsin Criminal Code, Sec. 943.50(3)

25. La. Code Crim. Proc. Ann. art. 215.B (West 1987).

26. W. Va. Code Sec. 61-3A-4 (1981).

27. Iowa Code Ann. Sec. 808.12, 2 (West 1980).

28. Okla. Stat. Ann. tit. 22, Sec. 1343 (West 1967).

29. *Ling v. Whittemore*, 140 Colo. 247, 343 P.2d 1048 (1959).

30. 369 Pa. 94, 151 A.2d 476 (1959).

31. 151 A.2d 476 at 478.

32. 166 Ga. App. 284, 304 S.E.2d 460 (1983).

33. *Phillips v. Smalley Maintenance Services Inc.*, 711 F.2d 1524 (11th Cir. 1983).

34. *Texas Dept. of Mental Health & Mental Retardation v. Texas State Employees Union*, 708 S.W.2d 498 (1986).

35. 57 N.C. 13, 290 S.E.2d 732 (1982).

36. 290 S.E.2d 732 at 738.

37. The court cited *Sutherland v. Kroger Co.*, 144 W. Va. 673, 110 S.E.2d 716, 723–24 (West Va. 1959) and *Bennett v. Norban*, 369 Pa. 94, 151 A.2d 476 (Pa. 1959) as examples of states applying the tort to illegal searches.

38. 151 A.2d 476 at 479.

39. *In re Deborah*, 177 Cal. Rptr. 852, 635 P.2d 446 (1981).

40. 108 Ga. App. 159, 132 S.E.2d 119 (1963).

41. 132 S.E.2d 119 at 123.

42. 178 Mich. App. 230, 443 N.W.2d 382 (1989).

43. 443 N.W.2d 382 at 384.

44. 25 N.Y.2d 560, 255 N.E.2d 765 (1970).

45. 255 N.E. 2d 765 at 768.

46. 255 N.E. 2d 765 at 770.

47. 255 N.E. 2d 765 at 771.

48. 64 Cal. App. 3d 825, 134 Cal. Rptr. 839 (1976).

49. 33 Conn. Supp. 66, 360 A.2d 899 (Conn. 1976).

50. *Restatement (Second) of Torts* Sec. 46 Comment d (1965).

51. *Pretsky v. Southwestern Bell Telephone Co.*, 396 S.W.2d 566 (Mo. 1965); *Smith v. Standard Oil, Div. of Amoco Oil Co.*, 567 S.W.2d 412 (Mo. 1978).

52. 291 NLRB 11 (1988).

53. 436 U.S. 180 (1978).

54. 407 U.S. 551 (1972).

55. 407 U.S. 551 at 567.

56. 326 U.S. 501 (1946).

57. 407 U.S. 551 at 569.

58. *Hudgens v. NLRB*, 424 U.S. 507 (1976).

59. 447 U.S. 74 (1980).

60. 335 Pa. S.493, 485 A.2d 1 (Pa. Super. 1984).

61. 485 A.2d 1 at 8.

62. 495 Pa. 158, 432 A.2d 1382 (1981).

63. Avery, *Federal Labor Rights and Access to Private Property*, 11 Indus. Rel. L. J. No.2, 145, 222 (1989).

64. 389 Mass. 581, 452 N.E.2d 188 (Mass. 1983).

65. *State v. Brechon*, 352 N.W.2d 745 (Minn. 1984).

66. Annot., 41 A.L.R. 4th 773, *Trespass: Demonstrations, Business Lands* (1985).

67. *Planned Parenthood of Monmouth v. Cannigaw*, 204 N.J. Super. 531, 499 A.2d 530 (1985).

68. 395 F.2d 730 (5th Cir. 1968).

69. 395 F.2d 730 at 732.

70. 395 F.2d 730 at 734, 735.

71. Note, *Regulation of Demonstrations*, 80 Harv. L. Rev. 1773 (1967).

72. *NOW v. Operation Rescue,* 914 F.2d 582.

73. 914 F.2d 582 at 586.

74. 18 U.S.C. Sec. 1961 *et. seq.*

75. 868 F.2d 1342 (3rd Cir. 1989), *cert. denied*, 493 U.S. 901 (1989).

76. 18 U.S.C. Sec. 1992.

77. *United States v. Dreding*, 547 F.2d 471 (9th Cir. 1976), *cert. denied*, 429 U.S. 1108 (1976).

9

Protecting Intangible Property

While it is difficult enough to establish reasonable means for protecting store merchandise, workplace tools, and other tangible property from theft, at least the legal rationale for protecting them is fairly simple—people stealing these things are thieves and can be prosecuted accordingly. These are things one can put one's hands on, and values can be readily established. But what if the property is a formula, customer information, engineering information, operating and pricing policies, designs, drawings, or blueprints? Are they still considered property by the law and can their theft or compromise be pursued successfully under civil and criminal laws? When is a piece of paper just a piece of paper and when will the law recognize that the paper really constitutes something of considerable value?

PATENT AND COPYRIGHT PROTECTION

Maybe the first thought is that most of these things are covered by patents or copyrights and that is the protection they need. To some extent, the thought is a correct one but the coverage provided by patents and copyrights does not do the entire job. For example, patent protection only includes processes, machines, articles of manufacture, and compositions of matter.[1] The United States Copyright Act, 17 U.S.C. Sec. 101–914 (1988), protects such things as literary, musical, and dramatic works, motion pictures, sound recordings, and computer programs, but it does not extend to ideas, procedures, processes, systems, methods of operation, concepts, principles, or discoveries. Separate and apart from the limited scope of patents and copyright coverage are problems with staying abreast of rapid developments in technology and the relatively brief life expectancy of some covered items such as computer software.[2] It is expected that case law driven by present legal uncertainties will help shape the scope of copyright protection.

TRADE SECRETS

That a lot of things in the intellectual property arena were not covered by federal statute was not a significant problem for a long time. But as rapid developments took place in technology, some of the technological "have nots" decided that the easiest way to do research and development was to take trade secrets from those that had them.[3] In the early twentieth century, there was limited recourse to the criminal law for such thefts; the only routes to be pursued were such theories as robbery or specific state criminal statutes.[4] Early civil trade secret cases go back to 1868, but generally speaking, the courts had a problem considering such subjects as property worthy of protection by the law.[5]

Criminal Law

Interest in reforming the criminal laws peaked in the 1960s as companies found that trade secret thieves were circumventing civil actions by leaving the country or were judgment proof. For example, thieves stole drug secrets from U.S. drug manufacturers and sold them to Italian drug firms or used them in Italian companies that the thieves already owned. They then sold the products around the world including in the United States. The thieves were operating on the knowledge that Italy did not grant patent protection on pharmaceuticals.[6]

Different states reacted to the problem in different ways. Some incorporated trade secrets into existing statutes on larceny or theft and others set up separate sections for the subject in their criminal codes. By 1970, twenty states had passed some kind of criminal law relating to trade secrets.[7]

Before analyzing a state criminal law case, it will be of value to get some understanding of just what "trade secret" means. There continue to be some variations among the states both on the criminal and civil sides, but it is safe to say that the best definition is still set out in the *Restatement (First) of Torts* Sec. 757 comment b (1939):

A trade secret may consist of any formula, pattern, device or compilation of information which is used in one's business, and which gives him an opportunity to obtain an advantage over competitors who do not know or use it. It may be a formula for a chemical compound, a process of manufacturing, treating or preserving materials, a pattern for a machine or other device or a list of customers.

What exactly falls under this definition varies slightly according to the jurisdiction, but generally it includes such things as engineering information, sources for raw materials, design manuals, operating and pricing policies, market research studies, computer software, drawings, and blueprints.[8] The Restatement goes on in Sec. 757 to list six elements to use in deciding whether or not the information in question meets the definition. These are:

- the extent of knowledge about the information outside the business;
- the extent of knowledge about the information among employees;
- the extent of employer measures to protect the secrecy of the information;
- the value of the information to the business and its competitors;
- the effort and money expended by the employer in developing the information; and
- the difficulty for others to acquire or duplicate the information.

In reviewing numerous cases, it becomes evident that the most critical area of court inquiry is into the extent of protection rendered by the business. This is true both in civil and criminal cases. For example, New Jersey covers the subject under theft and related offenses.[9] It first incorporates trade secrets into its definition of property and then defines trade secrets as:

the whole or any portion or phase of any scientific or technical information, design, process, procedure, formula or improvement which is secret and of value. A trade secret will be presumed to be secret when the owner thereof takes measures to prevent it from becoming available to persons other than those selected by the owner to have access thereto for limited purposes.

It should be noted that the New Jersey definition of property also includes "financial instruments, information, data and computer software, in either human readable or computer readable form, copies or originals." Other states also have directly addressed the computer technology theft problem and have modified their statutes accordingly, but the changes generally have been uneven.[10]

A review of a 1988 Texas trade secret criminal case will be helpful in understanding the law on the subject.[11] Texas has a separate theft of trade secret provision that reasonably tracks the Restatement and New Jersey statute language and states that it is a violation for anyone to knowingly make a copy of an article representing a trade secret without the owner's consent.

This case incorporates computer technology into the trade secret definition. The employer was engaged in the electronics business and was developing a computer software program that causes a device to respond in a specified manner to commands issued by voice. Work was being carried out in a Dallas speech research laboratory.

The laboratory was separated from other facilities and access was limited to only certain authorized personnel. Exterior gates were monitored by security guards around the clock and laboratory employees were required to wear a certain type of identity badge to gain access. Programs were stored in memory banks and access could be gained only through specifically assigned codes or passwords. Access was permitted only on a need-to-know basis.

An engineer with the company, Leonard, resigned and took a job as a vice-president with a smaller company that was also engaged in voice recognition and speech synthesis research and development. Over a period of time, several other employees followed Leonard to the new company. One of these employees believed he recognized information at the new employer's that belonged to the old employer. He informed his old employer's security people of this belief in the hope that it would help him get his old job back.

Security recruited this person as a "mole" and he was sent back to search his new employer's premises and equipment for further information. Among other things he took photos of tapes containing labels of certain programs he recognized from his former employment. Meanwhile, an internal investigation at the old employer indicated that only a few hours before Leonard left, someone made a copy of the entire directory assigned to Leonard. Within that directory were five programs identified as trade secrets.

To this point, security had been running its own operation but now it went to the district attorney and the case became a law enforcement matter. A search warrant was obtained based on the information made available by the company and a search at the new employer located the five programs. Leonard was arrested and admitted that he had copied the five programs and taken them with him but contended, among other things, that the five programs were not trade secrets and that there was no probable cause for the issuance of the search warrant.

In responding to Leonard's contention that the owner had not taken sufficient measures to protect its property and, accordingly, it did not have trade secret status, the court stated, "This voluminous record is replete with evidence detailing the strict security measures taken by the complainant to prevent any and all information emanating from the speech laboratory from falling into the hands of unauthorized persons."[12] Included among these many measures was a requirement that all employees sign non-disclosure agreements when hired. The court had no problem in finding that the evidence showed that the requirement that the owner must take measures to protect its secrets had been met by the first employer.

As to the search warrant, it must be remembered that law enforcement did not place or control the mole or direct private security in its operation. The government only became involved when the employer came to it with evidence already collected. As far as the court was concerned, there was probable cause for the issuance of the search warrant because the government acted on detailed information supplied by security people, managers, and the mole in the form of an affidavit.

A California criminal trade secret case, *People v. Serrata*,[13] is of interest because it covers the "measures taken" issue as well as an entrapment and preemption question. In this case, IBM had taken numerous steps to protect its trade secrets, including stamping all secret drawings "IBM Confidential," continually spot-auditing the files of randomly selected employees for the unauthorized possession of documents, requiring countersignatures when documents were checked out, and installing special magnetic locks on high security buildings. The court pointed out that it is clear that when an owner takes security measures to protect information from becoming available to unauthorized persons, it is reasonable to believe that such information is secret and the owner intended that it stay that way.

The defendant asked for a jury instruction on entrapment based on evidence that an IBM employee had induced the defendant to commit thefts. The court commented that since the IBM employee was not a law enforcement officer but only a private citizen in the employ of IBM, the entrapment defense was inapplicable. The thefts were well underway before the public authorities were called in by IBM to apprehend the thieves, and accordingly, law enforcement officers could not have been involved in inducing Serrata to engage in criminal activity.

Preemption has been covered earlier in discussions about the National Labor Relations Act and arbitration in their relationship to state tort actions. This does not end the subject, though, because the relationships between federal and state actions permeate many areas of the law. In this case, the defendant contended that the state trade secrets statute was preempted by federal patent law. The court pointed out that the trade secret laws were designed to accomplish an entirely different purpose than federal patent laws and that trade secret laws afforded protection only against disclosure or use by some improper means. Patents are disclosed and are available for the whole world to look at; trade secrets aren't. It is the dishonest disclosure of trade secrets that constitutes an offense.

Civil Actions

The civil side of the trade secret picture has had a somewhat similar uneven development. Probably the first cases involving the protection of trade secrets took place over one hundred years ago. The legal theme seemed to involve an attempt to enforce a degree of business morality and to protect information as a form of property.[14]

States struggled with such questions as whether information constituted property and whether it was necessary that the owner be deprived of the use of the property. Of course in many of these situations the owner went on using its erstwhile secrets, only they were not secrets anymore, and that caused the harm.

Some states adopted the Restatement of Torts protection for trade secrets and others adopted the provisions of the Uniform Trade Secrets Act, which was approved by the American Bar Association in 1980. Since 1980, nineteen or more states have adopted some form of the Uniform Trade Secrets Act.[15] While there might be a question as to whether customer information gets protection under the Uniform Trade Secret Act, there are no other significant differences between the Restatement and the Trade Secret Act. For example, the act provides that a trade secret is "the subject of efforts that are reasonable under the circumstances to maintain its secrecy."[16]

State civil court actions normally include requests for injunctive relief and, if filed in federal court, sometimes include patent or copyright infringement contentions. As to the injunctive relief, most practitioners believe that if the problem is not nipped in the bud the secret will be completely compromised by the end of normal litigation. The idea of the infringement allegation is that those elements not covered under one violation can be covered under the other.[17]

In a 1970 Massachusetts case, *J.T. Healy & Son, Inc. v. Murphy & Son, Inc.*,[18] the plaintiff sought an injunction against the defendants disclosing or utilizing trade secrets. The court stated:

The essential characteristic of a trade secret being secrecy, we cannot reconcile the findings that certain processes were trade secrets with some of the other findings which prove that they were not guarded at all. The purported conclusion that the two processes "were sufficiently guarded by means that were reasonable in all the circumstances" is unacceptable when it has to be considered along with the testimony and the findings that there was a company policy that the best way to guard a secret was not to excite undue interest.[19]

The court went on to say:

He cannot lie back and do nothing to preserve its essential secret quality, particularly when the subject matter of the process becomes known to a number of individuals involved in its use or is observed in the course of manufacture within plain view of others.[20]

The court further commented that eternal vigilance is necessary and calls for "constant warnings to all persons to whom the trade secret has become known and obtaining from each an agreement, preferably in writing, acknowledging its secrecy and promising to respect it."[21] Merely excluding the general public from observing the manufacturing process was not sufficient to meet the protection standard.

Arco Industries Corp. v. Chemcost[22] involved injunction requests on a patent infringement as well as on a trade secret violation. The subject of the litigation was grommets. As to the trade secret contention, the federal court observed that even if Arco had shown sufficient novelty of its grommet to justify a finding that it would have come under the Michigan definition of trade secrets, it would have lost because it had not been treated as a secret. In the court's judgment, the secrecy standard was over and above the usual privacy with which an ordinary business is conducted.

Arco had not screened off or restricted any areas in its plant and did not systematically screen visitors. Suppliers and customers were routinely shown through the plant. Management did not inform plant workers or visitors that anything in the plant was confidential. The court commented that a subjective intent to treat something as secret is insufficient as a matter of law to warrant trade secret protection.

In their article entitled "Protecting Trade Secret Information: A Plan for Proactive Strategy," the authors comment that while the courts will closely scrutinize security measures they will not normally require small businesses to meet the same standards as larger ones.[23] Again, as in most other areas of the law, the emphasis has to be on reasonableness. But generally, the courts will not give large businesses any sympathy if they fail to provide needed protection for what they contend are trade secrets. The theory seems to be that if one contends that something is a protectable secret one ought to be able to prove that he treated it that way.

FEDERAL LAWS DEALING WITH INTANGIBLE PROPERTY

Federal Common Law

With some special exceptions there is no separate federal common law and no tort law.[24] These trade secret cases are all state actions. But what happens in situations where there has been the theft of a formula and a state civil or criminal action will not solve the problem? Will it fall through the cracks? The next step is to explore the potential for relief under several federal statutes.

National Stolen Property Act[25]

In the early 1960s in New Jersey, prior to the passage of a state criminal statute relating to trade secrets, several employees at a laboratory removed and copied documents outlining manufacturing procedures. They sold these copied documents along with certain stolen cultures to individuals who were going to resell or use them for their own purposes in Italy.

While separate infringement actions were pursued, the business sought relief through the federal government under the National Stolen Properties Act.[26] The primary legal issue in the case was whether the transportation of papers describing the manufacturing process constituted the transportation in interstate or foreign commerce of "any goods, wares or merchandise, securities or money of the value of $5,000 or more, knowing the same to have been stolen, converted, or taken by fraud."

Keep in mind that the documents that were transported were copies of the originals and these copies were made by the employees off the work site. The court said it was not pursuaded that just because the intangible information was copied onto another paper didn't cause it to lose its status as "goods" for the purposes of the Act. However, the court went on to say that "the statute would presumably not extend to the case where a carefully guarded secret formula was memorized, carried away in the recesses of a thievish mind and placed in writing only after a boundary had been crossed."[27] In discussing the use of copies and the question of whether they constituted goods the court said, "It would offend common sense to hold that these defendants fall outside the statute simply because, in efforts to avoid detection, their confederates were at pains to restore the original papers to Lederle's files and transport only copies or notes."[28]

The court buttressed its holding by noting that the documents were transported with the cultures, which were tangible items, and that the documents helped explain the value of the cultures. The papers could have been relied upon simply as demonstrating the scope of the criminal enterprise and as enhancing the value of the microorganisms.

The key to this statute is proving interstate or foreign transportation of goods, and many of the things previously described as trade secrets meet the definition of goods.

Mail and Wire Fraud

But what protection is available in a situation in which the subject matter either does not involve goods or the materials are not transported in interstate commerce? Will any federal statute reach the situation described above if an employee memorizes a formula, leaves the workplace, and does not cross a state boundary or only reduces it to writing after he crosses a boundary? In exploring possibilities for gaining federal relief, some use has been made of the Fraud by Mail[29] and Fraud by Wire statutes.[30] For all intents and purposes, these are identical statutes except that one involves use of the mail and the other use of a wire.[31] Primary attention will be given to the mail fraud statute.

The mail fraud statute provides in pertinent part:

Whoever, having devised or intending to devise any scheme or artifice to defraud, or for obtaining money or property by means of false or fraudulent pretenses, representations, or promises . . . for the purpose of executing such scheme or artifice or attempting to do so [uses the mails or causes them to be used] shall be fined not more than $1,000 or imprisoned not more than five years or both.[32]

The wire fraud statute uses the same language, except that instead of "mail" it uses the phrase "transmits or causes to be transmitted by means of wire."[33]

In November 1988, Section 1346 was added to the law and it notes the term "scheme or artifice to defraud" includes a scheme or artifice to deprive another of the intangible right of honest services. This explains critical language in both the mail and wire fraud statutes, and therein lies a story.

The mail fraud statute first came into effect in 1872 and its purpose was to protect the integrity of the U.S. mails by not allowing them to be used as instruments of crime. The focus of the statute was on the misuse of the mails.[34] In numerous cases, particularly in the 1970s and 1980s, courts had no problem with the application of the law to "property," but continued to explore the meaning of "scheme or artifice to defraud." This new interest was one shared with the states as both sectors attempted to respond to the growing sophistication in criminal activity.

Intangibles increasingly were becoming the subject matter of both state and federal cases. Some intangibles arguably could be considered to be property and others could not. Still, at least for mail and wire fraud cases, some of the intangibles that could not be considered property were being covered under "scheme or artifice to defraud." Some of these intangibles certainly would not be considered "goods" under the National Stolen Properties Act and probably would not be considered trade secrets under state laws.

A review of a 1981 federal district court case, U.S. v. Kelly[35] illustrates the point. Kelly was employed at Sperry Univac in Pennsylvania to develop a system for computerizing the generation of sheet music. Kelly and another employee, Palmer, entered into a business relationship with another company to develop a so-called "allegro" system. Kelly and the others used the mails to help promote their new system. Univac discovered that their resources were being utilized, and following investigation by the company's security and the FBI, Kelly and Palmer were indicted for mail fraud. The essence of the charge was:

that by unauthorizedly utilizing their employer's computer time and storage facilities for the development of a private business venture, defendants defrauded
Univac of their loyal and faithful services as employees and used the United
States' mails in furtherance of their fraudulent scheme by causing the promotional
materials to be mailed.[36]

Kelly and Palmer were not taking any trade secrets and they were not
taking any property, so what was the theory of the violation? Before
considering the court's rationale, keep in mind that the purpose of the
mail fraud statute was to prevent the post office from being made an
instrument in some scheme to defraud. Here, the court stated that a
scheme "which is directed at depriving an employer of the honest and
faithful services of its employees or of its right to have its business conducted honestly may constitute a scheme to defraud with the meaning of
the mail fraud statute."[37]

It should be noted that Kelly's and Palmer's status as employees was
critical in making this decision. In that status they owed a duty of honest
and faithful service to their employer. This is part of the balance of rights
and duties in the employment sector. As an aside, it would be strange if
this duty was not seriously evaluated in a wrongful discharge case and at
the same time found to be a critical element in a federal criminal case.
These are the kinds of contradictions that can be created if the laws are
looked at in isolation.

The court in *Kelly* made several other points. Although a number of
mail and wire fraud cases involve government employees, the statute is
clearly applicable to the private sector. Further, the scheme does not
necessarily have to be directed against the employer's economic interests.
The *Kelly* court quoted from *U.S. v. Proctor & Gamble*,[38] in which the
court commented on the employment relationship as follows:

When one tampers with that relationship for the purposes of causing the employee
to breach his duty he in effect is defrauding the employer of a lawful right. The
actual deception that is practiced is in the continued representation of the employee to the employer that he is honest and loyal to the employer's interests.[39]

The *Kelly* court agreed that the mail fraud statute requires more than
a failure to render loyal and faithful service and noted that there must
also be a scheme to deceive, mislead or conceal material information. As
far as the court was concerned, this test was met because the company
had a policy against the use of its property for private ventures and Kelly
and Palmer knew of the policy, made extensive use of the computer
facilities, took steps to conceal their activities, and willfully failed to seek
authorization for their activity.

This represents one example of a situation outside the normal meaning
of trade secrets or property in which federal law can provide assistance.

But even within the definition of property, courts have included confidential and non-public commercial information such as customer lists, customer credit data, lists of services provided customers, and accounting data, as well as services of employees and good will.[40] In the *Carpenter v. United States* decision in 1987, the Supreme Court focused on the meaning of property and concluded that the Wall St. Journal had a property right in making exclusive use of confidential business information and that this information had been misappropriated with an intent to defraud.[41]

The wide-ranging use of the mail and wire fraud statutes took a body blow in the 1987 Supreme Court case, *McNally v. United States.*[42] Despite the fact that every court of appeals that had considered the phrase "any scheme or artifice to defraud, or for obtaining money or property" had read it in the disjunctive, the Supreme Court decided that it should be read to only cover situations involving money or property. The court said it was persuaded that Congress intended only to prevent schemes to obtain money or property. So much for the protection of non-property intangibles, but the court did say that if Congress decided to go further it must speak more clearly than it had. As already noted, Congress did speak shortly thereafter and basically restored the old circuit court and *Kelly* interpretations by stating specifically that "schemes or artifice to defraud" includes a scheme or artifice to deprive another of the intangible right of honest services.[43] Again, this covers both the mail and wire fraud statutes. The Supreme Court *Carpenter* case discussed above was decided during the period between *McNally* and the passage of Section 1346, and this timing explains the court's focus on property.

While the primary emphasis of this discussion has been on the definition and scope of the statutes' subject matter and "scheme" language, some attention should be given to how much, if any, actual mail or wire use is necessary to trigger a federal interest. In *United States v. Bohonus,*[44] a federal circuit court said, "One causes use of the mails when he acts knowing that the use of the mails will follow in the ordinary course of business, or where, though not intended, such use is reasonably foreseeable."[45] The court went on to note that mailings do not have to be an essential part of the scheme but they must be made, or caused to be made, for purposes of executing the scheme.

Appreciating that the *Carpenter* case represents a narrower view of subject matter than now is necessary, it is still worthwhile to consider *Carpenter* in terms of the use of the mails or wire in order to justify the finding of a violation. In *Carpenter*, Winans, the daily writer of a Wall Street Journal column, entered into a scheme with two brokers to give them advance information as to the timing and contents of his column. This permitted them to buy or sell on the probable impact of the column on the market. While there was evidence that the newspaper suffered no financial injury, the schemes apparently netted about $690,000. As already noted, the court found that the newspaper had a property interest in the information that was going into the column and considered it confidential. The writer misappropriated that proprietary interest by his pre-publication releases. The court noted that it was not necessary that the paper suffer any monetary loss. It was enough that the newspaper had been deprived of its right to exclusive use of the information. This took care of the subject matter issue.

How does the use of the mail and wire fit in? The *Carpenter* court stated:

Lastly we reject the submission that using the wires and the mail to print and send the *Journal* to its customers did not satisfy the requirements that those mediums be used to execute the scheme at issue. The courts below were quite right in observing that circulation of the "Heard" column was not only anticipated but an essential part of the scheme. Had the column not been made available to *Journal* customers, there would have been no effect on stock prices and no likelihood of profiting from the information leaked by Winans.[46]

This understanding that an integral part of the scheme would be the use of telephone, telex, mail, or other communications media is cited in numerous cases including fraudulent credit card schemes, schemes to defraud poultry breeders of payment for non-existent chicken feed, and automobile leasing schemes.[47]

As in all criminal statutes, intent is a critical element. However, the government proves intent if it proves that the scheme was reasonably calculated to deceive persons of ordinary prudence or comprehension.[48] Intent may be inferred from all the circumstances and need not be proved by direct evidence.[49]

Extortion and the Hobbs Act

What protection is available in a situation in which a multi-national company has its designs and drawings copied and stolen from a plant in a foreign country, and the thief arrives in the United States at corporate headquarters and demands $10 million for their return? If the demands are not met, the material will be sold to competitors. Certainly there is no statute that is so finely drawn that it would only cover this kind of situation, but there might be one that would include such a situation within its broader parameters and could be used to solve the problem. What might be involved would be some kind of patent infringement or theft of trade secret, but where would one file the civil action and what good would it do if filed? Probably a state criminal extortion statute has been violated, but would the state have authority over property located outside its jurisdiction? Is there a better legal tool?

The Hobbs Act seems to cover this very narrow set of facts.[50] The Hobbs Act reads:

(a) Whoever in any way or degree obstructs, delays, or affects commerce or the movement of any article or commodity in commerce by robbery or extortion or attempts or conspires so to do, or commits or threatens physical violence to any person or property in furtherance of a plan or purpose to do anything in violation of this section shall be fined not more than $10,000 or imprisoned not more than twenty years or both.

(b) As used in this section . . .
  (2) The term "extortion" means the obtaining of property from another, with his consent, induced by wrongful use of actual or threatened force, violence, or fear, or under color of official right.

Before attempting to resolve the question raised in the opening comments in this section, some attention should be given to the background of the Hobbs Act and some of its usual interpretations and applications. The Act was passed as a successor to 1934 anti-racketeering legislation, and for a number of years it was used in labor cases involving such matters as the use of force or violence by union officials against employers in order to obtain personal payoffs.[51] In 1973 in the *Enmons* case,[52] the Supreme Court put some parameters on the use of the Hobbs Act in labor matters by refusing to extend it to situations in which union violence was used to gain higher wages and other monetary benefits. Subsequent legislative attempts to plug this loophole have been unsuccessful.

While it had its roots in racketeering and its early application in labor matters, the Hobbs Act has been extended into many other areas. For example, as discussed in chapter 8 in connection with demonstrations, it has even been applied to situations involving aggressive picketing activities by activist groups. The oddity is that the Hobbs Act cannot be used in most labor picketing violence cases but is used in similar activities by non-labor groups.

The focus of this discussion will be on extortion because that is where the Hobbs Act is most commonly used and has most application to private security. One of the first questions has to be, then, what is the Hobbs Act trying to protect? The answer is property. Remember that the mail and wire fraud statutes covered non-property intangibles as well as property, so the Hobbs Act does not have the scope of coverage of those two statutes. But at the same time consider that property under such cases as *Carpenter*, a wire and mail fraud case, had a fairly broad meaning.

The Third Circuit in a 1985 case, *United States v. Local 560*,[53] commented that the Hobbs Act extends to protect intangible as well as tangible property. It cited other circuits that found such things as the right to solicit business accounts and the "right to make business decisions free from outside pressures wrongfully imposed" in that category.[54] The court went on to find that in a union setting the membership's right to democratic participation in the affairs of their union is properly considered extortable property for purposes of the Hobbs Act.

This *Local 560* case is also helpful in figuring out how certain activities fit into the legal scheme of things. It is primarily a RICO case and will be discussed under that section, but it is included here because the predicate acts necessary in the case for finding a RICO violation are Hobbs Act violations. It is also a labor case, and separate and apart from the *Enmons* limitations there are possibilities of conflict with federal labor statutes including the National Labor Relations Act and the Labor Management and Disclosure Act, which regulates internal union activity. How do the parts fit together?

The intent of the government in this RICO civil action was to remove the so-called Provenzano group from control over the affairs of Local 560. The government contended that the group had gained control through murder and extortion and an obvious Hobbs Act question was what property rights were involved. The government could not get its remedy unless it proved a RICO violation, and it could not prove a RICO violation without proving a Hobbs Act violation, and it could not prove that without proving an extortion of property.

The court acknowledged that if the rights involved in this case were National Labor Relations Act section 7 rights, the NLRA would be preemptive because of the remedial nature of that statute and the primacy of the NLRB in resolving unfair labor practice disputes. The court then cited *United States v. Boffa*[55] as establishing this position. *Boffa*, another RICO case, used mail fraud activity as its predicate acts but the philosophy on relationships with the NLRA is applicable.

The *Local 560* case went on to note, however, that the property here, the right to democratic participation in the affairs of the union, was not a Section 7 right under the NLRA. It did not involve wages, hours, and other terms and conditions of employment. But that does not take care of the whole labor area, because Section 530 of the Labor-Management Reporting and Disclosure Act (LMDRA) does cover union members' rights.[56] The court distinguished the two acts and noted that the Hobbs Act was created to help combat extortion and Section 530 focused on prohibiting physical assaults on members in connection with internal union affairs. Since the Hobbs Act had a greater reach than Section 530 it could not be preempted by it. The interest here is not purely academic to point out the intricacies of a particular case but to evidence the interrelationships between laws and the danger in looking at any of them in isolation. There has been considerable earlier discussion in chapters 2, 4, 5, and 6 about the relationships between the NLRA and Title VII and the NLRA and arbitration with state causes of action, and this is an added facet of the same interrelationship problem.

With regard to the other elements in the Hobbs Act scheme, it is axiomatic that the federal government will not get into a matter unless there is some federal interest. In mail and wire fraud cases, the federal interest is readily apparent—the mail is carried by a federal agency and telephones and telegrams are integral parts of interstate communications. The National Stolen Property Act is not triggered unless the goods moving in interstate or foreign commerce are valued at more than $5,000. The Hobbs Act talks about "in any way or degree" obstructing, delaying, or affecting commerce or the movement of any article or commodity in commerce. The extorter does not have to intend to affect commerce, and commerce can be affected if the resources of an interstate business would be depleted or diminished in any manner by the extortion.[57] The relative size of the extorted business is not in issue as long as it is involved in interstate activity.[58] The mail or wires do not have to be used and the monies or property do not have to move across state lines.

As to the actual extortion activity, there has to be evidence that the victim was fearful, the fear was reasonable, and the extorter made use of the fear to carry out the extortion.[59] There still are cases in which the requisite fear has been created by violence or threats of violence. The activist demonstration cases fall into this category. However, a large number of cases involve fear of economic loss. The economic loss to be feared is the threatened economic harm that the victim could reasonably believe would befall it if the extortionate demands were not met. "There must just be a reasonable fear of an economic loss sufficient to induce the victim to part with the property demanded rather than face the threatened consequent loss. In other words, the victim must reasonably think the threatened loss makes it worth his while to play the extortioner's game."[60] Economic loss has been an element in cases involving a wide range of concerns including loss of contract, loss of liquor license, loss of police protection, and kickback schemes.[61] Another element of interest is that the extortioner does not have to receive any benefits from the extortion. The law is interested in protecting the victim from loss and it is of no legal consequence whether the extorter was unjustly rewarded.[62]

A review of the *United States v. Inigio* case[63] will help pull some of these elements together, give some feel for the geographical scope of the Hobbs Act, and answer the questions raised in the opening comments in this discussion of the Hobbs Act. The Third Circuit in 1991 considered a case in which several former Du Pont employees copied and stole certain technology from its plant in Argentina and removed it to Italy. Several attempts were made to interest Mexican and Italian businesses in the technology. In addition, the leader of the group, Skerianz, approached

Du Pont people at its Delaware corporate headquarters and told them it could get all its technology back plus an agreement not to use it in return for $10 million. The theft had taken place in Argentina and the stolen documents were in Italy and had never entered the United States, but the attempted extortion had taken place in the United States. At a certain point in the investigation, the matter was turned over to the federal government and subsequently arrests took place in Switzerland. The parties involved returned to the United States for trial.

An initial question involved jurisdiction, and the court concluded that even though must of the activity took place outside the United States, there was sufficient impact on interstate commerce to warrant the court's attention. The guideline is depletion or diminishing "in any manner" the ability to conduct an interstate business. Du Pont's size was of no consequence in judging whether the activity met this test. Since it conducted a substantial amount of business in the United States, the loss of the $10 million had a potential for depleting or impairing its ability to carry out that business. In a footnote, the court observed, "We do not reach the issue of whether completely extraterritorial extortionate conduct involving a foreign corporation would satisfy the jurisdictional demands of Sec. 1951 if that corporation conducted only minimal business in the United States."[64] As U.S. businesses become more deeply involved in global activities, there should be an increasing interest in insuring that U.S. laws provide needed protection.

The fear of economic loss element was quite obvious in this case; the demand for $10 million speaks for itself, as this kind of money clearly made it worthwhile to play the extortioners' game.

One other point is worth mentioning. As often happens in criminal cases, one of the defendants contended he was entrapped. It has been mentioned at several earlier points that entrapment is a defense against government activity in criminal cases. It does not apply to private security people who are not acting as agents of the government. In this case, the court concluded that the contentions were without merit because there was no evidence of government involvement in the early stages of the investigation while Du Pont was gathering information. This regular use of the entrapment defense again evidences the need to understand the separate roles played by private security and law enforcement. A failure to understand these roles can jeopardize significant investigations. It is also interesting that one defense raised was that Du Pont had not properly protected its property in Argentina; but failure to protect secrecy is a trade secret defense and was given scant notice in this Hobbs Act case.

The Catch-All—RICO

Before discussing the intricacies of the Racketeer Influenced and Corrupt Organizations Act (RICO),[65] it is first necessary to understand its origin and purposes. In 1970, with its passage, Congress was taking a broadside attack on organized crime and, among other things, was attempting to prevent its penetration of businesses and use of those businesses as covers for its activities.[66]

Congress did not create any new substantive legal protections to meet its objective, but bundled together twenty-four pre-existing, separate types of federal crimes and eight state crimes and provided that if they were triggered in a certain way, the violators would receive not only substantial criminal penalties but would also be subject to civil actions including treble damages. The incorporated federal laws included mail and wire fraud, Hobbs Act violations, and actions under the National Stolen Properties Act. The state crimes included murder, kidnapping, gambling, arson, robbery, bribery, extortion, and dealing in narcotics or other dangerous drugs. The language of the statute was left somewhat generalized in order to provide flexibility in meeting developing schemes of organized crime. However, this lack of specificity has taken the scope of RICO far beyond Congress's original focus and RICO has generated an unusual amount of litigation.[67]

Its use is particularly attractive in the private security sector because by incorporating some state crimes into the federal scheme it gives a reach across state lines that previously did not exist, it provides more substantial criminal penalties, and it gives offended businesses an opportunity to recoup treble damages plus attorneys' fees in civil actions. RICO's criminal remedies are set out in Section 1963 and include forfeiture of both tangible and intangible property and imprisonment for up to twenty years. A civil action can be pursued under Section 1964(c) by any person injured in his business or property by any RICO violation.

With that as a background, it is time to take a closer look at the range of activity targeted by Congress. Section 1962 makes it unlawful for any person—not just mobsters—(a) to use money received from a pattern of racketeering activity to invest in or operate an enterprise; (b) to gain or maintain control over an enterprise through a pattern of racketeering activity; or (c) to conduct or participate in the operation of an enterprise through a pattern of racketeering activity. Subsection (d) covers conspiracies to violate subsections (a), (b), or (c).

Subsections (a) and (b) focus on using tainted money or prohibited tactics in getting into or maintaining control over an operation, and (c) point toward using prohibited tactics while functioning within an operation. The words and phrases repeated in the three subsections are "any person," "enterprises," and "pattern of racketeering activity." It makes sense to get a better understanding of what these terms mean before going further.

By definition, "person" includes any individual or entity capable of holding a legal or beneficial interest in property.[68] Under RICO the person is the individual or individuals who are trying to take over or operate a business for their own purposes—in other words, the "person" is the bad guy. The court in *Continental Data Systems v. Exxon Corporation* stated, "The RICO person is the wrongdoer."[69] A "person," of course, can be a corporation.

As used in the RICO statute, an "enterprise" can be a bad guy or a good guy, depending on circumstances. In the *Continental Data* case, the court said the RICO enterprise is a passive instrumentality, a mechanism through which the person performs his violative acts. In some situations the person controls the enterprise and the enterprise has liabilities, while in other cases, such as *Continental Data*, the person functions without the control or knowledge of the enterprise and the enterprise is not liable.

"Enterprise" can include illegitimate associations as well as legitimate businesses.[70] It can include a group of entities such as two partnerships and one individual or groups of individuals associated with various corporations.[71] It can also cover activities that are not part of a formally organized structure. For example, in *United States v. Young*,[72] the court found that an enterprise consisted of two or three leaders and several core individuals who were associated to run marijuana into the United States. Enterprises can include foreign businesses as well as those of the United States.[73]

For subsection (c) purposes, "person" and "enterprise" are considered by nearly all circuits, except the Eleventh, to be separate entities, but "person" and "enterprise" can be the same entity for subsection (a), the investing and use of money section.[74] This potential confusion is introduced at this time only to warn case readers of one of the distinctions between the different subsections. Some cases are filed as violations of all Section 1962 subsections and others are more selective and refer to only (a), (b), or (c).

A review of three cases will be helpful at this point. In *Busby v. Crown Supply, Inc.*,[75] Busby contended that his employer had used two schemes to defraud its salesmen of income. The salesmen were paid commissions based on the difference between the company's costs and the retail prices. Busby contended that the company was using false cost figures to diminish the amount of commission, and that the company instituted a rebate program that bypassed the salesmen. The RICO allegation involved subsection (a)—investing and using monies obtained through a pattern of racketeering. Busby's theory was that through the use of the false cost and rebate schemes the company was able to retain funds that had been fraudulently obtained and use them in its operation. For subsection (a) purposes, the company was not only the person but also the enterprise— both bad guys. This willingness by most circuit courts to look at the dual nature of a corporation insures liability when the corporation is actually the beneficiary of the racketeering activity. Of course an enterprise does not have to be a full-blown corporation, as the term includes informal groups as well. If it looks like it is the enterprise that is getting the benefit from the racketeering-obtained monies, then (a) appears to be the subsection of interest.

Subsection (b) usually involves the old-fashioned methods of violence and extortion in gaining or maintaining control over an enterprise. In *United States v. Local 560*,[76] the government framed its civil action in terms of the Provenzano group violating subsection (b) by acquiring an interest in and controlling Local 560 through extortion and murder. Local 560 was also one of the defendants in the case, so it was an enterprise that was subject to remedial action. The government also contended that there was a violation of subsection (c) because the Provenzano group participated in the conduct of Local 560's affairs.

Subsection (c) presents most of the legal problems, so the third case relates to that subsection. *Petro-Tech, Inc. v. Western Co. of North America*,[77] a 1987 Third Circuit case, involved a situation in which Petro-Tech, among others, filed a civil RICO action. Petro-Tech, an oil and gas drilling and well management company, had contracted with Western to do certain work in its well drilling operations. Western's business was highly competitive and it responded to its low profits by billing companies for services and materials it had not provided. According to Petro-Tech, several of Western's high-ranking officers knew of the practice and it was deliberate company policy. The predicate acts were use of the mail to solicit business and provide the over-billed payment requests.

Some of the RICO charges involved subsection (c), and the necessary question was whether the enterprise could be reached under this subsection. The focus of subsection (c) seemed to be on people operating illegally as employees or associates within the enterprise. Most courts were saying that the enterprise could be attacked through subsections (a) and (b), but for subsection (c) purposes the enterprise was just a neutral conduit. As a neutral it had no liability for the acts of its employees or associates.

The court acknowledged this position as a starting point and then addressed the issue of whether the corporation could be brought in under respondeat superior or aiding or abetting theories. The court concluded that both theories were foreclosed because they would make the enterprise responsible for the acts of employees or associates—something outside the scope of subsection (c). This is not to say that enterprises are generally unreachable under RICO, because the court at the same time stated that the two theories, respondeat superior and aiding and abetting, are appropriate for use under subsection (a) if the enterprise is benefitting from the racketeering activity of its employees or associates. Further, if the corporation was identified as a person acting in conjunction with the several individuals as an enterprise, subsection (c) could still be a viable vehicle for relief.

Determining whether RICO allegations under subsections (a), (b), (c), or even (d) are appropriate is primarily a matter of standing back and figuring out who is doing the crime, who is benefitting from it, and who is being victimized. It is then a matter of putting the right name tags on the parties involved. The person is the bad guy and sometimes the enterprise is a bad guy. If the enterprise is only a neutral and in a real sense just being used by employees or associates, subsection (c) is probably the way to go in most courts to reach the real culprits. The primary idea, though, is not to get lost in the legal intricacies of this rapidly developing area of the law. The fact that the various circuits have somewhat different interpretations of the same statute should not deter the search for relief. Most of the differences of opinion are in the fine-tuning and normally can be resolved through careful pleading. Further, most reluctant courts are finally convinced by the Supreme Court that RICO has to be given a liberal interpretation in order to meet congressional objectives.

In resolving subsection (c) issues, some courts have wrestled at great length over how deeply the person has to be involved in the enterprise's business. The Eighth Circuit seems to require some participation by the person in the operation or management of the enterprise.[78] The D.C. Circuit emphasizes participating in the conduct of the enterprise's affairs.[79] The Eleventh Circuit does not seem to get hung up in this fine-tuning, as in the *Young* case it tied the followers in with the leaders of the drug operation, on the premise that these followers knew what was going on within the enterprise and each participated in at least two off-loads of marijuana from the mother ships.

Courts keep asking for more guidance from the Supreme Court as to what these different phrases mean and the normal response by the Court is that RICO may be a poorly drafted statute but that it is Congress's business, and if Congress wants to correct it, it will. The Supreme Court adds that it does not intend to give the language a pinched or restricted interpretation but to give it the flexible range Congress seems to have intended.[80] This lack of certainty includes the meaning of the next subject for discussion—the term "pattern of racketeering activity."

Of course "racketeering" does not mean only organized crime activity. The cases have gone well beyond that and again the Supreme Court has said that if Congress wanted to retrench to that limited meaning, it could do so through new legislation. But, the term "pattern" is puzzling, as the statute only talks about two or more predicate acts. Predicate acts means violations of federal statutes such as the Hobbs Act or the mail or wire fraud statutes. The courts, again, have spent a lot of time analyzing its meaning without providing much direction. The Supreme Court has said that plaintiff or prosecutor must show that the racketeering predicate acts are related and that they amount to or pose a threat of continued activity.[81] "Related" seems to mean the acts must have the same or similar purposes, results, participants, victims, or methods of commission, or otherwise are interrelated by distinguishing characteristics and are not isolated events. Continued activity or "continuity," as described by the Supreme Court, is "both a closed- and open-ended concept, referring either to a closed period of repeated conduct, or to past conduct that by its nature projects into the future with a threat of repetition."[82]

With this vague guidance in mind, the Seventh Circuit in the 1990 case *U.S. Textiles v. Anheuser-Busch Companies*[83] established some check-points. In first considering the numbers and kinds of predicate acts, the court concluded that just a number of mailings or telephone calls themselves will not be enough to justify a RICO action even though they constitute a mail or wire fraud violation. The court felt that the draconian remedies provided by RICO could only mean that Congress did not intend RICO to apply in every garden-variety kind of case. Of course, one court's garden might be another court's very rich farm. If the case involved more than one victim, this court would have a greater interest. This is not to say there had to be more than one scheme, because the Supreme Court had already said that one scheme can do the job. But for this court, additional schemes would be added factors to consider. The court also noted that it would look at the total package and would consider the existence of distinct injuries. The presence of multiple injuries would help evidence the continued activity element the Supreme Court seemed to be looking for.

In a real way, this court and some others seem to be saying that while RICO certainly has a great range, it cannot be used to solve all problems. The treble damages and stiff criminal sentences provided for RICO violations seem to point toward criminal activity that presents a significant social threat.[84] So, as noted, proving a mail fraud case, for example, and having the requisite two or more acts will not necessarily prove a RICO case in all federal courts. The pattern of racketeering activity requirement seems to point toward resolving fairly significant crimes that are not only related but are or have a potential for being repeated.

With the understanding that there are some limitations on its use, it is still amazing to view the range of activities that have been the subject matter of RICO cases, particularly civil actions. As noted in chapter 8, RICO has been used to manage demonstrations as in the *Northeast Women's Center, Inc. v. McMonagle* case.[85] It was used on the civil side by the government to remove people from control over a labor organization, in *United States v. Local 560*.[86] In *H. J. Inc. v. Northwestern Bell*,[87] the allegations involved payments by Northwestern to members of a state rate-setting group. In fact, the primary use of the statute has been in the area of white collar crimes such as price-fixing, bank fraud, defense procurement fraud, and real estate and securities transactions, and it remains to be seen what parameters the courts will put on its use.[88]

Computer Fraud and Abuse Act

For the computer illiterate, the subject of computer crime conjures up images of some kind of rocket science. As a consequence, many security people have avoided dealing with the subject. In order to gain some perspective, it might be of value to consider the computer as a tool that is used in a crime. It then becomes akin to a camera, a copying machine, or even a ladder. Confusing technical language should not cloud the fact that often at the heart of the matter is the theft or compromise of intangible property.

As discussed earlier in this chapter, different aspects of computer crime have been attacked under copyright and trade secret theories as well as under traditional state criminal statutes. One commentator has noted that there are forty federal statutes and eleven areas of traditional state laws that have been used as a defense against these crimes.[89]

The federal government has tried its hand on the subject in the Computer Fraud and Abuse Act.[90] As might be expected, its primary focus is on government owned or used computer systems. However, there are two areas of the act that may be of interest to the private sector. One covers intentional acts of unauthorized access to the financial records of customers of financial institutions. There seems to be a question as to whether the act is violated by merely looking at such information or whether the information has to be downloaded to a hard copy.[91] The act also prohibits trafficking in passwords or similar access information that affects interstate or foreign commerce, but it is yet to be determined just how the impact on interstate or foreign commerce will be measured.[92]

It is too early to say whether this act will be a significant weapon in fighting computer crime but, at least, its another avenue that should be considered.

OBSERVATIONS

The dramatic developments in technology that have taken place over the past twenty or thirty years have given private security significant new concerns. When does an idea, a plan, or a process become property that will be protected by the law? What court do you go to to get the protection?

State criminal and civil laws will protect trade secrets but these courts will measure the existence and worth of the trade secret by the security steps taken by management in protecting it. These courts do not like to be used to do what a business should have done for itself—protect its own trade secrets. The courtroom is not the place to be first showing concern that the compromised property constitutes the heart and soul of the business. As far as the courts are concerned, if it's gold, treat it like gold.

Federal laws offer a wide range of protections, particularly if the criminal activity is carried out in part beyond the state's jurisdiction. Further, as in the mail and wire fraud cases, the protections will be extended beyond property to the intangible right of "honest services."

Choosing the appropriate source of legal relief requires analyzing the problem at hand and determining who is involved, where the activity is taking place, the mechanics involved in the compromise, and the relief desired. Are the expenses and time involved in pursuing a civil RICO action justified if the culprits are destitute and the compromised interests can be retrieved and protected through a Hobbs Act or mail fraud case? Would a wire fraud case be a more appropriate vehicle than a civil trade secret action, particularly if inadequate security measures had been taken to protect the property involved? To know the individual laws in isolation is interesting, but to understand how they interrelate and can be used to solve different problems is productive. It is also necessary to understand how roles can change. For example, if law enforcement is introduced, the game will be played under a different set of investigative rules.

Legislatures and courts normally will, over time, respond to societal changes. The congressional reaction in plugging up the loophole in the mail and wire fraud statutes created by the Supreme Court's decision in the *McNally* case on nonproperty intangibles is an example of quick relief.[93] The gradual establishment of parameters in the RICO statute is an example of slow relief. The thing to keep in mind is that these changes invariably involve the balancing of numerous rights, and what appears to make great sense to business will not necessarily be considered by the courts or legislatures to be good for the country as a whole.

NOTES

1. 35 U.S.C. Sec. 101.

2. R. Dorr & W. Eigles, *Resolving Claims to Ownership of Software and Computer Stored Data—The Importance of Temporary Restraining Orders and Preliminary Injunctions*, 5 Computer L.J. 1 (1984); V. Neumeyer, *Software Copyright Law: The Enforceability Sham*, 35 Loyola L. Rev. 485 (1990).

3. D. Fetterley, *Historical Perspectives on Criminal Laws Relating to the Theft of Trade Secrets*, 25 Bus. Law. 1535 (1970).

4. Annot., 84 A.L.R. 3d 967, *Misappropriation of Trade Secret* (1978); Sokolik, *Computer Crime—The Need for Deterrent Legislation*, 2 Computer L.J. 353 (1980).

5. Epstein & Levi, *Protecting Trade Secret Information: A Plan for Proactive Strategy*, 43 Bus. Law. 887 (1988).

6. Fetterley, *Historical Perspectives* at 1536, 37; Wolk, *Some Legal Aspects of Industrial Security*, 9 Prac. Law. No. 4, 87 (1963).

7. Vandevoot, *Trade Secrets: Protecting a Very Special "Property,"* 26 Bus. Law. 681 (1971).

8. Epstein & Levi, *Protecting Trade Secret Information*; Silberberg & Lardiere,

Eroding Protection of Customer Lists and Customer Information Under the Uniform Trade Secrets Act, 42 Bus. Law. 487 (1987).

9. N.J. Rev. Stat. Sec. 2C:20-1.

10. Sokolik, *Computer Crime*.

11. *Leonard v. State*, 767 S.W.2d 171 (Tex. App.-Dallas 1988).

12. 767 S.W.2d 171 at 176, 177.

13. 62 Cal. App. 3d 9, 133 Cal. Rptr. 144 (1976).

14. Epstein & Levi, *Protecting Trade Secret Information*, 43 Bus. Law 887.

15. Silberberg & Lardiere, *Eroding Protection*, 42 Bus. Law 487.

16. Uniform Trade Secrets Act §1(4), 14 U.L.A. 541, 542 (1980).

17. R. Dorr & W. Eigles, *Resolving Claims to Ownership*, 5 Computer L.J. 1.

18. 357 Mass. 728, 260 N.E.2d 723 (1970).

19. 260 N.E. 2d 723 at 730.

20. 260 N.E. 2d 723 at 730.

21. 260 N.E. 2d 723 at 731.

22. 633 F.2d 435 (6th Cir. 1980).

23. Epstein & Levi, *Protecting Trade Secret Information*, 43 *Bus. Law.* at 896, 897.

24. *Erie R. Co. v. Tompkins,* 304 U.S. 64 (1938); *United States v. Kin Buc., Inc.,* 532 F.Supp. 699 (D.C.N.J 1982).

25. 18 U.S.C. Sec. 2314.

26. *United States v. Bottone*, 365 F.2d 389 (2d Cir. 1966), *cert. denied.* 385 U.S. 974 (1966).

27. 365 F.2d 389 at 393.

28. 365 F.2d 389 at 394.

29. 18 U.S.C. Sec. 1341.

30. 18 U.S.C. Sec. 1343.

31. *United States v. Louderman*, 576 F.2d 1383, 1387 (9th Cir. 1978) *cert. denied*, 439 U.S. 896 (1978); *United States v. Barta*, 635 F.2d 999, 1005 (2nd Cir. 1980).

32. 18 U.S.C. Sec. 1341.

33. 18 U.S.C. Sec. 1343.

34. *McNally v. United States*, 483 U.S. 350 (1987).

35. 507 F. Supp. 495 (E.D. Pa. 1981).

36. 507 F. Supp. 495 at 497.

37. 507 F. Supp. 495 at 499.

38. 47 F. Supp. 676 (D. Mass. 1942).

39. 507 F. Supp. 495 at 500.

40. *U.S. v. Louderman*, 576 F.2d at 1386-88.

41. *Carpenter v. United States*, 484 U.S. 19 (1987).

42. *McNally v. United States*, 483 U.S. 350 (1987).

43. 18 U.S.C. Sec. 1346; *United States v. Berg*, 710 F. Supp. 438 (E.D. N.Y. 1989); *United States v. Martinez*, 905 F.2d 709 (3rd Cir. 1990).

44. 628 F.2d 1167 (9th Cir. 1980).

45. 628 F.2d 1167 at 1173.

46. 484 U.S. 19 at 28.

47. *United States v. DeBiasi*, 712 F.2d 785 (2nd Cir. 1983); *United States v. Castillo*, 829 F.2d 1194 (1st Cir. 1987); *United States v. Shrylock*, 537 F.2d 207 (5th Cir. 1976).

48. *United States v. Alston*, 609 F.2d 531 (D.C. Cir. 1979) *cert. denied*, 445 U.S. 918 (1979).

49. *United States v. Andrade*, 788 F.2d 521 (8th Cir. 1986) *cert. denied*, 479 U.S. 963 (1986).

50. 18 U.S.C. Sec. 1951.

51. *United States v. Iozzi*, 420 F.2d 512 (4th Cir. 1970); *Bianchi v. United States*, 219 F.2d 182 (8th Cir. 1955).

52. *United States v. Enmons*, 410 U.S. 396 (1973); Minamyer, *The Labor Activity Exemption to the Hobbs Act: An Analysis of the Appropriate Scope, Lab. L. J.*, 34 (1983).

53. 780 F.2d 267 (3rd Cir. 1985).

54. 780 F.2d 267 at 281.

55. 688 F.2d (3d Cir. 1982), *cert. denied*, 460 U.S. 1022 (1983).

56. 29 U.S.C. Sec. 530.

57. *United States v. Addanizio*, 451 F.2d 49 (3rd Cir. 1971), *cert. denied*, 405 U.S. 936 (1971).

58. *United States v. Inigio*, 925 F.2d 641 (3rd Cir. 1991); *United States v. Mazzei*, 521 F.2d 639 (3rd Cir.), *cert. denied*, 423 U.S. 1014 (1975).

59. *Callanan v. United States*, 223 F.2d 171 (8th Cir. 1955) *cert. denied*, 350 U.S. 862 (1955).

60. *U.S. v. Inigio*, 925 F.2d at 650.

61. *Northeast Women's Center, Inc. v. McMonagle*, 868 F.2d 1342 (3rd Cir. 1989), *cert. denied*, _____ U.S. _____, 110 S. Ct 261 (1989).

62. *United States v. Trotta*, 525 F.2d (2nd Cir. 1975), *cert. denied*, 425 U.S. 971 (1976); *United States v. Hyde*, 448 F.2d 815 (5th Cir. 1971), *cert. denied*, 404 U.S. 1058 (1971).

63. *U.S. v. Inigio*, 925 F.2d 641.

64. 925 F.2d at 649, footnote 7.

65. 18 U.S.C. Sec. 1961 et. seq.

66. 18 U.S.C. Sec. 1962 (a)(b)(c).

67. Atkinson, *RICO Sec. 1961–68, Broadest of the Federal Criminal Statutes*, 9 J. Crim. L. & Criminology 1 (1978).

68. 18 U.S.C. Sec. 1961 (3).

69. 638 F. Supp. 432 (E.D. Pa. 1986).

70. *United States v. Turkette*, 452 U.S. 576 (1981); *Russello v. United States*, 464 U.S. 16 (1983).

71. *First Federal Savings & Loan Ass'n v. Oppenheim, Appel, Dixon & Co.*, 629 F. Supp. 427 (S.D. NY 1986).

72. 906 F.2d 615 (11th Cir. 1990).

73. *United States v. Parness*, 503 F.2d 430 (2d Cir. 1971).

74. *Busby v. Crown Supply, Inc.*, 896 F.2d 833 (4th Cir. 1990); *Haroco v. Amer. Nat. Bank & Trust Co.*, 747 F.2d 384 (7th Cir. 1984), *aff'd on other grounds*, 473 U.S. 606 (1985).

75. Busby v. Crown Supply 896 F.2d 833 (4th Cir. 1990).

76. 780 F.2d 267 (3rd Cir. 1985).

77. 824 F.2d 1349 (3rd Cir. 1987).

78. *Bennett v. Berg*, 710 F.2d 1361 (8th Cir. 1983) *cert. denied*, 464 U.S. 1008 (1983).

79. *Yellow Bus Lines v. Local Union 639*, 913 F.2d 948 (D.C. Cir. 1990); *United States v. Scotto*, 641 F.2d 47 (2nd Cir. 1981).

80. *H. J. Inc. v. Northwestern Bell*, 492 U.S. 229 (1989).

81. *Sedima, S.R.P.L. v. Inrex Co.*, 473 U.S. 479 (1985).

82. *H. J. Inc v. Northwestern Bell*, 492 U.S. 229, 241 (1989).

83. 911 F.2d 1261 (7th Cir. 1990).

84. *Marshall-Selver Constr. Co. Inc. v. Mendel*, 894 F.2d 593 (3rd Cir. 1990).

85. 868 F. 2d 1342 (3rd Cir. 1989) *cert. denied* 493 U.S. 901 (1989).

86. 780 F. 2d 267 (3rd Cir. 1985).

87. 492 U.S. 229 (1989).

88. C.P. Blakely & S.D. Cessar, *Equitable Relief Under Civil RICO*, 62 Notre Dame L. Rev. 526 (1987).

89. C. Chen, *Computer Crime and the Computer Fraud and Abuse Act of 1986*, 10 Computer L.J. 71 at 75, 76 (1990).

90. 18 U.S.C. Sec. 1030 (1986).

91. C. Chen, *Computer Crime and the Computer Fraud and Abuse Act of 1986*, 10 Computer L.J. 71 at 79 (1990); D. Griffith, *The Computer Fraud and Abuse Act of 1986: A Measured Response to a Growing Problem*, 43 Vanderbilt L.R. 453 at 476 (1990).

92. C. Chen, *Computer Crime and the Computer Fraud and Abuse Act of 1986*, 10 Computer L.J. 71 at 79 (1990); D. Griffith, *The Computer Fraud and Abuse Act of 1986: A Measured Response to a Growing Problem*, 43 Vanderbilt L.R. 453 at 480, 481 (1990).

93. *McNally v. United States*, 483 U.S. 350 (1987).

10

The Special Nature of Some Security Functions

Private security covers a great deal of legal territory and while much of it has been discussed in earlier chapters, there are other areas that have not been reached. An attempt has been made to approach problems by first identifying the parties involved and the factors that enter into the balancing of rights of those parties. These parties included employees, organized and unorganized employers, invitees, trespassers, and owners and operators of businesses. The balancing elements were set out for criminal and civil laws as well as administrative laws such as the National Labor Relations Act. But there are other parties such as students and schools who have a whole range of rights and obligations that have not been considered in depth. Further, there are a number of businesses that, because of their nature, are highly regulated by the government and they have not received any special attention. Not all of these parties and interests can be discussed, but this will be an attempt at covering a few of them.

STUDENTS AND SCHOOLS

Before analyzing any cases, it will be helpful to identify the kinds of students and the kinds of schools that are involved. Are they public school students or private school students? Are they high school students or college students? Responses to these questions are critical in resolving the tensions that exist between the students' demand for more freedom and a school's obligation to provide a safe environment conducive to acquiring a good education. For example, first amendment freedoms will not carry much weight with a court if a private school is involved. Further, pleas by fourteen year old high school students for more freedom do not have the same impact as similar pleas by twenty year old college juniors.

Searches

Some time was spent in chapter 1 explaining the different roles played by private sector security and law enforcement. Within that discussion there was a further refinement of the roles played within government by administrators and law enforcement people. It will be of value now to refocus on the *New Jersey v. T.L.O.* case,[1] which considered a fourth amendment search issue.

The setting was a public high school and the issue was the balance between the students' right of privacy and the considerable interest of teachers and administrators in maintaining discipline in the classroom and on school grounds. The court recognized that schools have a legitimate need to maintain an environment in which learning can take place. The court went on to say:

the accommodation of the privacy interests of schoolchildren with the substantial need of teachers and administrators for freedom to maintain order in the schools does not require strict adherence to the requirement that searches be based on probable cause to believe that the subject of the search has violated or is violating the law. Rather, the legality of a search of a student should depend simply on the reasonableness, under all the circumstances, of the search.[2]

Some states have passed legislation in this search area that applies to students. For example, Iowa provides specific tests for school officials to follow, but they appear to be geared toward the reasonableness standard. Within that context, officials must consider the age and sex of the student and the nature of the suspected violation. No searches are to be conducted if they involve strip or body cavity searches, use of a drug-sniffing animal to search a student's body, or searches by an official of a student of the opposite sex.[3] This kind of statute can put a lot of flesh on the *T.L.O.* bones.

Rules and Regulations

Switch the scene now to a public college campus and the subject matter from the fourth amendment to the first amendment and a freedom of association issue. The public college still has a right and an obligation to institute rules that serve legitimate educational objectives and students have some rights to privacy and freedom of association. What happens if these rights and obligations come into conflict, for example, in a case where the college limits the rights of students to entertain members of the opposite sex in their rooms?

While it was done under a test of state constitutional provisions, a New Mexico court considered the same elements that would have been present in a federal case.[4] The court recognized the board of regents' authority to create conditions of quiet seclusion in university dormitory rooms that would be conducive to safety, study, and reflection. The court noted that even if the university's regulation that limited visitations in dormitory rooms infringed upon the students' right of association, that association right was not an absolute right and was subject to restrictions. In the court's judgment, the regents' regulation was neither arbitrary nor unreasonable.

Disciplinary Action

What laws pertain to disciplinary action, and how are they applied? Again, the focus is on state-sponsored schools and constitutional protections. The courts have said a student may exercise his first amendment rights involving freedom of expression if he does so without materially interfering with the requirements of appropriate discipline in the operation of the school and without colliding with the rights of others. But conduct by the student, in class or out of it, that for any reason materially disrupts classwork or invokes substantial disorder or invasion of the rights of others is not protected by the guarantee of freedom of speech. Some actions, such as fighting and cheating, while not protected by the first amendment, also deserve attention. Since a student may have a claim under state law to a public education, a property interest under the fourteenth amendment, he cannot be deprived of it without due process of law, and that means some kind of hearing. It does not have to be a full-dress judicial hearing; all it has to do is provide an opportunity for both sides to present their cases.[5]

There is no question that starting in the 1960s college students both in public and private settings gained more and more freedoms. These gains were made more through societal than legal pressures, particularly in the private sector. Of course, as students gained more control over their campus lives, administrators had to lose some of their ability to regulate student affairs.

Injuries to Students by Third Parties

But what happens in this new atmosphere if a student is injured by a third person in a campus incident? Will the university or college be liable even though it has withdrawn from its former role as a quasi-parent? Or will the school be relieved of liability?

As noted in chapter 2, courts have gone in several different directions in responding to the question. All agree that prior to the 1960s, the university had a special relationship with the student, and although there was no guarantee of safety, there was a high degree of duty owed to protect students. The relationship was akin to that between guest and hotel or traveler and common carrier. Did new student freedoms change that relationship?

An Illinois court in 1987 considered a situation in which a university student was injured during a fraternity party.[6] In resolving the issue of whether the school owed a duty to the student, the court commented that it was the school's job to provide an education and not to be a custodian or babysitter. The school was not an insurer of the student's safety. Further, in this court's judgment the university had neither contracted to provide protection or security nor assumed added responsibility because it had equipped its building with security devices and provided security personnel. Using a landlord-tenant analogy, it found that the university had no duty to protect its "tenants" from harm caused by intentional or criminal acts of third parties. And, of course, if there is no duty there is no need to determine whether a duty has been violated.

Other courts have voiced different views. In 1991, a Delaware court came down the other way and found a duty and a violation of the duty.[7] Again, the injury took place in a fraternity incident. But this time the court made an analogy to shopping mall cases. This area of the law was discussed at length in chapter 7, and it is to be remembered that a number of states have recently created duties in situations involving injuries at malls by third parties. Prior to that time, mall owners and operators were not liable for such injuries.

After an extensive review of court cases treating the school-student relationship, the court stated:

In sum although the University no longer stands *in loco parentis* to its students, the relationship is sufficiently close and direct to impose a duty. . . . The university is not an insurer of the safety of its students nor a policeman of student morality, nonetheless, it has a duty to regulate and supervise *foreseeable dangerous activities* occurring on its property. That duty extends to the negligent or intentional activities of third parties. Because of the extensive freedom enjoyed by the modern university student, the duty of the university to regulate and supervise should be limited to those instances where it exercises control. Situations arising out of the ownership of land . . . , involving student invitees present on the property for the purposes permitted them are within such limitations. (Emphasis added.)[8]

It is interesting that the creation of the duty in the mall cases came about because of the increased attractiveness of those locations for criminal activity. In the university cases the duty is not being created but is being watered down because of the new freedoms granted students. The question in the mall cases is how high to go up in duties and the question in the college cases is how low to go down. Both of these legal developments are caused by societal changes and the need for the law to react to those changes.

Dissemination of Information

There are additional unique concerns created by the student-school relationship. The *Porten v. University of San Francisco* case[9] discussed in chapter 8 in the section on dissemination of information was looked at as a potential tort and potential violation of the privacy provision of the California constitution. The fact that the case involved a student-university relationship did not distinguish it from other cases. But now a new concern enters: the Family Educational and Rights of Privacy Act (FERPA)[10] and its impact on the dissemination of school records.

FERPA provides for the withholding of federal funds otherwise available to educational institutions having a policy or practice of permitting the release of educational records. In short, a school must keep certain records confidential as a condition to receiving federal funds. The funding aspect of this statute gives it strong enforcement leverage.

In 1991, a federal district court in Missouri considered a situation in which a university had refused a student journalist's request to inspect and copy criminal investigation reports maintained by campus security.[11] Campus security performed functions that included searches of students' rooms and the investigation of suspected criminal activity on campus by students and non-students. Its reports covered such subjects as sexual assault, robberies, burglaries, and other crimes. Security forwarded such reports to law enforcement authorities for use in their investigations. The university distributed a policy statement indicating that such reports would be withheld from the public and the media.

The student journalist claimed that there had been delays in filing these reports with law enforcement and because the police were unable to promptly investigate crimes, she, as a student on campus, was deprived of proper protection. She claimed she had a right to the reports under a Missouri sunshine law. The university claimed that it was prohibited under FERPA from giving her the reports.

The court concluded that the state's open records statute was applicable to all state bodies, including the university, and the school's criminal investigative records were not protected from disclosure any more than police records. Further, FERPA did not provide a defense because it did not prohibit disclosure, it just penalized for disclosing. In any event, as far as this court was concerned, the reports were not educational records covered by FERPA. In the court's judgment an individual's status as a student at a state university should not entitle him or her to any greater privacy rights than the general public when the privacy interest relates to criminal investigations and incident reports.

There undoubtedly will be more activity in this area. The issue is complicated because it involves state laws that provide open access to criminal records, state-sponsored activities, and possible conflict with a federal statute, FERPA. This is a relatively narrow area of interest and while it generates considerable heat, it should not be applied to a broader range of circumstances. These media-attractive cases point up the need to first identify the players and the rules the game is being played by.

GOVERNMENT-REGULATED BUSINESSES

The government's interest in some businesses is so significant that it has created a whole range of regulations that dictate to some extent how they carry out their security functions. Transportation, the manufacture of controlled substances, banking, and security are just a few examples. While each area might justify a book in itself, a cursory treatment here might at least give a feeling for some elements that distinguish them from the non-regulated world.

Transportation

Chapters 3 and 4 dealt with the National Labor Relations Act, but no reference was made to the fact that railroad and airline employees are covered by the Railway Labor Act.[12] This statute was passed in 1926 to cover railroads and amended in 1936 to apply to carriers by air. While the National Labor Relations Act is not applicable to rail and air disputes, NLRB cases are sometimes used as reference points in resolving similar problems under the Railway Labor Act.[13] So within the transportation industry, an over-the-road truck driver might be covered by the NLRA and a railroad brakeman might be covered by a different act. Further, the same truck driver might not be covered under the Fair Labor Standards Act relative to maximum hours, if his or her duties substantially effect safety of operation. Under such circumstances the secretary of transportation has the power to establish qualifications and maximum hours of work.[14] The government's interest in protecting the safety of the public is at the bottom of many of these differences.

The Department of Transportation is divided into different administrative groups including the Federal Railroad Administration, Federal Highway Administration, and Federal Aviation Administration. The Coast Guard, Maritime Administration, and Urban Mass Transportation Administration are also within the DOT. Following one case through one of those departmental administrations will help frame the special role the government can play in the private security sector.

The Federal Railroad Safety Act of 1970 gave the secretary of transportation authority to establish rules and regulations for railroad safety.[15] The Federal Railroad Administration adopted regulations authorizing railroads to administer breath and urine tests to employees who violated certain safety rules.[16] In *Skinner v. RLEA*[17] the Supreme Court considered whether these rules violated the fourth amendment, which is the search and seizure amendment.

These drug-testing rules were applied to private sector employees, so how would the fourth amendment get into the picture? The *Skinner* court answered it this way: "Although the Fourth Amendment does not apply to search or seizure, even an arbitrary one, effected by a private party on his own initiative, the Amendment protects against such intrusions if the private party acted as an instrument or agent of the Government."[18] This case raises many of the points made in chapter 1, but this time there is a distinction. Here, the private employers were acting only according to authorized but not required regulations. Was this enough to make the private employer an instrument of the government?

The court noted that the government had removed all legal barriers to the testing. It preempted state laws covering the same subject matter and superseded any provision in a collective bargaining contract. The government also indicated a strong preference for the testing and an interest in gaining the results of the tests. In the court's judgment, all this evidenced a significant involvement of the government in the testing process. Thus, the private employer found itself with fourth amendment obligations. Once involved, though, the private employer was not burdened by law enforcement obligations but was put in the same capacity as the school administrator in *T.L.O.* and the work-related searchers in *Ortega*.[19] These cases were discussed in some detail in chapter 1. The watchword for assessing the constitutionality of the searches in those cases was "reasonable," and the *Skinner* court went on to use the same test in evaluating the Federal Railroad Administration regulations. The court found that the regulations were reasonable within the meaning of the fourth amendment. As noted in chapter 6 under "Drug Testing," the *Skinner* case has been used as a guideline for drug-testing programs in the private sector. If the Federal Railroad Administration drug-testing plan could pass fourth amendment muster, it should be acceptable for less stringently tested private sector drug programs.

Similar regulations have been established by the Federal Highway Administration[20] and they are in the process of being challenged in several federal courts. Others will be implemented for pipeline facilities.[21] These regulations generally incorporate the Procedures for Transportation Workplace Drug Testing Programs published by DOT.[22] Congress has been concerned about the continuous court testing of these regulations and bills have been introduced into the Senate and the House to give them statutory status.[23] Nearly four million transportation workers are impacted by these drug-testing regulations, so it is an area of some importance.

While drug testing is a good example of government impact on private employees in transportation, there are other areas that are also affected. For example, DOT becomes involved in advisory standard settings. Cargo security advisory standards have been issued and they cover such things as lock and key control for security cribs and the use of electronic surveillance.[24]

Manufacturers of Controlled Substances

Regulations under the Controlled Substances Act[25] deal with registering businesses that manufacture, distribute, or dispense controlled substances.[26] These regulations provide, in part, that applicants and registrants shall provide effective controls and procedures to guard against theft and diversion of controlled substances. The Drug Enforcement Agency (DEA) uses these regulations to determine whether businesses are meeting their security obligations. Separate and apart from physical security items such as fencing, alarm systems, and procedures for handling visitors, the regulations speak directly to employee screening, employee responsibility to report drug diversion, and illicit activities by employees.

In the employee screening area, the regulations note that there is a need to know certain information about employees in order to provide overall controlled substance security. The regulations go on to say that:

It is, therefore, assumed that the following questions will become a part of an employer's comprehensive screening program:
> Question—Within the past five years, have you been convicted of a felony, or within the past two years, of any misdemeanor or are you presently charged with committing a criminal offense? (Do not include any traffic violations, juvenile offenses or military convictions except by general court martial.) If the answer is yes, furnish details of conviction, offense, location, date, and sentence.[27]

While it is unusual in employer-employee relationships to find a requirement that an employee must report rule violations by other employees, these regulations state that it is:

the position of DEA that an employee who has knowledge of drug diversion from his employer by a fellow employee has an obligation to report such information to a responsible security official of the employer. . . . A failure to report information of drug diversion will be considered in determining the feasibility of continuing to allow an employee to work in a drug security area. The employer shall inform all employees concerning this policy.[28]

It could be, then, that within a large manufacturing complex that is only partially involved in producing controlled substances, there will be two sets of rules—one set driven by DEA standards and another by the normal pressures of the workplace. If differences exist in the rules by which employee conduct is measured, the reasons for those differences should be understood. As evidenced here, in some circumstances the differences are created by government regulation.

Banking

The banking industry introduces a whole new vocabulary and articulation of rights and duties of employees and management in their relationships with customers. The purpose of these comments is not to explore all of these new areas but to take a small cross section of the regulated side of the business in order to understand why bank security people might take certain security measures.

There are four federal supervisory agencies: the Comptroller of the Currency with respect to national banks and district banks; the Board of Governors of the Federal Reserve System with respect to Federal Reserve Banks and state banks that are members of the federal reserve system; the Federal Deposit Insurance Corporation (FDIC) with respect to state banks that are not members of the federal reserve system but the deposits of which are insured by the FDIC and state savings associations; and the Director of the Office of Thrift Supervision with respect to federal savings associations.[29]

Each of these supervisory agencies has been required to promulgate rules establishing minimum standards with which each bank or savings and loan association must comply with respect to the installation, maintenance, and operation of security devices and procedures to discourage robberies, burglaries, and larcenies and to assist in the identification and apprehension of persons who commit such acts.[30]

As an example of such regulations, the Board of Governors of the Federal Reserve System established security regulations for federal reserve banks and state member banks.[31] These regulations require the Federal Reserve and member banks to develop and provide for the administration of a security program. Within that program there must be a number of enumerated items such as training and periodic retraining of employees in their responsibilities including the proper use of security devices and proper employee conduct during and after a robbery. Minimum standards are set out for surveillance systems and robbery and burglary alarm systems.[32]

Certainly there is value in non-banking security people observing how banks conduct their security business and some of the procedures might be applicable to their own functions. But it has to be understood that the motivation for implementing a policy might be different. The bank might be required to do so by regulation.

Security

Businesses are not regulated only by the federal government; in some situations states and local governments play a major role in how organizations conduct themselves. The security business is a good example. More than forty-five states are involved to various degrees in regulating different aspects of these businesses.[33] Licensing requirements can apply to private investigators, security guards, guard dog service handlers, polygraph operators, private alarm contractors, and other security-related personnel. Areas of interest include age, experience, personal character, and training.

Some aspects of the different state programs are of interest in that they help separate private security from law enforcement. The California *Taylor* case was discussed in chapter 1 because it highlighted some of the distinctive features of each. The court commented that just because California licensed security guards and regulated their activity the guards were not transformed into state agents. Though security guards are required to take a course in the exercise of power to arrest, the state emphasizes in its training literature that "a security guard is not a police officer. Guards do not have the same duties as police officers; they do not have the same training; and they do not have the same powers according to law. A security guard arrests with the same power as any other citizen."[33]

Other states also make a point of distinguishing private security from law enforcement. The Tennessee Private Protective Services Licensing and Regulatory Act prohibits the use of law enforcement representations on private security badges, insignia, vehicles, or equipment, and has restrictions on wearing police-style uniforms.[34] Arkansas, in its private security training programs, includes instructions on the legal authority of private guards.[35]

The impact of regulations on the status of the regulated private entity is of interest. The Supreme Court in the *Skinner* case found that the private sector was burdened by fourth amendment obligations because of the Federal Railroad Administration's drug testing regulations, and the *Taylor* court found that California private security regulations did not make private security people agents of the state. Where is the line? Again it is hard to say, but in the *Skinner* case the government not only told private employers what to do but how to do it. In *Taylor*, the government was only providing general parameters and not getting into the day-to-day operations of the private sector. Further, it kept insisting that the private sector was not to act as the agent of the government. What it amounts to is that there are regulations and then there are regulations.

OBSERVATIONS

Students are not employees of their schools and in only a strained way are they customers. Schools generally are not looked upon as businesses oriented toward making a profit. The relationship is between students interested in getting an education and schools interested in providing it. In attempting to balance conflicts between these unique interests, some courts make analogies to invitee-owner relationships even though the factors in the balance are not exactly the same. The interest in selling the product, education, is not so much generated by a desire for profit as a desire to satisfy societal obligations. Most of the legal conflict in balancing student-school rights has taken place in the public sector because that is where most of the laws exist. Private sector relationships are more often developed in reaction to societal pressures including the happenings in state-sponsored schools.

A significant part of business has to submit to government regulation because of the government's interest in protecting the public. These protections sometimes are manifested in specific regulations that are not found in the normal employee-employer relationships. While the usual workplace rule might be tested in an arbitration setting, these rules and regulations are challenged in federal and state courts and the benchmark is not a collective bargaining contract but the federal constitution or a state statute.

Private security people all have the same fundamental objectives, but it has to be recognized that differences in legal pressures created by differences in businesses might cause them to emphasize different means in reaching those objectives. Just because a means is used by one does not necessarily indicate that it should be used by all. Each security person has to recognize the nature of his or her own business.

NOTES

1. 469 U.S. 325 (1985).
2. 469 U.S. 325 at 341.
3. Iowa Code Sec. 808 A.2 (1986).
4. *Futrell v. Aherns*, 88 N.M. 284, 540 P.2d 214 (1975).
5. *Jenkins v. Louisiana State Board of Education*, 506 F.2d 992 (5th Cir. 1975); *Tinker v. Des Moines School District*, 393 U.S. 503 (1969); *Goss v. Lopez*, 419 U.S. 565 (1975); *Nash v. Auburn University*, 812 F.2d 655 (11th Cir. 1987).
6. *Rabel v. Illinois Wesleyean University*, 514 N.E.2d 552 (1987).
7. *Furek v. University of Delaware*, 594 A.2d 506 (Del. 1991).
8. 594 A.2d 506 at 522.

9. 64 Cal. App. 3d 825, 134 Cal. Rptr. 839 (1976).

10. 20 U.S.C. 1232 et seq.

11. *Bauer v. Kincaid*, 759 F. Supp. 575 (W.D. Mo. 1991).

12. 49 U.S.C. Sec. 151–163.

13. *Brotherhood of Railroad Trainmen v. Jacksonville Terminal Co.*, 394 U.S. 369 (1969), *reh'g. denied*, 394 U.S. 1024 (1969).

14. *Beggs v. Kroger Co.*, 167 F.2d 700 (8th Cir. 1948); 49 U.S.C. Šec. 3102.

15. 45 U.S.C. 431 (a).

16. 49 C.F.R. Part 219 (1989).

17. 489 U.S. 602 (1989).

18. 489 U.S. 602 at 614.

19. *New Jersey v. T.L.O.*, 469 U.S. 325, 337, 342 (1985); *O'Conner v. Ortega*, 480 U.S. 709, 721, 725 (1987).

20. 49 C.F.R. Sec. 391.81 et seq. (1988).

21. 49 C.F.R. Sec. 199.1 et seq. (1988).

22. 49 C.F.R. Part 40 (1989).

23. S. 676 and H.R. 3301.

24. 49 C.F.R. Part 101 (1978).

25. 21 U.S.C. Sec. 801; 21 C.F.R. Part 1301 et seq. (1973).

26. 21 C.F.R. Sec. 1301.90 (1975).

27. 21 C.F.R. Sec. 1301.91 (1975).

28. 12 U.S.C. Sec. 1881.

29. 12 U.S.C. Sec. 1882.

30. 12 C.F.R. Part 216 (1991).

31. 12 C.F.R. Sec. 216.3.

32. C.P. Nemeth, *Private Security and The Law* 24 (1989).

33. *People v. Taylor*, 222 Cal. App. 3d 612, 271 Cal. Rptr. 785 (1990).

34. Tenn. Code Ann. Sec., 62-35-127, 128 (1987).

35. Ark. Code, Ann. Sec. 17-33-101, 208 (1977).

Conclusion

The first step to finding one's way through the legal maze impacting private security is to be objective. One of the most serious illnesses to be suffered by any private security person is tunnel vision. An early symptom of this disease is a tendency to talk in terms of "we" and "they." "We" usually turns out to be a small group of security people and "they," often, is the rest of the world. This mind set prevents any possibility for being objective, and without objectivity there is no possibility for understanding and working within the laws that apply to private security.

Objectivity leads one to understand that there are numerous players involved in most security problems and these players have different rights and obligations. Employees are people critical to the well-being of a business who have certain rights and obligations that may vary depending on whether they are organized or unorganized. Businesses can only exist with satisfied customers and these customers also have certain rights that determine how they can be treated.

Further, it has to be recognized that all businesses are not the same and legally acceptable security activity sometimes will vary with the nature of the business. What might make sense in an explosives plant might not make sense in a suburban office building. In addition, the way some businesses conduct their security activities might be dictated by federal or state regulations. Understanding security's role within all these configurations is critical to making legally sound decisions.

However, just knowing the names and roles of all the players will not do the job unless problem-solving decisions are reasonable. Being reasonable, then, is the second step. The reasonable person theme runs through all facets of the law, but the problem is that the reasonable person keeps changing. To evaluate rights and act as a reasonable person based upon 1950s standards will not do the job in the 1990s. This is not to say that present-day standards and values are correct, but they have to be understood in order to get the job done. One does not have to *be* today's reasonable person, one just has to know how he or she thinks.

To make objectivity and reasonableness effective tools in getting through the maze, they should be used with the understanding that the laws are often in a state of change. The law reacts to changes in society, and private security has to monitor these trends. For example, the current ineffectiveness of unions' organizing efforts does not mean that employees are now more satisfied with employers. It just means that employees do not believe in the collective solution to workplace problems anymore and are now taking their individual complaints to court. It should be recognized that that is where more and more work-related confrontations will take place.

The problem is that the shift to the new arena of wrongful discharge has not brought with it all the rules under which the old game was played. Arbitrators had established a common law of the workplace under which employees were recognized as having obligations as well as rights. Some courts have not grasped all the factors in the employee-employer balance and tend to treat employees as they would customers in a customer-owner relationship or individuals in an individual-government relationship.

One wonders how many courts considering wrongful discharge cases will ponder the words of the Supreme Court in *United Steelworkers v. Warrior & Gulf Navigation Co.*, 363 U.S. 574 (1960), when it said:

The labor arbitrator performs functions which are not normal to the courts; the considerations which help him fashion judgments may be indeed foreign to the competence of courts. . . . The parties expect that his judgment of a particular grievance . . . will reflect such factors as the effect upon productivity of a particular result, its consequences to the morale of the shop, his judgment whether tensions will be heightened or diminished. . . . The ablest judge cannot be expected to bring the same experience and competence to bear upon the determination of a grievance because he cannot be similarly informed.

Is a carefully crafted balance of workplace rights destroyed just because there is no bargaining agent? Does the individual employee in the unorganized sector have a bigger bundle of rights than an organized employee? Shouldn't an employer have the same right to run a productive business irrespective of whether it is unorganized or organized? And shouldn't a judge as well as an arbitrator consider such a factor in establishing a balance of rights?

This is an example of one shift and adjustment, or lack of adjustment, to the shift. There are numerous others that, from a private security vantage point, can be looked upon as either good or bad. Shoplifting statutes and search standards for government sector administrators have placed private security in a better position to adjust to increased thefts and use of drugs. RICO interpretations have given business a new weapon in curbing sophisticated white collar crime. On the other hand, the establishment of *Weingarten* rights and the extension of liability to mall businesses for injuries inflicted on customers by strangers might seem onerous and unnecessary burdens.

Unfortunately, confusion is added because of the failure of legislatures and legal forums to understand some of the basic distinctions in rights and roles as they attempt to readjust balances. For example, the failure to understand the different roles played by law enforcement and private security has created problems in the arbitration area. Further, some courts in the interest of providing relief for customers injured by strangers might unintentionally be forcing employers into the law enforcement business. Current events dictate that there has to be cooperation between private security and law enforcement, but private security should never be forced into becoming an agent of law enforcement, unless private security assumes a law enforcement role.

As law enforcement agencies increasingly contract out functions such as transporting prisoners to private security firms, more attention will have to be given to the laws that will bind such firms in these new functions. Will these private security people be engaging in law enforcement work requiring the application of law enforcement legal standards or will they be performing work similar to that of school and workplace administrators requiring the use of a less stringent standard?

The point is that, for better or worse, change is a constant factor in the law. These legal changes are made in response to changes in society. Some, for example, are in response to perceived imbalances of rights caused by overly aggressive security people, some might merely represent a search for a deep pocket to compensate an innocent victim, and some represent attempts by the government to protect the safety and security of the public.

Objectivity, reasonableness, and trend-watching put one in a position to sort out what is legally important from the unimportant in their job function. This is the hallmark of a knowledgeable private security person. The report of a shoplifting case might be of academic interest to a manufacturing plant security person but of considerable significance to one employed in a retail business. A change in *Miranda* warning requirements might get passing notice by a private security person, but the same person at an organized site will be vitally interested in changes in the law regarding *Weingarten* warnings.

It is of considerable importance that decisions not be made merely because they are legal. A decision should be made because it is practical and solves a problem. If it meets that yardstick, it can then be tested against the law. What might be legal might be dumb in terms of employee or customer relations.

In sum, there are numerous laws that instinct alone might not recognize and specific knowledge will be required. But all the legal knowledge in the world is not going to do any good unless the decision-maker is objective and reasonable, and applies good, common sense.

Good luck with the maze.

Bibliography

Atkinson, J. *RICO Sec. 1961-68, Broadest of the Federal Criminal Statutes*, 69 J. Crim. L. & Criminology 1 (1978).

Avery, D. *Federal Labor Rights and Access to Private Property: The NLRB and the Right to Exclude*, 11 Indus. Rel. L.J. 145 (1989).

Bazyler, M. *The Duty to Provide Adequate Protection: Landowner's Liability for Failure to Protect Patrons from Criminal Attack*, 21 Ariz. L. Rev. 727 (1979).

Blakely, C.R. and Cessar, S.D. *Equitable Relief Under Civil RICO*, 62 Notre Dame L. Rev. 526 (1987).

Bornstein, T. & Gosline, A. *Labor and Employment Arbitration*, Sec. 24:02 (1991).

Comment, *The Protection and Recapture of Merchandise from Shoplifters*, 46 Ill. L. Rev. 887 (1952).

Comment, *Industrial Due Process and Just Cause for Discipline: A Comparative Analysis of Arbitral and Judicial Decisional Processes*, 6 UCLA L. Rev. 603 (1959).

Comment, *Shoplifters Beware*, 11 Drake L. Rev. 31 (1961).

Craver, C. *The Inquisitorial Process in Private Employment*, 63 Cornell L. Rev. 1 (1977).

De Guiseppe, J. Jr., *The Effect of the Employment-At-Will Rule in Employee Rights to Job Security and Fringe Benefits*, 10 Fordham Urb. L.J. 1 (1981).

Dertouzos, J., Holland, E., & Ebener, P. *The Legal and Economic Consequences of Wrongful Termination* (1988).

Dorr, R. & Eigles, W. *Resolving Claims to Ownership of Software and Computer Stored Data*, 5 Computer L.J. 1 (1984).

Elkouri, F. & Elkouri, E. *How Arbitration Works*, (4th ed. 1985).

Epstein, M.A. & Levi, S.D. *Protecting Trade Secret Information: A Plan for Proactive Strategy*, 43 Bus. Law. 887 (1988).

Fairweather, O. *Practice and Procedure in Labor Arbitration* (1983)

Gregory, D.L. *Reducing the Risk of Negligence in Hiring*, 14 Employee Rel. L.J. 31 (Summer 1988).

Jacobs, R. *Defamation in the Workplace*, Lab. L.J. 567 (September 1989).

J. Jones, P. Ash & Soto, C. *Employment Privacy Rights and Pre-Employment Honesty Tests*, 15 Employee Rel. L.J. No. 4 (Spring 1990).

Jones, E.A. "Truth," *When the Polygraph Operator Sits as Arbitrator (or Judge)*, Proceedings of the 31st Annual Meeting of National Academy of Arbitrators, 75, (1978).

Keeton, W. Page et al., *Prosser & Keeton On the Law of Torts* 5th ED. (1984).

Larson, A. *The Law of Workmen's Compensation* (1991).

Lipson, M.E. *Compounding Crimes*, 27 Hastings L.J. 175 (1975).

Minuti, M. *Employer Liability Under the Doctrine of Negligent Hiring*, 13 Del. J. Corp. L. 501–532 (1988).

Nemeth, C.P. *Private Security and the Law* (1989).

Note, *Labor Law–Federal Preemption—The Aftermath of Sears*, 27 Wayne L. Rev. 313 (1980).

Note, *Protecting Employees-At-Will Against Wrongful Discharge: The Public Policy Exception*, 96 Harv. L. Rev. 1931 (1983).

O'Connor, D.T. *Accommodating Labor's Section 7 Rights to Picket, Solicit and Distribute Literature in Quasi-Public Property with the Owner's Property Rights*, 32 Mercer L. Rev. 769 (1981).

Olsen, T. *Wrongful Discharge Claims Raised by At Will Employees*, 32 Lab. L.J. 265 (1981).

Perritt, H.H., Jr. *Employee Dismissal Law and Practice*, Sec. 1.12: Current Status of the Employment-At-Will Rule in 50 States (2d ed. 1987).

Sager, T. & Trigg, H. *A Legal Framework for Implementing and Enforcing a Comprehensive Substance Abuse Policy and Program*, Eastern Mineral Law Foundation Eighth Annual Institute (1988).

Shattuck, C.A. *The Tort of Negligent Hiring and the Use of Selection Devices*, 11 Indus. Rel. L.J. 42 (1989).

Shepard J., & Duston, R., *Thieves at Work: An Employer's Guide to Combating Workplace Dishonesty* (1988).

Shepard, J., Duston, R. & Russell, K. *Workplace Privacy*, A BNA Special Report (1987).

Silberberg, H.J. & Lardiere, E.G. *Eroding Protection of Customer Lists and Customer Information Under the Uniform Trade Secrets* Act, 42 Bus. Law. 487 (1987).

Sokolik, S.L. *Computer Crime—The Need for Deterrent Legislation*, 2 Computer L.J. 353 (1980).

Susser, P.A. *Electronic Monitoring in the Private Sector: How Closely Should Employers Supervise Their Workers*, 13 Employee Rel. L.J. 575 (1988).

Tysse, G. & Dodge, G. *Winning the War on Drugs: The Role of Workplace Testing* abridged edition (1989).

Vandevoort, J.R. *Trade Secrets: Protecting a Very Special "Property,"* 26 Bus. Law. 681 (1971).

Wolk, I.L. *Some Legal Aspects of Industrial Espionage*, 9 Prac. Law. No. 4, 87 (1963).

Yelonsky, M. *Business Inviters Duty to Protect Invitees from Criminal Acts*, 134 U. Pa. L. Rev. 883 (1986).

Index

About the Author

LEO F. HANNON spent six years as a special agent with the Office of Naval Intelligence in Washington, D.C. and ten years as an attorney with the National Labor Relations Board in Philadelphia, Pennsylvania. In 1969 he joined the E. I. Du Pont de Nemours and Company Legal Department in Wilmington, Delaware, as a labor and security lawyer. For sixteen years he was managing counsel for Du Pont's labor, benefits, and security group. He retired from Du Pont in December 1990.